To Peter and
with best wis[hes]

John Dewehurst

GENERALLY SPEAKING
'Then Hurrah for the Life of a Soldier'

The subtitle is from a soldiers' song, words and music by J. S. Cook, sung by members of the 1st Foot (The Royal Regiment) on their way to Gallipoli to embark for Constantinople and the Crimea in 1854. With cholera rife in Gallipoli, it was a sentiment some of them might shortly call in question.

GENERALLY SPEAKING

'Then Hurrah for the Life of a Soldier'

JOHN AKEHURST

MICHAEL RUSSELL

© John Akehurst 1999

The right of John Akehurst to be identified
as the author of this work has been asserted by him
in accordance with the Copyright, Designs
and Patents Act, 1988

First published in Great Britain 1999
by Michael Russell (Publishing) Ltd
Wilby Hall, Wilby, Norwich NR16 2JP

Typeset in Sabon by The Typesetting Bureau
Allen House, East Borough, Wimborne, Dorset
Printed and bound in Great Britain
by Biddles Ltd, Guildford and King's Lynn

All rights reserved
ISBN 0 85955 253 5

TO SHIRLEY
TO WHOM I OWE SO MUCH
(BUT TELL HER SO RARELY)

Contents

	Foreword	9
1	In the Beginning	11
2	Officer Cadet	25
3	Subaltern	38
4	Malaya	53
5	Malaya – Operation Sword	63
6	Malaya – Third Year	73
7	Hong Kong, England and the TA	85
8	Introduction to the Staff	99
9	Company Command and Back to Camberley	112
10	Battalion Command	124
11	More Colleges	138
12	The Dhofar War	151
13	Brigadier Staff	166
14	Divisional Command	172
15	Staff College Yet Again	183
16	Field Army and Inspector General	195
17	Winding Up	207
18	Retired	225
19	Reflections	241
	Index	251

Foreword

In compiling this book I have made use of occasional diaries, regimental magazines and records, and had frequent recourse to the memories of my wife and my friends, but I have rarely been a consistent or conscientious diarist. Mostly I have had to rely upon my own memory. An American ambassador, speaking in London, said: 'As I get older I find I have an increasingly vivid and more precise memory of events that never happened.' I am myself burdened with this problem and therefore apologise for any inaccuracies in the narrative. I am sure there are plenty, but I assure the reader that I have committed no deliberate falsehoods. The book is as accurate as I can make it.

It took some years to decide whether to have a go at this work. One friend questioned how I dared because he thought I was not sufficiently interesting. He is probably right, but a number of others have been of the opinion not only that progress from private to general throughout the duration of the Cold War has a potential value of its own, but also that the places and events of which I have had first-hand knowledge, and many of the people I have met during my service, warrant recording. I hope they are right. I have tried to avoid esoteric military matters and prosaic day-to-day things of purely personal significance, and only to include matters which I hope will be of wider interest. I am acutely conscious that the personal pronoun is heavily used but in a book of memoirs this is probably inevitable. I cannot see a way round this and am sorry if it grates.

I am profoundly grateful to Major Michael Barthorp who has been endlessly patient and encouraging, probably spending as much time in writing detailed constructive comment and advice as I did in writing the first draft. Shirley, my wife, who has supplied valuable opinions, corrections of memory and much detailed editing, has never been overtly appreciated for her help with this book or for all the other things that the ideal wife provides, but I am deeply thankful, really I am.

Warminster 1999

I
In the Beginning

Most of us can recall certain moments or events which changed or shaped our lives. One of mine has a name – 'Corporal Pyne', a man who was personally responsible for my obtaining a commission by deception. Happily it is now a bit late for the Ministry of Defence to take action on this fraud; at least I hope they have more pressing issues to which to devote their time and dwindling budget.

The story needs a long introduction. In 1947, disillusioned with civilian life after short spells as a bicycle mechanic, a prospective golf professional and a bank clerk, I signed on at Maidstone for 'Five and Seven', the jargon then for five years with the Colours and seven on the Reserve, which was the Regular soldier's contract of the day.

I was an only child, born in Chatham and constantly in trouble for most of my first eighteen years. My mother's was a big family and I seemed to have dozens of cousins. My grandmother claimed that of them all I was by far the naughtiest and most difficult. To my embarrassment she enjoyed boring listeners with tales of my childhood pranks and sins. How, for instance, a taste for the hard stuff began when I was two – at my grandparents' hotel, the Maiden's Head in Uckfield. My pram had been carelessly parked close to some beer crates full of near-empty bottles. The next thing anyone knew was that the bottles were empty and I was plastered. Other tales included my cutting out the flowers from a pretty settee cover and, later, my sundry misdemeanours on the train when commuting to a prep-school in Dover. Pleasing, however, was a *Daily Mail* cutting dear to my mother's heart. The occasion was a children's angling competition off the Deal Pier. The report in the *Mail* included the passage: 'I asked young John Akehurst, aged 7 and not much bigger than a fair sized fish himself, how he was getting on. "Fine," he boasted, "I caught ten great big ones! But they all got away."'

My education was much disrupted by the Second World War. My father grew to be somewhat at odds with my mother and preferred to live alone to pursue his job as a bank manager in Deal, Kent, and other interests about which my mother had dark and probably justified suspicions. Even as war loomed he claimed that Deal, just across the Channel from potential fighting, was too close to danger for women and children. He used this as an excuse to evacuate my mother and me to what he considered to be safer places. On 2 September 1939 we were driven perilously through the night with shaded headlights to the hotel in Uckfield, where the next day I can clearly remember Chamberlain's sepulchral voice emerging from the 'beehive' radio to tell us that we were now at war with Germany. A few minutes later the mournful but scary notes of the first air raid warning of the war brought the order from my grandmother to don gas-masks and await Armageddon. We children were disappointed that Armageddon held off. We stayed at Uckfield for some months and I attended a term at each of two schools which had been evacuated there from London. One of them was 'Harrow High School', which sported a particularly bright blue and yellow cap, but that is all I can remember about it. I cannot even remember the name of the other school.

Eventually, in early May 1940, my mother's argument that evacuation was hardly justified by the phoney war persuaded my father that we should return to Deal. This was the signal Hitler had been waiting for to invade France and we had ringside seats for the evacuation from Dunkirk and some of the bombing of the coastal towns and the Downs shipping that followed. I then spent a term or two at Alleyn's School which, for some logic known only to its management, was evacuated to Walmer for safety, where it moved into buildings from which another school had left for Devon. It, in turn, then fled elsewhere and we were evacuated again; this time to an aunt's family house in Leatherhead, where we spent the height of the Blitz under one of the Luftwaffe's main routes. It seemed that German pilots who were too windy either to get to London, or to drop their bombs on their appointed targets, thought Leatherhead a sensible and safer alternative. There were some very uncomfortable and occasionally frightening nights spent packed like sardines in the cold, damp shelter in my uncle's cellar. I attended City of London Freemen's School in Ashtead for only a week before a parachuted land-mine destroyed it and closed another educational chapter for me.

After grandstand views of the Battle of Britain and the early part of London's ordeal we returned yet again to Deal, where I was provided with the services of Jimmy Dick, MA, an elderly Scottish academic, as personal tutor for a few months. He only taught the three Rs and

French but we made remarkable progress in these subjects, which was a mixed blessing when at the age of eleven I was sent to a boarding school at Cranbrook, partly because my mother wanted me out of the way of the frequent air raids and the cross-Channel shelling. This latter was disconcerting because except at night when one could often see the flash from the Cap Gris Nez area the great shells arrived without warning and were big enough to demolish a house. We were critical of Mr Churchill because when the Germans began their big gun attacks he directed that retaliation should be made available. Thereafter it was hardly ever the Germans who initiated firing, but always our own guns firing at the Calais area.

I began in the lowest class, named Form 2 for some reason which escapes me, and was behind in such subjects as history and geography but about two years ahead in Jimmy Dick's areas. Confidence in the latter made me an insufferably conceited little prig which brought down upon me some very ugly bullying. This plus homesickness were not the best starts to my first settled period of education. Most of the bullying, which included such delights as being tied to the wire springs of my bed and made to spend the night there with the mattress on top of me, was at the hands of a particular tyrant called Brian Luck, who was bigger and stronger than I. A friend persuaded me that, win or lose, the matter could only be resolved by challenging Luck to personal combat. The challenge was issued and the next few days were spent in a ludicrous argument about whether the form of the conflict should be wrestling or boxing. My tormentor knew as well as I did that he could punch the living daylights out of me, whereas I felt I might be able to avoid his fists by tying him up with some lethal stranglehold. Eventually we submitted to arbitration and our peers came up with the compromise of 'all-in wrestling', which meant, in effect, no holds barred. I can remember little about the details of the fight, except that most of the bruises and blood were mine, but the end was a stalemate of tangled arms and legs. The result was declared a draw, hands were shaken, and, happily, that was the end of the bullying.

Cranbrook, in the Weald of Kent, afforded glimpses of the war and we enthusiastically maintained maps of our armies' progress after the tide turned. 1944 was enlivened by the V1 'Doodlebug' flying bomb attacks. The school was on one of the routes for these weapons and on the very first night we heard the unusual sound of their passage directly over us. One of them cut out soon after passing and duly crashed to earth with a mighty explosion. None of us knew about the things and speculation was rife among the boys that Britain had invented a new ray which caused the internal combustion engine to cut out. Because so many passed above us it became routine that during meals a boy who could raise a note from a bugle would be stationed outside the dining hall looking east. On the approach of a flying bomb he would blow his bugle and all the diners would fall to the floor and fight for space under their tables. These spaces were available in about the same proportion as the *Titanic*'s lifeboats. I was one of the bugle blowers and found myself on duty when a V1 cut out a bit short of the school. It was my job to sound the warning 'G's. I learned then to admire the cool with which young drummer boys in earlier wars could get sounds out of their bugles when confronted with imminent contact with the enemy. Somehow the lips are loth to form in the usual way. Happily the threatening bomb passed well overhead and exploded about a mile away but I won few marks for steadiness under fire.

Later in 1944 substantial numbers of the airborne glider and parachute force heading for Arnhem and Nijmegen provided an exciting spectacle on their way to Holland, but that was more or less the end of the Second World War for us, although food, sweets and clothes rationing seemed to go on for ages after it.

With the end of bullying came comparative peace and a surge of self-confidence with which I embarked upon a career of studied rebellion and indiscipline. I have always felt that those of us who were at school during the war were saddled with elderly teachers well past their sell-by date who served on only because the younger, more vigorous, and in my view more understanding, members of their profession were away at war in the services, broadening their minds to become outstanding teachers when they returned. The old men responsible for us were a constant challenge to me, as I suspect I was to them, and there could only be one winning side.

One incident which rankles to this day was 'The Backscratcher Affair'. In order to supplement the abysmal school food boys would go into the little town as often as they could afford it and buy beans on toast or something similar from one of the two available cafés. Mark Hudson, my closest friend, and I went to Miss Bryant's Tea Rooms one afternoon to find it already full, so we had to queue. The line was formed beside the artifacts that Miss Bryant had on display and for sale and one of these was a stick with a small ivory hand at its end. Intrigued, I picked it up and asked Mark if he knew what it was. He did, so I tried it out, stuffing the thing down the inside of the back of my collar. At that moment we were called through to a vacant table and because Miss Bryant was watching I could not withdraw the wretched implement and went for my beans with it lodged down the inside of my shirt. Came the time to pay and we were still under close observation, so I thought I would make discretion the better part of valour and return the thing the next day. Unfortunately it had been missed and the finger of suspicion pointed at us. By the time we got back to school the lady had already telephoned the Headmaster who met us and challenged us with having stolen the backscratcher. I confessed at once and tried to explain what had happened and that I really had no intention of depriving Miss B permanently of what to me was a perfectly useless object. Russell Scott, the Head, already no great admirer, told me to stop 'prevaricating' (the word is ingrained in my memory – I had to look it up in a dictionary afterwards) and administered summary justice in the shape of eight strokes of his own 'backscratcher'. I was labelled a thief, nearly expelled, and a letter of outrage was sent to my father. I suppose I should blame bad luck rather than Scott, but it still hurts.

I was constantly in all sorts of trouble and the only things that really captured my imagination were flouting authority, games, the Corps and English. The result of this turmoil was that I held the record for strokes received from the cane, was the most senior boy not to be a prefect, but was the Sergeant-Major (No. 1) in the Corps. This last came about mainly because Lieutenant-Colonel H. F. Saunders, MBE, the old warhorse who taught my favourite subject, English, also ran the Corps and the Dramatic Society and perhaps recognised some talent undiagnosed by my housemaster and most of the rest of the teaching community. Despite my reservations about it all I did take part in practically everything that was on offer, including singing in the choir, being an altar server, playing parts in all school plays and joining in all the sports that were available, even winning cups for fives and swimming.

Exam results reflected this muddle. In School Certificate (O Level), I scored three distinctions, three credits and two failures, history and geography – mostly because they were taught so badly (that at least is my opinion). I settled for English, French and Latin for Higher Certificate (A Level). Saunders managed to convey enthusiasm for language and literature but was not much good at preparing his pupils for exams. In order to avoid having to set and mark exams himself halfway through the two-year course he entered me at the end of the first year for the exam proper 'for practice'. In the event I scraped the lowest possible pass mark, at which my father rubbed his impoverished hands together with glee and declined to pay for another year 'just to get higher grades'.

Thus it came about that I left school, both to my own and my father's relief, at sixteen, and had to decide how to earn enough cash to run a motorbike, my pride and joy, and take full advantage of the temptations that independent transport offered. A predecessor at Cranbrook had been Lord Rootes, who had risen from being a bicycle mechanic to running the nationally powerful Rootes Group of car manufacturers and retailers. Here was an inspiration, my father thought, for me to become a tycoon and cushion his later years; so he apprenticed me to a bicycle shop. I quite enjoyed taking such intricacies as the Sturmey-Archer three-speed to bits and putting it together again, but the combination of boring routine, permanently filthy hands, and no obvious prospects made my time as a mechanic very brief indeed. There followed a short attachment to J. O. Lovelock, the professional at the Royal Cinque Ports golf club, but this, too, was doomed. Mr Lovelock commended the way in which I ran his shop and his accounts but advised me not to think of trying to earn a living by actually playing. My enthusiasm has endured but my handicap has never been in single figures and I still describe the game as the best fun you can have with your clothes on.

Having enjoyed and been fairly successful in the Corps at school I began to entertain thoughts of joining the Army, although, in truth, I knew practically nothing about it nor had I any relatives serving in it whom I could interrogate. I had no idea of the effects of rapid demobilisation after the war, the country's residual worldwide roles, the demands of Empire and administering the newly-won peace, the prospects for an Iron Curtain and an Atlantic Alliance to counter it, and the need for National Service to provide comparatively inexpensive manpower for all these tasks, and at the same time to offer a counterweight to the political spectre of high unemployment. I was still six months short of the minimum age limit for signing on, and conscription was at least a year away, so I accepted further advice from my father and became a clerk in his bank 'to make me realise', he said, 'that it was not the sort of job that I should like'. I found it boring, although in those days it was enlivened by a great deal more personal service to the customer than one can find today. Looking back now, the working practices seem extraordinarily antiquated and the average bank clerk of today would find them hard to believe. There was one typewriter in the branch and no other mechanical aid. All the customers were well known and their current accounts were contained in two huge ledgers, A to M and N to Z. Every transaction was recorded in ink and at the end of each day there was a 'callover'. This involved the manager calling out every name in the ledger and the clerks then replying with the details of any cheque or voucher relative to that name, where it was duly ticked off in the ledger as having been checked. This could be quite entertaining because most customers had nicknames derived from their initials, puns on their names, or references, seldom complimentary, to personal characteristics. To save time and postage one of the earliest daily duties of the junior clerk was to take fistfuls of cheques drawn on the other four of the big five banks round to their respective branches in the town and collect cheques drawn on ours. The next job was to join the other clerks in adding and subtracting every one of the day's transactions in every account and entering the result by hand. A balance would thus be struck and if it came anywhere near the red it had to be brought to the manager's attention. Overdrafts were few and mostly modest at that time.

The work was dull, but there were many compensations. I enjoyed evening golf, and often set off on weekend jaunts to Central London to learn in detail its geography, an exercise which has often proved its value over the years. Occasionally I rode to Stratford-on-Avon to soak in some Shakespeare and pursue June, my first love, who was a receptionist at the Swan's Nest Hotel. Ah, the bliss of punting on the Avon on a warm summer's evening, declaiming Elizabethan poetry, and achieving my first kiss. Nevertheless I could not face a lifetime in banking – indeed my father always wished he had chosen some other profession himself – so on 12 August 1947, the day I was seventeen and a half, which was the earliest at which one could join, I rode to Maidstone, the nearest Army recruiting office, and there offered my services to the King. At that time, when multitudes were trying to get out of the Army and replacements for them were conscripted largely against their will, a lad who wanted to join voluntarily was a rare bird, worthy of polite reception. 'Right, lad,' said the smartly dressed but gnarled sergeant-major whose ribbons bore witness to distinguished war service, 'I expect you would like to begin with a spot of leave.' 'Sounds good' I said, in my innocence, not realising that the arrangement was designed for the Army's benefit, not mine, and that there would be no pay to accompany this 'spot of leave'. I was sent home without even any travelling expenses and directed to return on 16 September. I asked what would happen then, and was told that I would be posted just up the road to Invicta Lines where after a little interesting training I could go home for the weekend.

After one last anguished visit to Stratford I duly reported, as ordered, at 1000 hrs precisely. The prospect of Invicta Lines and early leave, together with the issue of uniform, confined my total luggage to a toothbrush, a pair of pyjamas and a spare hanky. My grandmother had always taught us that whenever the opportunity offered, or before any event which might be protracted, we should make use of any available facilities. There happened to be some such not fifty yards from the recruiting office, so in I went in pursuit of Granny's recommendation. Emerging to enter the office I found myself in the company of a number of pale and unhealthy-looking Kentish miners who were summoned either to be conscripted or avoid it with the authority of the official dispensation for miners. Immediately we were ushered before a team of doctors whose first demand was a specimen. My prudence of a few minutes before was suddenly my undoing (or at least restricted it to that), and delayed my enlistment by half an hour or so.

It turned out that of all the throng who arrived that morning only two of us were volunteers. After passing a superficial medical we were both welcomed into his office by a very elderly major (he must have been nearly forty) who expressed his delight at our patriotism. On reflection I suppose patriotism probably did have something to do with it, together with the exciting prospects of wearing uniform, travelling, shooting, and perhaps even killing someone if I was lucky. The pay, at four shillings (20p) a day, could not have been a powerful incentive. The major invited us to sign a form and swear an oath of allegiance to His Majesty and then handed out the 1947 equivalent of the King's Shilling, which amounted to 6/8d (35p). The other recruit, whose name was Jack Standen and who wanted to join The Duke of Cornwall's Light Infantry because an uncle had served in that regiment in the First World War, was then asked to leave. 'Young man,' said the major, 'your education is superior to that of Private Standen, so you will be i/c draft.' This sounded exciting – to be in charge for a journey of even half a mile was authority indeed. 'Here is your railway warrant,' he said. 'Where to, sir?' said I. 'To Hollywood' came the reply, with a misleading whiff of stardom. In fact, Palace Barracks, Hollywood, just outside Belfast, Northern Ireland, was the base of the 28th Training Battalion, an organisation which gave six weeks' exceptionally tough basic infantry training, followed by another twelve weeks of preparation to be an infantry officer or NCO.

Standen, it turned out, although he lived only eight miles from Maidstone, had never been to London nor had he ever seen the sea; so when it came to 'i/c draft' responsibilities I probably had the edge on him. After a little wide-eyed sightseeing in London, for which I was able to be a competent guide, we set off from Euston and crossed the Irish Sea from Heysham to Belfast – my own first departure from mainland Britain. We landed on a cold, dank morning and, in due course, after drawing uniform and equipment and being inoculated, vaccinated and generally messed about, we began our basic training. This was largely conducted by a war-experienced sergeant of the Wiltshire Regiment and three similarly experienced corporals. Ours was Corporal Wood of the Royal Norfolks, an impressively competent leader with self-confidence and no little intelligence. Our platoon was made up of Regular and National Service recruits from all walks of life throughout the United Kingdom. There was every possible variety of motivation, education, background and fitness. Charlie Small, for instance, was a current British amateur weightlifting champion and a useful man to have as a friend.

One, later to reach national fame as leader of the Liberal Party and for other reasons, was Jeremy Thorpe, who during his short stay with us was very much the dominant personality. For example, our platoon commander, a Second Lieutenant Ogle of the King's Royal Rifle Corps, seemed to have but one job, which was to take the weekly current affairs lecture which the Government of the day had made compulsory. At his first attempt Jeremy, in the nicest possible way (for he was a kindly and very amusing man), so tied up the wretched Ogle with his knowledge and his wit that our commander surrendered and the next few sessions were taken by Jeremy himself. Then came a morning when he went sick, telling us that in his opinion military service and Thorpe were not mutually compatible. We all wondered what he told the doctor that morning, but we never saw him in uniform again. I happened to meet him in a London restaurant some time later but it was at the height of his legal and political troubles and I funked asking him how he got out of the Army.

After six weeks some of the platoon were weeded out as lacking the potential to be officers or NCOs and were sent to join battalions of their regiments. Others, including me, were made acting unpaid lance- corporals which boosted our self-confidence but gave the Regular sergeant and corporals the opportunity to disengage themselves from some of the more onerous and unattractive duties and delegate. Those of us who remained were now allowed to wear the cap badge of the regiment of our choice, in my case the exploding grenade of the Royal Fusiliers. I had no territorial or family claim to that famous regiment and went for it solely because Saunders, the schoolmaster whose influence had led me to the Army, was proud to have served with it in the First World War. Eventually we survivors, after eighteen busy weeks, during which we had become competent and supremely fit infantrymen, who had marched, it seemed, the length and breadth of Ulster, paraded for our passing out. Prizes were presented. Charlie Small, Royal Fusiliers, was Best Recruit, Andy Nelson of the Inniskilling Fusiliers was the Smartest Recruit and I was Best Shot. This honour was marginally due to my own reasonable eye with rifle and the Bren light machine gun, but mostly because some generous fellow had put a few of his shots inadvertently on my target in the final rapid fire practice with the Bren, thus considerably enhancing my score!

Now, at last, we were allowed seven days' leave which included travel time. Deal was about as far from Belfast as one could get and I was home for less than four days before returning to a very new situation in Northern Ireland. The route back was via Stranraer and Larne and on the long, long train journey to Stranraer I was introduced to poker by some of my peers. It was a salutary and expensive experience which I have never repeated. We crossed to Larne on the *Princess Victoria* ferry in really rough weather and I had the impression at one stage that I was the only person aboard who was not seasick. I have always felt sorry for those who suffer from this affliction, and count myself extremely lucky that I am not numbered among them. A few days later the *Princess Victoria* was lost in a storm with dreadful loss of life.

The objective for those of us who sought Regular commissions was the Royal Military Academy at Sandhurst and at that time there were two ways of getting there, both of which included passing the three-day Regular Commissions Board tests. The first was simply to hold Higher Certificate, which gave direct access to the RCB, but in my case there was a potential danger to this route. The RCB would demand a school reference, about which I lacked confidence for the good reasons which I have described. The second route was to take another three-day test called War Office Selection Board, or WOSB pronounced 'Wosbee'. Success here qualified one to train for a National Service commission at an officer cadet school for about five months. Applicants for Regular commissions attended for a few weeks and then took RCB. Those who passed moved at once to a holding unit at Aldershot to await the next Sandhurst term, those who failed returned to continue their quest for a temporary commission.

WOSBs were hard pressed and there was a waiting period of three or four months, which was spent in our case at a holding unit called Cadet Company at Helen's Bay, thirteen miles east of Belfast. My record as a soldier this far had been reasonably good, but now it all began to come unstuck. A fellow soldier at Palace Barracks, Paul Adamson, was a bit of a Lothario and had endeared himself to a very pretty Belfast girl called Sadie. He was not a potential officer and at the end of the course was posted to Egypt to join the South Staffords. He asked me to console the bereft Sadie, a favour which I undertook with great enthusiasm. Falling in love, of course, is not to be missed, but it complicates the life of a busy soldier, especially when the last train back to camp is at 2245 hrs and there are temptations to miss it and accept walking the thirteen miles through the night. This leaves one less than alert, and at Cadet Company alert one had to be. Turnout had to be immaculate, drill precise, and training continued apace. The officers and NCOs were of high quality, especially an Irish Guards sergeant called Whelan.

Early in 1948 we were required to find a guard of honour for Princess Margaret at Stormont House and Sergeant Whelan's job and ambition was to produce perfection. He was a tall ramrod of a man with a fierce, but twinkling, eye, a bristling moustache and a full command of the vocabulary of his kind. On one frosty morning he was even more dissatisfied with our performance than usual and gave vent to a *tour de force* which none of us who was there has ever forgotten. There were thirty or so cadets on parade and he marched along all three ranks, jabbing his pace stick at everyone in turn, and calling each a different insulting expletive, mostly unrepeatable. It was a wonderful exhibition of the Guards NCO's art, and in a rare show of indiscipline we all put our rifles between our knees and clapped, making Sergeant Whelan apparently apoplectic, but surely he must have been delighted. On another similar occasion he fell to his knees on the square, adopted the praying position with his hands together, cast his eyes to heaven and shouted: 'Heaven protect me from these idiots!'

Due to some administrative oversight the officers' mess, which only had four members, was deprived for a few weeks of a cook, and for reasons which were never explained to me and by a thoroughly undemocratic process I was chosen to fill the vacancy. This I did with some trepidation, especially as having to get up at some unearthly hour to start breakfast played havoc with my love life. The officers generally expressed themselves satisfied with my efforts but not so Sergeant Whelan when he took his turn as orderly officer, one of whose duties was to inspect the mess kitchen. I stayed up all night blacking the stove, polishing the saucepans, scraping the tables and indulging in all manner of probably unhygienic practices to give the kitchen and its contents the immaculate appearance necessary for one so demanding as Sergeant Whelan. Satisfied at last, I lit a cigarette, leaned back against a shelf, and admired my handiwork. This, sadly, was the moment Whelan chose to burst in unannounced, and within seconds I was being hustled into the guard room under arrest for 'smoking and idling in the officers' kitchen'. The outcome was a short period of confinement to barracks, which not only jeopardised the love life even further but was the start of a period of distress. Soldiers confined to barracks had to parade for inspection several times a day and it was easy for pernickety inspectors to find fault with them, leading to further confinement. Consequently, once started, it was not easy to complete one's punishment. One became very tired and this contributed to the major disaster which was about to befall me.

There came a night when all the senior people in the camp went to Belfast for the evening and it was known that they would be returning on the train which would arrive at the station, ten minutes' walk away, at 2315 hrs. I was on guard at the front gate at that time, where a sentry box was provided. This was, of course, long before the 'troubles' (everyone, including us, was too frightened of the 'B Specials', policemen who all seemed to be huge and fierce) and there was thought to be no serious threat. It was bitterly cold, so I sneaked a chair and blanket from the guardroom, sat on the chair, threw the blanket over my head, and stuck my rifle into the sentry box roof by its bayonet. I heard the train come in and thought to myself that I now had five minutes before I should need to beware of the returning officers. Muttering repeatedly to myself that I must stay awake for these five minutes had, unfortunately, a similar effect to that ascribed to counting sheep. The next thing I knew was one Captain Cockram of the Royal Sussex being exceedingly rude about my alertness. At Commanding Officer's Orders the next day he proved himself articulate too, describing vividly the removal of the blanket to reveal 'a startled sentry vociferously proclaiming himself to be wide awake'. My fourteen days in the 'nick' were more than fully deserved, indeed I was lucky to get off so lightly, but the most serious effect was the entry on my conduct sheet which would accompany me soon afterwards to WOSB. At that time only about one in ten were passing and anyone with a conduct sheet like mine would not stand a cat in hell's chance. The worst snag was that one only got one go, and failure for me, a Regular soldier, would mean a posting to 1st Battalion The Royal Fusiliers and the prospect of another four and a half years in the ranks, followed by who knew what career.

So now, at last, we come back to Corporal Pyne and his pivotal effect on my life. Corporal Pyne was a regular Royal Fusilier and the company clerk. He was a betting man and ran a book on which cadets would pass WOSB. The combination of the low success rate and his careful appraisal of the candidates enabled him to get good odds and he was known to be a good judge. Now, Corporal Pyne, perhaps for reasons of solidarity as a fellow Royal Fusilier, had decided that I was worth backing to pass, and found an embarrassing number of takers. But this was before my heinous offence. After it he could no doubt see his wagers going down the drain and proving expensive.

In due course thirty of us went off to somewhere near Chester to be put through our paces with lecturettes, discussion groups, initiative tests, and a long interview at the end. I went through the various events with enthusiasm but dreaded the interview, at which I felt sure my conduct sheet would come up and all would then be lost. I was astonished, therefore, when I was not questioned about it. Naturally I was not going to raise the subject myself. When the results were announced I learned to my surprise and delight that I was one of only four out of the group who passed. I couldn't believe my luck. On return to Helen's Bay a few days later I asked Corporal Pyne if he could think of any reason for my amazing good fortune. With a sly and self-satisfied smirk he fished out of his in-tray my documents, which had just been returned from WOSB. Where there might have been a conduct sheet there was a note, illegibly signed but given a rubber stamp of authority, expressing regret that the said document had been mislaid and would be forwarded when found. A temporary sheet was enclosed but no offences were recorded on it.

Corporal Pyne, if you are still alive and this story should find its way to you, please get in touch and I will buy you the best dinner you ever had!

Happily this marked the end of a long period in which it seemed that whenever I took a chance or transgressed I got caught. With hindsight it seems that plenty of chances were still taken but what the police call the 'detection rate' slumped, and from then on I survived my time as a cadet more or less unscathed.

2
Officer Cadet

Eaton Hall, leased from the Duke of Westminster's estate near Chester, was the grand setting for an officer training establishment. The Hall itself housed the headquarters and the cadets were accommodated in huts whose ugliness cut any delusions of grandeur in their new potential officer status down to size. The site has now reverted to the Duke who has controversially rebuilt the Hall to a modern design and, sensibly, removed the huts. I can remember little of the few weeks I spent there but etched upon my memory are three things, the Adjutant, the Regimental Sergeant-Major (RSM) and boxing.

The Adjutant is only remembered because of his name, Hedley-Dent, and the obvious nickname to us all – Badly Bent. He seemed a martinet and his inspections were universally dreaded. Badly Bent was backed by a fearsome RSM, a tall, dominant guardsman with a remote but powerful personality and piercing eyes. One lived and drilled with the constant fear that RSM Copp would single one out for personal admonition. This took the form of bringing those awesome eyes to within inches of the miscreant, staring him into petrified jelly, and coldly demolishing him with acerbic phrases. In our time the only discomfiture was the fact that the winner of the Belt of Honour of an earlier intake, for whose passing out we all had to rehearse, was a cadet destined for the Royal Electrical and Mechanical Engineers. One of the belt winner's privileges was to have his regimental march included in the final march past. The REME marches were the jolly and catchy ditties 'Lilliburlero' and 'Auprès de Ma Blonde' to which we marched with a spring in our step, but for Mr Copp they lacked the dignity and *gravitas* which a regimental march deserved and he very obviously suffered this part of the parade with distaste.

Boxing was a sport which had never appealed to me other than as a spectator and when all new cadets were detailed to attend the gymnasium for a trial before a forthcoming inter-company competition I was not overjoyed. The cadet responsible for conducting the trial was a champion of something or other and my test lasted about fifteen seconds in the vertical position and some minutes in the horizontal. Failure to be selected for the company boxing team was no disappointment, but I revelled in the quality cricket that occupied most of my sporting time at Eaton Hall.

Before long the call came for those who aspired to Sandhurst to attend the Regular Commissions Board and to make their way to Knepp Castle, south of Horsham in Sussex, for the purpose. We faced this with more confidence than the WOSB because the pass rate for those who were already under officer training was over 90 per cent. The tests were generally similar to those of the WOSB but with two significant differences. The first was that the major-general commanding gave every candidate a personal interview of about half an hour, and the second that you had to undergo an educational test on various academic and general knowledge subjects. The uneasily named Major-General Pratt was known to set unusual tests and situations in order to observe the candidate's reaction, such as interviewing while lying in his bath, so we were all prepared for anything. Summoned to his presence within a few minutes of arriving, I was filled with apprehension that my conduct sheet had caught up with me at last, but this was not the case. General Pratt told me that I was the youngest candidate of the group and that he did not want me to have any feelings of disadvantage. I was not to be the 'Cinderella' of the party and to boost my confidence he wanted me to know that throughout his time at RCB he had never failed the youngest aspirant of each group.

My next and full interview with the commandant came shortly before the announcement of results and our departure. I entered his office full of all the right things to say and not to say, only to be told told that I could have the run of the office and its bookshelves and drawers for a few minutes and was then to sit behind the grand desk. He, the general, would sit before me and *I* was to interview *him* as if *he* were the candidate. The only useful discovery in a panic-stricken and cursory search of the office was the general's entry in his copy of *Who's Who*. I cannot remember what I asked, although I do recall his description of a somewhat dubious relationship with his platoon sergeant when serving, for some unknown reason, as a young officer in New Zealand. What I did not realise at the time was that his interview technique was a very clever way of getting the interviewee to ask all of the questions he wanted to be asked himself and perhaps a few that he would prefer to avoid. It was an effective approach and it came as no surprise to learn later that after retirement Pratt was appointed to a psychological chair at Cambridge.

Interview complete, I was treated to advance information about my results. Apparently I had just scraped through the educational test, by virtue of some generous marking, but it was the opinion of the testing officers for the rest of the programme that I should be deferred for another attempt later. The general told me that it was most unusual for him to overrule his team of examiners but he was damned if a whippersnapper like me would spoil his record about the 'Cinderellas' and he would therefore allow me to go to Sandhurst and jolly well justify his confidence.

Those of us from Eaton Hall were so delighted that our progress towards the career of our choice had cleared its penultimate hurdle that we left for London in a euphoric haze that only tumultuous celebration could assuage. We set about so doing with some panache. Unfortunately we did it so effectively that we missed the last train to Chester and found ourselves paraded before Badly-Bent for punishment on return. Not that we cared much because a day or two later we were packed off to Mons Officer Cadet School at Aldershot to join up with potential Regular officers from all over the Army to await the next Sandhurst term. At Mons we found ourselves in the care of the Royal Army Education Corps and another famous RSM. Chalk and cheese one might say.

The stay at Mons was for about three months and our unit was called 'Sandhurst Company'. Its commander was a Major Fowler of the RAEC and he and his officers, all from the same Corps, had the unenviable duty of bringing us to a common academic standard ready for the intellectual challenges of Sandhurst. There was no common starting point and I fear that few of us learned very much, although the regime was a pleasant relaxation after the rigours endured so far. Or at least it would have been but for endless drill parades. These came under the direct supervision of RSM Brittain, a portly Coldstream Guardsman with a voice which today would have brought noise pollution complaints from any Aldershot residents within half a mile. After starring in *They Were Not Divided*, a war film about the Guards Armoured Division, which he described as 'my film', he became a national figure and appeared frequently on television. An expression of the time, 'dead rej', fitted him to a T, indicating as it did a smart but unimaginative soldier of no great brainpower working permanently to rule. There were endless stories about this intensely regimental and dedicated but unrefined man, mostly apocryphal I think, but adding up to a portrait of his character. It was alleged, for instance, that he would don football clothes before filling in his football pools coupon, that when answering a telephone call from an officer he would begin by saying 'I'm saluting you, sir; I shall be grateful if you will acknowledge', and his household was allegedly run with a rod of iron. He was a very good drill instructor indeed and could spot an individual error from an extraordinary distance, as I was once to discover.

We were marching on to a passing-out parade rehearsal and my mind was elsewhere, having just received a *billet doux* from the Irish girlfriend, who, despite the separations brought about by Captain Cockram and Sergeant Whelan, was still in close touch. Suddenly the whole parade, about 300 strong, was called to a halt by the RSM and ordered to face its front, whereupon came the command: 'The third man in the rear rank of Sandhurst Company, COME HERE!' I wondered idly who this luckless soul might be until the whispers of those about me made this all too clear. There followed a few minutes which no doubt gave everyone else entertainment but for me were simply awful. A series of bellowed orders, immediately followed by 'AS YOU WERE' because the response was idle, slow, or simply wrong, eventually found me standing quivering before the awesome Mr Brittain. My turnout was then taken apart item by item, with one particularly galling detail. I was intensely proud of my Royal Fusiliers cap-badge, now a good nine months old, and had worked like mad to polish it to a glistening smoothness. Brittain added this treasure to my list of sins by saying that I could wear a badge as well worn as that when I had been in the regiment for twenty years. The outcome of all this was appearing before Major Fowler the next morning charged with thirteen offences, all written out in detail to describe varying degrees of 'idleness', which was the guardsman's all-purpose expression for dissatisfaction about anything. 'Idle boots', 'idle trousers', 'idle haircut', 'idle about turn' etc etc were all grist to the mill of idleness. Major Fowler was not unduly moved and awarded the standard three days' 'restrictions' (cadet equivalent of confinement to barracks) which was the norm for any failure on the drill square.

There is one more story about Brittain, which I did not hear myself but was assured that it really happened. He was taking a parade one morning when he suddenly remembered that he had forgotten to order sandwiches for some expedition later in the day. He summoned a cadet and ordered him to proceed to his married quarter and convey the necessary instruction. As the messenger fled from the square, and was a good hundred yards from the RSM, the voice bellowed after him at maximum decibels: 'Come straight back here, and don't f--k the wife!'

My road to Sandhurst had had its ups and some near-disastrous downs but it would be quite wrong to assume from my description of it that the downs exceeded the ups. When I leapt from our lorry onto the New College square in the world-famous grounds of RMA Sandhurst I was a supremely fit and well-trained infantry soldier whose enthusiasm for the Army was far from diminished.

The course lasted for eighteen months and was divided into three terms, dubbed Junior, Intermediate and Senior. Progress through these terms took one from the dregs of that society, chased unmercifully from reveille to lights out, through steady progress if not to relaxation at least to being treated, when a senior, as reasonably mature and responsible. Throughout there was a common spirit of all being of an age and in the same boat, and many lasting friendships were formed. The routine was mostly consistent. The day began with breakfast roll call, a parade on which one was inspected and woe betide anyone not perfectly turned out. The morning was usually devoted to military instruction, including endless drill, the afternoon to sport of one's choice, and the three hours between tea and dinner, when most cadets were already exhausted by their day's activities, to academic education, for which there were many possible courses to match academic levels and, to some extent, personal preference. In the latter category, for instance, I was able to volunteer for Russian, meteorology and photography, all of which were both useful and enjoyable.

A common view, which I shared, was that much of the time spent on drill, about one third of the military instruction, could have been better occupied. The end-product on the Sovereign's Passing-Out Parade was very impressive indeed but subsequent generations have shown that similar perfection can be achieved in rather less than half the time. Similarly the military instruction was broadly based upon the organisation and handling of the division, as the lowest level at that time at which all arms and services were brought together. Despite the logic of this there was a common gripe among unit commanding officers of the day that newly-commissioned officers could no doubt handle higher formations in war but knew precious little about commanding platoons and troops, which would be their first duty after leaving.

Once again one encountered a renowned RSM, probably the most outstanding of them all. J. C. Lord, of the Grenadiers, had been captured at Arnhem and had been awarded the MBE for running an other ranks' prison camp in Germany with astonishing efficiency and discipline, winning the respect and, despite unyielding standards, the affection of all the men with him, and building with it their pride and self-confidence. When liberated he met the incoming troops with an immaculate Guard of Honour. Such an achievement spoke of a very special man, and this Jack Lord certainly was. Even now, nearly a half century later, I can remember his first words soon after our arrival: 'Gentlemen, my name is Lord, Regimental Sergeant-Major J. C. Lord, Grenadier Guards. So far as you are concerned J. C. stands for Jesus Christ. When we are on parade I address each of you as "sir", and you address me as "sir". The only difference is that you mean it, and I don't. In other words, you're "sir" to me, sir, but I'm "SIR" to you, sir, and don't forget it. When you are not on parade you address me as Mr Lord, plain Mr; but when we are on parade I'm Lord God Almighty. Now, listen in for the word of command gentlemen.' Lord had romance in his soul. On one occasion with nearly a thousand cadets and fifty instructors on parade he commanded silence, told us how lucky we were to be revelling in God's sunshine on a fine morning, and directed us to 'listen to the sounds of Sandhurst'. These were simple things like traffic from the London Road, cawing of rooks, quacking of ducks on the lake, the hum of motor mowers, the chiming of a clock. But it was a very unusual foray for a Guards RSM and one could not imagine it of a Copp or a Brittain.

Lord on parade was terrifying, but off it a courteous man of singular dignity who earned the highest admiration of us all for his professional standards and conduct. The only time his parade mask was seen to crack was when the Adjutant's horse, tended by a groom while Major Earle was inspecting the parade afoot, bolted, heading straight for the ranks of cadets before it. This was a severe test of discipline and courage under fire. Some wavering was observed as a ton and a half of horse bore down at high speed. Had it continued on its chosen line there might have been serious casualties, but daunted by the (nearly) steadfast khaki lines it turned right and made for the nearest sports pitch where it grazed quietly in the outfield until recaptured. Lord tried to maintain a serious face to match the appalling disruption of an adjutant's parade but could not hide some twitches at the corner of his mouth as the Adjutant gave forcible and noisy vent to his opinions about the conduct of his horse and its groom.

Society was closely ordered and we were issued with a personal book of the Academy's rules, which covered every possible contingency. Compliments to be paid to officers, for instance, took up three full pages. Saluting when in uniform was straightforward, but less so were how to pay respects when in plain clothes (with or without hat) or sports clothes, or how to acknowledge civilian lecturers, and what to do when riding a bicycle. All cadets were issued with a heavy khaki bicycle, extraordinarily prone to punctures, and naturally there were appropriate drill movements. Getting aboard happened in response to the commands: 'Wheels half right turn', 'Prepare to mount', 'Mount'. The equivalent to saluting was to 'ride to attention,' and any newly joined lecturer was noticeably astonished when a passing cyclist would suddenly freeze in an upright position and freewheel past him. The lecturer was required to respond with a 'good morning' or some sort of spoken courtesy, but most of them made do with an airy wave of the hand.

We had to admire, and perhaps envy, Officer Cadet Riley Lord, a rich young man, when, at the end of an exercise on the Hog's Back at lunchtime on a Saturday, he persuaded another cadet to wheel his bicycle back to Sandhurst, and had a light aircraft land on the main road to whisk him off to York races.

Bounds were carefully defined and it was forbidden to enter any public house within three miles of the Academy. A small group of us in my intake and company prevailed upon the landlord and his pretty daughter at The Queen in Blackwater to allow us the use of a back room whenever we rang ahead to book it. We always approached warily through their back garden, and left, perhaps more noisily, at some later time bearing little relationship to licensing hours. Cadets had to wear hats when going out, which was claimed to be the gentlemanly way to dress, but was actually to make anyone breaking bounds more readily identifiable. Given the haircuts inflicted upon us, identification of a cadet was probably easier when hatless. At weekends we had to book out and report in on our return, when a duty under-officer (a cadet in his senior term) would record the time and the letters 'SPD' or Sober and Properly Dressed. Some latitude in the condition required to match this description was often allowed to the more senior cadets, but never to juniors.

Old traditions died hard and some of the establishments and practices enjoyed quaint old-fashioned names. The café, NAAFI or canteen was known as the 'Fancy Goods Store' or 'FGS'. This dispensed sweets and a few useful artifacts like pens, pencils, paper and newspapers but had the main role of boosting the calories at a time when Britain was still severely rationed and army meals generally varied only between the appalling and the disgraceful. Such fare today would generate immediate mass mutiny. It was noticeable that boys from boarding schools adjusted to this far more readily than their day-school peers. The FGS was usually staffed by ladies well past their prime but New College in our time experimented with employing two comely girls named Bunny and Vera. The experiment did not last long. The clientele of the café suddenly doubled and many cadets found the next event pressing upon them long before they reached the end of the queue. It was alleged that the girls could be tempted into clandestine meetings after hours, and further that they both became pregnant, but this was probably untrue and based on wishful thinking.

One of the characteristics of the daily programme was that precious little time was allowed for the frequent changes of dress as we moved from drill to PT, or weapon training to classroom. Not only were fresh clothes required, they had to be clean and smart. Most graduates retain into their dotage the ability to dress quickly and accurately and to be suitably organised for the purpose.

Punishments, other than minor impositions available to cadet courts under senior under-officers, were happily inflicted infrequently. 'Restriction of privileges' was similar to confinement to barracks with extra drills thrown in. Extra drills were tiresome because they happened on Saturday afternoons when one would have preferred to be playing something, or taking leisure elsewhere. In my time I managed to avoid RPs and only suffered four extra drills. These came about because the well-meaning schoolmaster who was mainly responsible for my being in the Army had thought it supportive to get the Army and Navy Stores to send me a bottle of whisky. Unfortunately one of the rules in the book decreed that no alcoholic drink for personal consumption should be allowed to enter the Academy's grounds and when the Army and Navy van delivered my whisky to the company sergeant-major in person in his office there was hell to pay. My total denial of any responsibility was ignored by my rather stuffy company commander, Major Bill Broke-Smith, RA, who gave me a severe rocket before imposing the penalty. I felt aggrieved but there was no redress.

Japes, legpulls and any avoidance or violation of authority which could be kept from authority's knowledge represented fair game. At the end of our intermediate term we conducted an exercise which found the national press but, fortunately, no disciplinary action, Our intake in Marne Company sought a way of getting back at Neil McCance, our company senior under-officer who, in our opinion, could benefit from a touch of enlivening before going off to his regiment, The Royal Scots. John Riggall, a colleague, and I wrote an operational order to the effect that on the morning before his intake's passing-out parade a squad would assemble at 0600 hrs to kidnap McCance, tie him to his bed, and mount it upon a farm cart which had been snaffled by another, similar team and towed by car to the company lines. The whole *équipage* would then be towed to the entrance hall of the Arcade Cinema, near the entrance gates to the RMA grounds, where it would be left to take its chance. Tabloid newspapers were alerted to be present and advised that a kangaroo court might decide that death by hanging was the right punishment for a certain miscreant. If this occurred sentence would be carried out from a lamp post near the Sandhurst gates soon after dawn. I am proud to say that the whole operation went like clockwork. It achieved entries in several newspapers including an article in the *Mirror* headlined: 'Senior Under-Officer, Do Not Disturb' which was the wording of a placard we attached to the head of McCance's bed. In fact he did not suffer unduly, being untied by a postman and taken back to the company in a Royal Mail van, arriving before we did.

John and I also wrote a pantomime at that time about which I can remember nothing other than a couplet which ran:

> From ashes to ashes and dust to dust,
> If the RSM don't get you the Adjutant must.

Leave was quite generous, more, one thought, for the permanent staff's benefit than ours. On one of them I went back to Belfast to visit Sadie, and on another invited her to stay with us at Deal. As a diversion during this visit my father suggested a trip to Calais with Mr Ellis. This gentleman had been a bank customer before the war when he ran a thriving fish and chip shop. Unfortunately an early hit-and-run bomber had scored a direct hit on his shop. Ellis was not injured but suffered a breakdown and when taken into police custody was marching down Deal's High Street singing patriotic songs and scattering pound notes to the wind. He was taken to the mental hospital at Chartham, near Canterbury, but released soon after the war's end. With his Yorkshireman's eye for business opportunities he dropped fish and chips and took up scrap metal, which he managed from a yard in Dover Harbour. This was so successful that he bought a motor boat and started trips across the Channel, one of which Sadie and I were invited to join. The sea was choppy and half way across the boat ran out of fuel. This was the signal for Ellis to reload with jerricans of petrol and at the same time prepare a snack of fried chips on a Primus stove in the well of the boat. The overpowering smell of these activities compounded by the rolling of the boat were altogether too much for Sadie, and she spent most of the crossing hanging over the side.

Our arrival in Calais was deliberately timed to be immediately behind the daily ferry from Dover, because Ellis recognised that all the *douaniers* would descend on the ferry and disregard our little motor boat, which we then took up a narrow creek to be moored while lunch was taken. Having studied French at school for a decade or more I thought myself capable of communicating in the language, but confronted by a docker on the quayside and invited by Ellis to tell him to throw us a rope I was speechless. I could not think of the French word for rope. Eventually I asked him to throw us '*une ficelle,*' a string, which worked but it was a lesson about the limitations of classroom language instruction and the need for practical experience. After tying up we discovered the real reason for Ellis's trip. We were invited to carry cartons of instant coffee, which had been hidden under the decking, to a nearby café, in return for which, during our lunch of, yes, egg and chips, he negotiated a quantity of Parker pens (imitation I suspect) and perfume. Sadie and I sat up on the prow of the boat for the return journey, happily unaffected by *mal de mer* although sadly I never saw Sadie again after her return to Northern Ireland. I fear that life in the fast lane was too daunting a prospect for her.

I am presently engaged in collecting the names and addresses of as many surviving members of our intake as can be found for a possible reunion lunch 'Fifty Years On'. There were over three hundred of us in 1949 and at our only other gathering 'Forty Years On' about eighty dined together at an Oxford college where one of our number was bursar. I was then the only one still serving. Within a year or two we were all of an age, and yet at around sixty our appearances varied from fortyish to at least eighty. One of our number fell dead as he arrived; I hope for better luck than this when we meet again, although it is apparent and hardly surprising that about one in ten has already moved on to the great parade ground in the sky. I hope RSM Lord is there to knock them into shape, but that he will have retired before I arrive.

I am reminded of the remarkable mix of backgrounds of those who made it to Sandhurst and how little that mix intruded in our daily life. There are many claims that the Army was and is an élitist organisation whose officers have all enjoyed a privileged public school education. Even half a century ago this was not true and only about half our numbers came from such schools. This was actually quite surprising because whereas public school education was largely dedicated to producing leaders and preparing them for rigours such as came with Army life, state education was not so orientated. Sandhurst brought everyone to a common level. Certain regiments sought graduates from certain schools perhaps but the class divisions ended there and were rarely apparent during the course.

In the last few months one's thoughts turned to the future and to which regiment or corps would be lucky enough to secure one's services. Cadets were given three choices, one of which could be subdivided into a particular infantry regiment, a group of regiments, or 'any infantry vacancy'. Whether or not one achieved one's first choice depended entirely on one's position in a final Order of Merit. I, naturally, had made The Royal Fusiliers my first choice and had been interviewed and accepted by the Colonel of the Regiment at the headquarters in the Tower of London. I remember being asked if I had the necessary 'private income' for the regiment. With fingers crossed I answered in the affirmative, interpreting this to refer to my only income – that of a private soldier – and was not asked to quantify it. Major-General Harter said that I was acceptable to the regiment but warned me that there might be only one vacancy and perhaps not even that. In the event Tony Teague, who won the Sword of Honour and passed out more than a hundred places ahead of me was accorded the only vacancy. My next choices were: 'Any regiment in the East Anglian Brigade' (because I had heard there would be vacancies there), and 'any infantry vacancy', followed by Royal Army Service Corps and Royal Army Ordnance Corps.

The regiment into which one was to be commissioned was not made known until receiving a letter from the War Office about a week after leaving Sandhurst. It was prudent, however, to order some uniform during the final term because the interval between the commissioning letter and having to report for duty could be short. A number of military tailors had small shops locally in Camberley and I decided to go to all of them in turn to be measured for No 1 Dress – the blue uniform which was the formal dress of the day, and then to choose the one I liked best. Moss, Flights, Gieves, Hawkes and others were efficient but very formal and dull, but Mr Cracknell of Conway Williams was much more friendly. He warmed his hands on an electric fire before taking measurements and readily offered a cigarette to the customer. This, I felt, was a gentlemanly approach and in due course promised Cracknell my custom. The *modus operandi* this followed, as with most tailors of the day, was that they freely extended credit on the surety of a monthly banker's standing order and the prospect of this being increased with each forthcoming promotion until, hopefully, many years later the account might be settled in full. The permanent state of indebtedness of almost all of us in our early years certainly assured the tailor of loyalty, but cash flow problems from this somewhat haphazard system forced many of them, including 'Conway Bill', into closure in the seventies. This was sad because they were excellent tailors and it was a pleasure to do business with them.

At last, on 16 December 1949, we marched gratefully off the square and up the steps into the central Doric portico of Old College, to the strains of 'Auld Lang Syne' and pursued by the Adjutant on his horse. For reasons which I cannot now remember I had no partner arranged for the Ball that evening but one of my friends asked me to take his pretty sister. He further asked me to try to wean her from her unsuitable boy friend who, horror of horrors, was an oboe player. In this mission I failed and Jane is still happily married to her oboe player. I had approached my role with enthusiasm but was hampered by the fact that Jane had to be back in Beckenham to take a School Certificate paper at 0900 hrs in the morning. This meant borrowing a terrible old car, driving it through freezing fog well before dawn and then returning in time for the last breakfast roll call. This final indignity had been imposed after an earlier intake had disgraced itself with 'high-spirited' behaviour after their Ball. This had been a shambles, with some newly commissioned second lieutenants having to be propped between their friends in order to stay upright, but it would have been disloyal folly on my part to have missed ours. Little do the commuters on my route that morning know how close they came to injury as, fresh from the revelry, I steered a large and unfamiliar car over black ice. Jane passed her exam but probably gave little credit to me and no doubt celebrated later with the oboe player.

On Christmas Eve came a letter from the War Office whose first paragraph read:

> His Majesty having been graciously pleased to appoint you to a Second Lieutenancy in The Northamptonshire Regiment, I am directed to inform you that you will ultimately proceed to BETFOR for service with the 1st Bn, You will be prepared to proceed overseas by sea on or after 30th January 1950. Initially you will report on 12th January in person to the Adjutant, East Anglian Brigade Training Centre, at Meanee and Hyderabad Barracks Colchester.

It is no reflection on the fame of the regiment, solely of my own ignorance, that I had never heard of the Northamptonshire Regiment and do not think I had ever even visited the county, which, as a little-travelled Man of Kent, I believed to be fairly adjacent to the North Pole. I was also mystified about the whereabouts of BETFOR. No one at home could enlighten me and no such place was listed in the index to my atlas, so I telephoned Mr Cracknell of Conway Williams to inquire. He gave me the good news that by happy chance his firm was the appointed tailor to the Northamptonshire Regiment, and that BETFOR stood for British Element Trieste Force.

3
Subaltern

The Assistant Adjutant at Colchester, to whom we presented ourselves on a bitterly cold day, was Captain Geoffrey Morgan of the Essex Regiment which was the resident battalion running the Training Centre, a well-built officer with a forbidding moustache who seemed much older than he was. Having reported, the four of us who were joining were shown to a room containing four steel beds, four chairs and some hooks on the wall. In the centre was a beautifully blacked stove which looked as if it had never been host to hot coals. With the room came a clueless National Service batman who, despite the cold, told us that he had been warned not to expect fuel for at least a week. We made our way to the mess where we got as close to the roaring fire in the anteroom as was possible. Almost immediately in came a major who, after introducing himself, told us that halfway across the anteroom carpet there was a clearly defined seam. This represented the nearest point to the fire that subalterns were allowed to approach. The other side of the divide was reserved for captains and above. I think it was almost unique in the Army at that time that in the Essex Regiment subalterns were required to call captains 'sir' and not by their Christian names.

There was little to enthuse about during that month. We were attached to training companies, but not allowed to instruct or interfere in any way. The only event to relieve the gloom of the barracks was a night patrol we mounted to try to obtain some coal from a dump in a dark corner. We effected the theft but discovered a careful quartermaster had sprayed the dump with whitewash. Fortunately this did not help him to identify the thieves. So our dull existence continued until the end of the month and but for this one excursion we might well have wondered whether we had picked the right career.

There were two of us, Peter Worthy and I, destined for the Northamptonshire Regiment and together we were sent to report to the Regimental Depot at Northampton, where our initial impression was less than inspiring. At that time depots such as ours were only used for the purpose of discharging those soldiers whose service, after call-up for the war, was complete. Quite rightly it was felt undesirable for these men, many of them thoroughly disillusioned by peacetime soldiering, to meet the fresh-faced new boys, who would certainly have lost any motivation they might have had. We were greeted as we entered the barracks by RSM Clements. After our experiences of the RSMs of the Brigade of Guards this was an eye-opener. Clements was hatless, wearing a pullover and gumboots, and carried under his arm a basket of chicken food which he was taking to his small squad of hens.

Happily things got better after that. We were cordially welcomed by the small depot staff and the Regimental Secretary and in the evening a number of retired officers living in the area came in to dine and to welcome us. They could not have been more gentlemanly and kind and we began to think that perhaps we were doing the right thing after all. After dinner we were offered the choice of billiards or bridge. I chose the former and admitted that I could not play the latter. 'You'll have to learn, my lad,' said one of the genial old boys, and I took him seriously. When we reached the battalion I mentioned this gap in my training to the Quartermaster, John Lovesey, and for months he and his wife, Nell, had two of us round every week for supper and bridge instruction.

The following day we visited the regimental chapel in the Church of the Holy Sepulchre in Northampton, one of the best-preserved early Saxon round churches, and were regaled with its history by the vicar, Revd Philip Rowson.

Eventually we were sent to Harwich for a night ferry to the Hook, where we boarded the 'MEDLOC' military train, which for two days bore us through Germany, still, especially at Cologne, bearing the scars of war, down beside the Rhine and into Austria. At Villach we stayed the night in the Post Hotel before taking a bus next morning through the snowy Dolomites to Trieste. The road twisted and curved through the mountains with the bus's horn blaring at every bend then, suddenly, from bitter winter we emerged onto the sunny coastline and marvelled at the brilliant blue of the Adriatic.

At last we reached 1st Northamptons in Rossetti Barracks and there found the anteroom occupied by a number of officers who were making and testing a cocktail to be offered to American guests that evening. It was clear that the testing had been in progress for some considerable time and there was a degree of confusion and disagreement. We were invited to give an opinion with our untainted palates and thought it was awful, but had the tact not to say so.

1st Northamptons had recently arrived in Trieste after its two Regular battalions, the former 48th and the 58th, had amalgamated into one while serving in Austria. It was typically one of the old county regiments of the infantry of the line, now decimated by mergers and disbandments. Perhaps not one of the famous names, but with a long history of distinguished, steadfast and at times supremely gallant service the world over. It was particularly proud of having saved the Duke of Wellington's day at the Battle of Talavera in the Peninsular War, and it had fought well in France, Africa, Italy and Burma in the recent war. It was neither pompous nor pretentious, but commendably efficient, and most of its Regular officers and soldiers would claim it to be well above average in the field, if fairly run-of-the-mill on the drill square. Spit and polish were not high among its priorities, although its soldiers at that time claimed to be among the hardest-worked 'area-cleaners' in the Army. Barracks and accommodation were indeed spotless. It was, essentially, a family regiment, and reading back through its history and its casualty lists one came across the same names time and time again through several generations. Having no forebears in the regiment I used to joke that one was not fully accepted until one either married into it or, at least, became a godfather to its members' offspring two or three times. In fact this remark was grossly unfair; the Northamptons were friendly and we were made to feel welcome.

Trieste had been a Free Territory before the war but in 1945 it was claimed by both Italy and Jugoslavia. The dispute had threatened to come to blows in 1946 and an enterprising Major-General Morgan, stationed there, had taken some soldiers out at dead of night with supplies of yellow paint and daubed rocks to define a line to separate the contestants until some political agreement might be reached. This took until 1954 when the 'Morgan Line' was agreed to be the boundary, as it still is. The *status quo* when we were there was guaranteed by 5,000 British and 5,000 American soldiers. The barracks of the respective garrisons were well separated but we met each other frequently in the town, which, mainly because of the free-spending style of the Yanks, offered a swinging night life. We used to argue that the girls of Italy and other nations who descended on Trieste came for American money and British personality. The Americans probably got much the better of this deal, although their social lives were much more restricted and closely supervised, but the British did not do badly.

There were wonderful facilities for low level training. We could exercise more or less anywhere we liked outside the town itself. The hinterland offered rugged, hilly and rocky country with plenty of cover for all manner of tactical settings and we had access to infantry landing craft to practise sea landings on the coast. All this was right up the street of our Commanding Officer, Lieutenant-Colonel D. J. B. Houchin or 'Houch'. He had recently been the innocent party in an acerbic divorce and was a lonely and embittered man who spared little time for anything beyond his duty. The battalion he came to command was at full strength, thanks to National Service, and reasonably well organised, but the senior management had all been through an exciting war and were not wholly enamoured of peacetime soldiering. The sergeants' mess held a great deal of experience and was in quite good order, but from Houch's point of view the battalion's weakness lay in some of its company commanders. Past the first flush of youth, they were hard-drinking men and all too often the worse for that. With gin at 6/8d (35p) and whisky at 8/- (40p) a bottle, the temptation was all too readily at hand. I flinch when I think how much alcohol we all used to consume in those days. In a mess today few officers will take any drink at all at lunchtime, but then some of our seniors would think nothing of three or four pink gins before, wine with, and 'something to ease the digestion' post-prandially. I know now that Houch felt there was nothing much he could do to train these men who were set in their ways and attitudes.

His solution to this problem was to have a care for the sergeants' mess through the RSM, but to concentrate his considerable attention on the subalterns, particularly the Regulars. He had seen plenty of action during the war and was closely interested in his profession in general and tactics in particular. He was severe and few of us could find much affection for him as he ran us with a rod of iron. There was always written work to be done, which he corrected himself, often with unkind, pungent comment, and most of the many exercises which he set personally were aimed at company and platoon level, particularly the latter. We used to moan about it all, particularly about Houch's pointed and rude criticism, but we were trained well and many of us have been grateful for that for the rest of our lives. The Army of the day had post-war blues and few commanding officers at that time had anything like Houch's drive, energy, enthusiasm and tactical sense. Feckless by nature as I was then and dangerously easygoing and irresponsible, I am sure that under almost any other commanding officer my career would have shuddered to an early halt.

On the first morning we were briefed by the Adjutant, Major Wake Clark, and then sent to join our companies. I was to go to B Company, commanded by Major Ted Kitchin who had won an MC at Anzio. I was warned that he had a wound scar on his cheek. If it was livid it meant a bad night before and one would best keep one's mouth shut. This morning it was livid. I was told to draw three maps and three compasses and then take 5 Platoon on map reading for the next two or three hours. Accompanied by an elderly and reprobate platoon sergeant (on whose conduct sheet punishment was recorded for the thought-provoking offence of 'urinating on church parade'), I went into a barrack room in which some thirty soldiers were seated on their beds waiting to assess their new boss. Most were young National Servicemen, but there were half a dozen hardened villains who were waiting impatiently to escape from the Army after their war service. Under normal unblemished circumstances they would have been out by now but as one of them succinctly put it: 'Time in nick don't count.' Time spent in corrective establishments, which would only be for serious offences, was added to the normal date for demobilisation. There were one or two likeable rogues, but also one or two recidivists whose aim was to get out but not to make life easy for newly joined officers. I scrubbed the map-reading instruction as being simply too difficult and ran a wide-ranging discussion about life in the Army instead.

Trieste was an admirable station in which to begin one's commissioned life. Training was hard but mostly interesting. The unit was efficient and would have given a good account of itself in war. There was plenty of sport, and exciting social opportunities off duty. I had two and a half years there and would no doubt have fretted at its size – about twenty-five miles long and only three miles deep – had I not been able to get away several times.

The first escape was back to England for rifle shooting at Bisley. The regiment had had a first-class reputation for 'bullet-pushing' since 1881 and was highly successful in non-central Army competitions (shot on one's own local ranges with results posted back and entered centrally), but had not been at home to send a team to the Army central meeting at Bisley since before the war. Major Nick Ogle, a shooting fanatic, was keen to start this up and by way of reconnaissance entered one officer and four soldiers for the 1950 event. I was lucky enough to be the officer and it was decided that I would take my little team to our Territorial Army battalion based in Peterborough for three weeks' training beforehand. This was my first of many encounters with the TA, which at that time was enthusiastic but starved of resources and parts of it were considered by many to be not much more than an official drinking club. We were welcomed and given plenty of ammunition and range time so that for three weeks we were able to practise shooting from dawn to dusk. We were accommodated at a Royal Air Force Volunteer Reserve camp. There was little time for anything other than shooting but an unusual though not particularly difficult achievement was playing cricket for a team of Royal Air Force Reservists against some WAAFs and scoring a century.

On one of the weekends the TA Battalion, 5th Northamptons, held its own annual rifle meeting. The morning went well but the protracted lunch, at which even the Commanding Officer's cocker spaniel was less than sober, led to calling off the afternoon's shooting 'for safety reasons'.

Bisley itself was good value; we did not win any cups but did creditably and won a number of money prizes for places. The following year we could not go because of pressure on the timetable (or was it cost?), but in 1952 we sent a large team and it was useful that I knew my way around.

Another visit away was to the Oberammergau Passion Play, when the senior subaltern, Terence Stephenson (now Knox), and I stayed at the Army Leave Centre at Ehrwald, beneath Germany's highest mountain, the Zugspitze. We resolved to go to the summit of the mountain but missed the last cable car down and had to walk. In our blazers and cavalry twill trousers we were given pitying looks from earnest Germans festooned with ropes and with crampons on their boots. 'Mad dogs and Englishmen' read their faces. We hired bicycles to go to an American ice show in Garmisch-Partenkirchen, intending to freewheel the ten downhill miles there and return by trail. Unfortunately we missed the last train and arrived back with the dawn after a gruelling uphill struggle pushing our bicycles. The Passion Play itself was a wonderful and moving experience marred only by having to sit on concrete benches for five hours. I believe it is much more comfortable nowadays.

Other times away from Trieste included courses at Hythe on platoon weapons and, later, infantry signals, and a field firing expedition for the whole battalion to Schmelz, high in the Austrian mountains. Houch decided to enliven this enterprise by moving us to Villach by transport but then marching the whole battalion the sixty miles to the training area in four stages. It smacked of pre-war service in India as we marched out every morning headed by the band, who then motored ahead to escort us for the last mile into our overnight base under canvas. I missed the march up to Schmelz because I had damaged my knee playing cricket but Houch wanted to take his new Vauxhall car and invited me to drive it up for him. My duty was to deliver his sandwich lunch at every midday halt and three times this went well. The fourth occasion was disastrous. I had discovered that it was easy to disconnect the speedometer and use the car for unauthorised exploration of Austria before lunch. Unfortunately on one of these wide-ranging forays I lost the route to be followed by the marching troops and only caught up as they were falling in again for the afternoon's hike. Houch was not best pleased to have been deprived of his sandwiches but got retribution in spades three weeks later.

His final live firing exercise, set as usual at platoon level, was to be undertaken by each platoon in turn. They would advance five miles or so up a long valley, coming under carefully aimed fire a dozen times on the way. Houch took the platoon commanders on a reconnaissance detailing exactly what was to happen at every stage – this for safety reasons and so that the subalterns would do the right thing and they and their platoons learn all the right lessons. My troublesome knee had deprived me of training up to that point but it was mending, I was bored, and I decided to limp along on the recce with the others just to watch and sympathise with my friends. As a mere spectator I did not pay close attention to Houch's instructions, but seeing that I could manage to walk the course he ordered me not only to take part with my platoon, but also to be the first to go. At dawn next morning we awaited the signal to start. Houch arrived about fifteen minutes late. For some reason, probably connected with his lateness, he was in a foul temper and covered his own embarrassment by giving me a rocket for not being ready, which I was. Unnerved by this I reacted to the first firing by attacking the position left flanking, not right as had been directed on the recce. Houch was incandescent with rage. He marched us back to the start point and in front of my platoon tore me to shreds. He was so vitriolic that the platoon, although it was all my fault, sympathised with me. They did brilliantly for the rest of the performance and happily no more was said.

It is hard to credit now, when a battalion is established with paymasters, professional clerks and other specialist attachments galore, that in those days the subalterns had all manner of administrative responsibilities which their successors of today are spared. They were responsible, for instance, for managing the pay and the company accounts, with the help of a National Service clerk who probably had no specialist knowledge or experience and had to learn quickly. No soldiers had bank accounts and they were paid in cash at a weekly parade, having declared what, if anything, they wanted to save. The soldier would march to the table, the pay clerk would read out what he was to receive, the subaltern would sign an entry in his paybook and hand over the cash, and the recipient would then salute, turn about and march off. The company accounts were not particularly complicated but were minefields to those who were ignorant of double-entry accounting. An added hazard was the availability of cash in the company safe. It was forbidden to take any of this cash, even in exchange for a cheque or IOU, but the temptation was often much too great for the impecunious, and rates of pay were derisory. A second lieutenant's pay was thirteen shillings (65p) per day and many mess bill charges such as extra messing, mess guests and maintenance were obligatory. There was an awful day when the rate of exchange changed suddenly. At nine in the morning we were all told, without warning, that accounts were frozen with immediate effect and that a paymaster would be coming round to check accounts and cash during the morning. There was immediate panic, and at a hastily assembled meeting the subaltern account holders discovered that thanks to illegal cheques and IOUs there was only enough cash to support one, or possibly two, of the funds. Hurried arrangements were made to pool the cash for the first company to be checked, and then to keep the paymaster diverted while the cash was surreptitiously whisked to the next company and, so on. All was well in the end but there were some hairy moments.

There were some interesting personalities in the battalion and any number of characters. The company commanders, despite some of them being of indifferent quality, all had individuality and gave us plenty to gossip about. Among the subalterns my particular friends were Michael Barthorp and John Wetherall and between us we emerged, largely undetected, from any number of adventures and scrapes. Michael, a pessimist by nature, often hypochondriacal, was never loth to express disapproval of almost anything that displeased him and highly articulate when doing so. He seemed to be permanently deeply in love with girls who failed to write to him and went into deep depression every time he found his letter-rack pigeon-hole empty. Love was not always unrequited and eventually, against hot competition, he won the hand of Penelope, one of the next Commanding Officer's pretty daughters, so life was not all bad for him. Certainly today he looks back on Trieste with considerable nostalgia as he sits in Jersey writing first class and deeply researched books on military historical subjects in his exceptionally elegant English. He has always been wonderfully good company.

John Wetherall was a larger than life character in every way, including physically. He exceeded 6 ft 6 ins and weighed well over seventeen stone even then. Weight was always a problem and in later life there came a time when he was proud of dieting to get back onto the reading of his bathroom scales which stopped at twenty stones. Like Michael he was the third generation of his family to serve in the Northamptons and was always intensely loyal to it. He had a sharp sense of humour, the quickest of wits, and a penetrating voice which he would sometimes exercise before mature consideration. A famous story is of the Brigadier, after a morning inspecting the battalion, coming to the officers' mess with the Commanding Officer and, as his last duty before lunch, checking the officers' mess bill book in the anteroom. It was as he was saying to Houch 'I don't like the look of Wetherall's mess bill' that John himself happened to come through the door as the first one in to lunch. Instantly came the remark 'Neither does Wetherall', which earned him a stern interview with the Adjutant later. John stayed in the Army for over twenty years but, sadly, died suddenly in 1997, some years after retiring from his second career as a stockbroker. He was still serving the regiment on various committees and as its museum curator and was hugely popular. At his funeral, although he had retired as a major of no particular distinction, the village church was packed with some 200 mourners and many more had the service relayed to them by loudspeakers outside in the churchyard.

Plenty of sport was played and we had a particularly good cricket team, although our home matches had to be played on a tarmac square with coconut matting for a wicket. A fast bowler could be quite frightening because although the bounce was true a ball left the matting like a rocket. Naturally there was plenty of swimming and a very popular venue was a long promenade to the west of the town where the sea came right up to its wall. Here there were sunbathers galore at a time when the bikini was just coming into fashion, giving rise to its nickname 'The Meat Slab'.

On our first afternoon in the battalion we went out to watch the weekly cross-country race and Peter Worthy and I were appalled to see most of the other units' runners come in followed by a straggle of Northamptons. Eager to ingratiate ourselves we commented on this all too loudly and were immediately invited to take charge of the team. This we did, with some success, and the following year we won the Command competition; but cross-country in Italian heat is a crucifying sport and I hated it. I tried to get out of it at the beginning of that year but fell out badly with the second-in-command, Major John Rawlins, who ordered me to continue. The standard now was quite high and I remember the last and deciding race for having been particularly gruelling. We won but I came last of our team of ten (fortunately only eight counted for points) and was violently sick soon after crossing the line. I wanted to get my own back on Rawlins and when, soon afterwards, he gave a farewell party in the officers' mess and only offered wine or soft drink I wanted to make it as expensive for him as I could. The mess sergeant, Reynolds, was an ally but next morning I was summoned to the presence of the Commanding Officer. 'Major Rawlins tells me that although he did not offer it he was billed for one and a half bottles of sherry at his party last evening. On questioning the mess sergeant he was told that you were the only officer who demanded and drank sherry. You will apologise to your host and you will pay for the sherry.' Suffering, as I was, from a severe hangover this was a bitter pill indeed.

My memories of our escapades as young officers cause me to wonder how any of us survived to maturity without serious disciplinary action or, indeed, court martial. In my own case the new confidence that I could take chances with a fair prospect of not getting caught led to taking ever greater chances. I will pass lightly over riotous parties with hospitable (and wealthy) Americans to celebrate my twenty-first birthday. They were so good on the actual birthday that we sought out some different ones the next night for another twenty-first. And again the night after that! I will refer but briefly to an historic climb, while far from sober, up one wall, over the roof, and down the other, of the officers' mess, some sixty feet high. Looking at this more than forty years later filled me with awe. I will, though, give two accounts which may give the reader cause to wonder, as I do myself, how this feckless young officer ever reached the higher ranks of his profession.

One of our duties was occasionally to patrol the Morgan Line with half a dozen soldiers and this was popular for two reasons. One was that we were authorised to open fire on any border-crosser who failed to halt when challenged. I don't think this ever actually happened but it added spice to the duty and we tried all sorts of ploys, such as leaving one soldier behind during the patrol to hide himself and lie in wait in the hope of persuading some wretched Jugoslav that the coast was clear. This was as near to active service as most of us had come at that stage. The other attraction was that many of the patrols began and ended at a little *trattoria*, or pub, at Draga St Elia, where we could refresh ourselves after our exertions on the steep and rocky hillsides. The special attraction here was the barmaid and daughter of the house, Velleda Lupidi. Though only a young teenager Velleda was very, very attractive, both in looks and personality. We were all in love with her and visits to Draga were a popular diversion, whether patrolling or simply in spare time. So far as I know no one ever so much as touched Velleda, although we all helped her to pursue her ambition to learn English whenever the opportunity offered. With this in mind I once took my platoon to camp near Draga for a week for field and signals training. This infuriated my fellow subalterns who 'sent me to Coventry' for a few days to express their displeasure at my taking this unfair advantage.

The battalion mounted a guard at an ammunition dump near Sistiana, some ten miles west of the town, and it was the duty of the orderly officer to visit this guard once during the night at a time determined by drawing a card in the adjutant's presence. There came a night when I was orderly officer and had drawn the 'lucky' time of ten o'clock to go to Sistiana. Michael Barthorp was at that time newly appointed as transport officer and the mess sergeant, Reynolds, who is mentioned above and a great regimental character, was battalion orderly sergeant for the day, which meant that he would accompany the orderly officer for the visit. None of us had cars and Michael was keen for any excuse to drive. Over dinner we hatched a plot that he would dress as a private soldier and drive me in the usual

Land-Rover to visit the guard. To launch this idea we had drinks in the mess before leaving and were thus suitably primed, we thought, for our escapade.

All went well until coming back through the town we suddenly had the ludicrous idea that we would check out various nightclubs 'to make sure that our soldiery was behaving itself'. I hasten to add that this was not one of the orderly officer's appointed duties, but we set about it with energy and enthusiasm. It seemed reasonable that we should refresh ourselves in every establishment that we 'inspected' and quite soon Reynolds, with prescience, secured our agreement that 'he should return to barracks by taxi, to make sure everything was all right'. We continued our self-inflicted task until there came a time when it became apparent that although I was still reasonably sober Michael was clearly unfit to drive. Coming out of a nightclub called the Notturno, and standing behind the Land-Rover, Michael agreed that I should drive and went to hand over the keys. Unfortunately he missed my outstretched hand and the keys fell, not only to the ground, but through the grating covering one of the nauseous Trieste drains.

Michael felt unwell but rolled up his sleeve and fished in the disgusting contents of the drain, while I looked on with wrinkling nostrils. At this point a couple of streetwalkers came to see what was going on and with the Italian equivalent of 'Want a hand, dearie?' held a torch so that Michael could see as well as feel what his hand was in. A new complication now was the arrival of two 'Snowdrops', or American military policemen. Thank God they were not British redcaps, who would never have accepted whatever it was we said that sent them on their way. Michael went back into the Notturno to wash his arm and to telephone the barracks for help, which duly came in the shape of a towing truck driven by one Craftsman Davies. My last memory of that awful night is of steering the Land-Rover on tow and simultaneously holding on to Michael's collar while he registered his opinion of Trieste drains by retching out of the passenger door.

The warrant officers and sergeants of the battalion had mostly served in the war and many had been with the all-Regular regiment in India in the thirties. Service with the Raj was their idea of 'proper soldiering' and they wanted to recreate it if they could. One would hear tales of action on the North West Frontier and of famous marches to and from places such as Jhansi and Razmak just as often as of Dunkirk, Anzio or the Irrawaddy. They had a strong sense of duty and took tremendous pride in their regiment.

Part of my education as a subaltern came from the company sergeant-major of B Company, 'Willie' Wilmott. He had distinguished himself in the bitter fighting at Anzio and was now a mature CSM of integrity who exercised authority with a dry style and wit. He may not have been imposing in appearance but his manner brooked no flippancy or lack of respect from anyone. On one morning three of us platoon commanders came into the company office and Wilmott said, 'Good morning, Mr Turnill, good morning, Mr Wetherall, sir,' but ignored me completely. I offered 'Good mornings' of my own but achieved nothing more than a grunt. Later that morning I betook myself for a haircut and, on return, was greeted with 'Good morning, Mr Akehurst, sir.' One of his favourite expressions was in response to any flippant remark by a young officer: 'No time for levities, sir.'

On another occasion, towards the end of a Houchin exercise that had called for considerable endurance, the company captured a hill and occupied it for the night. At dawn there was the usual 'stand-to', when everyone had to take up his defensive position and be alert. Teddy Turnill was very tired and failed to rise. When Willie came round on his morning visit he saw this prostrate figure on the ground still wrapped in its blanket, and gave it a firm kick. Teddy spluttered from his sleep to be greeted with 'I'm sorry sir, I thought you was dead.'

While in Trieste I had occasion to return to England for Easter leave and flew from Milan to London and back in an Elizabethan aircraft of British European Airways. On the return journey I sat next to Stirling Moss, the racing driver, who was going out for talks with Ferrari. On landing only the brakes on our starboard side worked and the aeroplane slewed off the runway to the right across a field, and came to rest with its nose in a hedge. Moss and I congratulated ourselves on being the only passengers, who were mostly Italian, who did not scream and panic.

It was at about this time that Houchin left to command a Territorial Army brigade in Wales and was succeeded by Lieutenant-Colonel Robert Osborne-Smith, a very different character. He was an outgoing, warm-hearted man with a strong personality, Thespian talents, and a marked sense of fun. He was also a very good cricketer and played golf to single figures.

Each spring the three battalions in Trieste took it in turns to set up a range camp at Basovizza up on the hinterland behind the city. These would continue for three or four weeks and while we camped there everyone would fire the compulsory annual practices, and shooting teams would prepare for their competitions. The 1952 camp had special significance for me. Earlier that year Sir Henry Gurney, the High Commissioner in Malaya, had been ambushed and killed. His replacement was General Sir Gerald Templer, who was appointed High Commissioner, and Commander-in-Chief of the forces fighting in the Emergency against the largely Chinese Communist terrorists. This hugely dynamic, forceful and determined man soon made his policies clear, and one of them was to make maximum use of local forces so that when the terrorists were beaten it could be seen as far as possible to have been achieved locally and not just by the Colonial power. He therefore quickly set about creating a Home Guard, expanding and reorganising the police force, and not only expanding but also importing new British officers for the Malay Regiment. He asked the War Office to send out sixty young, well-reported officers as soon as possible.

On a wet and miserable Saturday at our range camp no firing could be carried out and a number of us were playing cards in the great marquee that was our officers' mess. On this occasion it was solo whist, not bridge, and the Quartermaster, John Lovesey, was playing in our group. I remember this so clearly because he had a delightful mongrel dog called Patch who was highly intelligent and knew his master only too well. When John was winning, as he usually was, Patch would sit beside him waiting for the occasional comforting pat. On this day John was losing and Patch was cowering in a corner. Suddenly an orderly room clerk came into the marquee and started putting individual letters in each officer's pigeonhole in the mess letter rack. These letters described very briefly Templer's policy for the Malay Regiment and said that commanding officers were not permitted to withhold applications for secondment. The enclosed proformas, which simply said 'I do/do not wish to volunteer my services for the Malay Regiment', were to be submitted by all officers immediately. There were many discussions over the weekend but on Monday morning Terence Knox, Peter Worthy and I were the only ones who volunteered. In my case it was not because I was unhappy in Trieste, indeed I was assiduously courting the Commanding Officer's other daughter at the time, but a combination of the miserable weather, a feeling that perhaps two and a half years in one small station was a long enough tour, but mostly the prospect that action against terrorists on the other side of the world would be exciting and the sort of thing that soldiers ought to want to do.

At that time I was battalion signals officer and one of my duties was to set up a telephone network throughout the camp. This was operated by a central exchange housed in a warm waterproof lorry that offered cover from view from senior officers who might object to idle hands. I therefore made it my duty to man the exchange myself from time to time. One morning, while fulfilling this mission, I took a call from brigade headquarters down in the town. 'The Brigadier would like to talk to Colonel Osborne-Smith.' 'One moment, sir' said I. I then rang the CO's number and continued to listen as operators were briefly meant to on those old exchanges, to establish that the two parties were in touch with each other. On this occasion they were, but the Brigadier's first words were 'Now, Robert, about these officers for the Malay Regiment.' This was altogether too much for this exchange operator, and to my shame I continued to listen in. This served me jolly well right, because the Brigadier's next words were: 'I think Knox is too good to go, but surely you can spare Akehurst and Worthy without too much difficulty can't you?' The Commanding Officer agreed and I have often wondered if my designs on one of his daughters had anything to do with the decision, or, if not, whether at least the decision afforded him and his wife some satisfaction, or even relief.

The outcome was that in July 1952, some weeks later, while at Bisley, a posting order was received, directing me to proceed to Malaya in August.

4
Malaya

Some thirty of the officers who had volunteered for the Malay Regiment boarded a BOAC Argonaut airliner at London Airport in August 1952 for their three-day journey to Singapore. Each leg of the boring and noisy flight took six to eight hours and there were night stops at Karachi and Rangoon. In Bahrein, where the *khamsin,* that occasional dry, burning and dusty wind from the Saudi desert, was at full blast, we were introduced to the temperatures which awaited us for the next three years. When the aircraft door opened we were assailed, not only as if opening an oven door to see how the roast is doing but also by what is now the familiar and unmistakable Middle Eastern reek of fuel and airport servicing. We sat exhausted in a tatty lounge where ceiling fans gently disturbed the stifling air, drinking pints and pints of squash. To those of us who had not previously been east of Suez it was a daunting experience.

At last we arrived in Singapore where the opening oven door let in another gust of heat, but this time heavy and humid. Acclimatisation takes about three weeks but the most noticeable climatic effect in the days before widespread air-conditioning was the lack of seasonal change. Those who stayed without breaks for leave in temperate zones or visits to the cool Central Highlands seldom realised the change in themselves, but often others could see in Europeans irritability, a loss of stamina and a tendency to butterfly-mindedness.

We moved to the depot of the Malay Regiment at Port Dickson where we were extensively briefed on the regiment and the Malays with their local and Muslim customs, kitted out with uniform including the stiff, oval, brimless *songkok*, and introduced to pay and banking arrangements. It was a comfort after some years of comparative poverty to learn that secondment pay and local allowances would give our finances a useful boost, and that an interest-free loan would be available to buy a car. We spent about a week at the depot and soon realised that Templer had good reason to send for younger officers. The British officers there were mostly on their last tour before retiring and had a style not dissimilar to that of the archetypal Somerset Maugham planter. Routine was important, initiative deplored, and it seemed that like uneconomical cars they needed regular and frequent refuelling. We were glad to get away to our various battalions, where although the average age of the officers was well above what was desirable and the younger reinforcements were clearly needed, at least in most of them there was an air of operational urgency and a commitment to defeating the enemy.

Captain Alan Peckham of the Buffs and I were posted to Butterworth to join 5th Battalion The Malay Regiment, then operating throughout the States of Kedah and Province Wellesley. The camp, at that time housing the battalion headquarters, was conveniently close to the ferry to Penang and consisted mostly of wooden huts, roofed with *attap* palm leaves. The rifle companies were in operational bases up to sixty miles away. We were told by Lieutenant-Colonel Seton Dickson, the Commanding Officer, that we were to spend two or three weeks attached to a rifle company getting operational experience before going to Kota Bharu on the north east coast for a six weeks' language course. Many of the senior Malays could speak English to a varying degree of fluency but few of the soldiers could and to command them properly a good working knowledge of Malay was going to be important.

I was sent to Kuala Nerang, out in the heart of Kedah, to join C Company commanded by Major Ian Craig-Adams who, coincidentally, had also been to Cranbrook School and encouraged towards the Army by the same master as I. He was nearing his forties and substantially overweight, but physically strong and possessed of plenty of stamina and seemingly hollow legs. I was given my jungle kit and the next morning with the whole company I embarked on my first jungle patrol.

There were more than twenty British, Commonwealth, and Malay infantry battalions in Malaya at that time and standards varied widely between them. Early in the campaign it seemed that attempts to learn from the most successful tactics and consequently issue central tactical doctrine had been less than adequate. The Emergency had been running for four years and much of the earlier ones had been spent in reacting to terrorist initiatives by waiting for an incident and then dashing out to try to follow up the perpetrators, usually fruitlessly and often into an ambush. This had been changing fast in the year or so before we arrived; central planning and an overall strategy were beginning to come into effect. This is not a book about the Malayan Emergency, there are plenty of those, but suffice it to say that intelligence was at last earning the prime importance it deserved and the terrorists had been increasingly forced back into the jungle by the sheer weight of numbers against them. They then became very dependent upon food supplies and significant effort and resources were now being devoted to food denial. One of the measures was to collect all the village farming people scattered throughout the country and concentrate them in 'New Villages'. These were then sealed inside barbed wire fences, with no one allowed outside them after dark. Entry and exit were monitored by close searching of the people and their bicycles and farming implements. This meant that the Communist terrorists (or CTs or bandits as they were generally called) had to come in to wired, protected areas to get their supplies, thus exposing themselves to ambush and disruption. This policy was hugely expensive and unpopular but was probably the single most effective weapon in the campaign and eventually it worked.

At Kuala Nerang there was little intelligence about where CTs might be and the patrol programme was simply based on moving through likely areas and hoping for contact. The chances of this on favourable terms were almost non-existent because by this time the CTs had become very skilful at concealing their camps and their movement. A statistic at the time said that over 900 patrolling man-hours were devoted to every terrorist contact. Most of the CT effort was defensive, with occasional offensive sorties, and they were adept at picking up the signs, sounds and smells of approaching security forces. Not, with C Company 5 Malay, that this was difficult. We walked long distances, but mostly along existing tracks and with no serious attempt at subtlety or stealth. I was not much impressed. The Malay soldiers were by now well experienced in jungle skills, tracking and movement and, competently led, could be silent, alert and aggressively brave. They were not natural fighters like, for instance, the Gurkhas, and this is why effective leadership was so important. The men, all of whom were Muslims but of varying enthusiasm for their religion, were mostly of *kampong* (village) origins and averse by nature to hard work or initiative. The country Malay is, or at least was, a friendly, easygoing, cheerful, lighthearted and lazy person but he could be trained and led into becoming a keen, smart, clean, resourceful and reasonably aggressive soldier. These potential talents were being wasted in C Company and, I suspect, in many other companies too. The next year or so would see a big difference throughout the country. For myself I learned what I could about countless new skills and practices. We carried rations for five days. After that time we either took an airdrop or, more usually, returned to base. How to assemble one's equipment and pack it comfortably was an early lesson but there was much else that was new. Communications by radio, hand signals, how to make a comfortable dry bed for the night, mess tin cooking, when to cut and when to duck the jungle foliage, navigation and learning to look through the vegetation and not at it. All these were intensely interesting and equally important to have in one's personal armoury.

The next adventure was the language course. This was run by a pre-war Guards RSM, now a major, Norman Staniforth. He had been imprisoned by the Japanese when RSM of a Malay Regiment battalion in early 1942 and spent his captivity perfecting his command of the Malay language. At its basic colloquial level it is one of the easiest languages in the world. There is little grammar, no declension, no definite or indefinite articles, tenses are created by the addition of a word to the basic verb, plurals by simply saying the single noun twice and there are no changes caused by gender. One can become colloquially competent just by learning vocabulary. Refinements do exist, creating a different style called *Bahasa Dalam*, or Inner Language, but it is only for the most formal use and unnecessary to learn for day-to-day conversation.

Kota Bharu in Kelantan was an idyllic place, untroubled by terrorism and made famous by Neville Shute in *A Town Like Alice* for its *Pantai Chinta Berahi* or Beach of Passionate Love. It was the home base of 3rd Battalion The Malay Regiment and occupied only by a very small staff and the families of the battalion which was in Pahang on operations. There were no distractions from learning the Malay taught by the overwhelmingly enthusiastic Staniforth. He encouraged us, as strongly as he could, to practise the language at every possible opportunity and recommended that we should go in to the little town on as many nights as we could afford it. There were several *ronggeng* (Malay style of dancing – no touching!) bars, but Staniforth promoted one in particular where he had schooled the girls into giving language practice to his students. In Kelantan there are many people of mixed Malay and Thai descent and the girls were both charming and pretty, so our linguistic exercises were not only practical but also a delight.

Having passed the course, and thus the colloquial test for a little language pay, we were about to depart when Staniforth told me that he was at the end of his tour and was about to go off on three months' leave, possibly not to return. He had applied, he said, for a promising student on the course to remain at Kota Bharu, swot up the language further for the next month, and then teach the next course coming in. He had chosen me for this and I was therefore to stay where I was until receiving further instructions. When Seton Dickson heard of this plan he exploded, saying that it was an ideal job for an elderly officer difficult to employ elsewhere but that he wanted his signals-trained officer back with the battalion by the day before yesterday. All this occupied about three weeks which I spent pleasantly brushing up Malay, but Dickson prevailed and back to 5 Malay I went. With hindsight this was absolutely the right thing, although I confess to rather enjoying the Shangri La style of Kota Bharu and being mildly regretful at the time.

The next two and a half years were exciting and eventful, with a year and a half in battalion headquarters followed by a year on jungle operations with a rifle company. To describe them in diary style would, I feel sure, be time-consuming and boring to the reader. I shall confine myself to what for me, were the highlights.

At first I was just signals officer and enjoyed the challenge of keeping in voice touch with those out in the jungle. I was then made intelligence officer as well and thus became what might now be called operations officer. All this was marvellous experience for a young lieutenant, enhanced I have to say by working for a commanding officer whose experience had not really prepared him for this appointment. He had to devote much of his time to administration because of a distinctly dodgy quartermaster, who later left under a very dark cloud. In effect I had virtual operational day-to-day command of the battalion – and loved it.

With a year still to go in 1954 I was beginning to feel self-conscious and deprived to have jobs that rarely took me out to the sharp end. There came a day when the General Officer Commanding, Major-General Hugh Stockwell, whom I had last met when he was Commandant at Sandhurst, came to visit the battalion forward tactical command post which was established in a garage behind the police station in Kulim. He asked if I was enjoying the work and I said that indeed I was but that I did not want to finish my tour without spending time with a rifle company on operations. The general was extremely forthright and ticked me off severely for complaining, telling me to get on with what I was told to do. Others knew better than I where I could be of most use. He was of course right, but two weeks later I was moved to D Company, where I began by being second-in-command and then, briefly, commanded. The policy was to 'Malayanise' the Army as quickly as possible to prepare it for the national independence which could be seen clearly on the not too distant horizon. The effect of this on me was that in six months I went from company commander to second-in-command to platoon commander in that order, while one of my erstwhile Malay platoon commanders went from lieutenant to major. This was perfectly logical and fair policy. It caused no resentment other than in losing the valuable pay of captain when I reverted to my true rank of lieutenant. But this is to move two years ahead.

The day of the Queen's Coronation in June 1953 was an eventful one for me too. One of our companies had suffered a fatal casualty to a single shot fired in the jungle. They were miles from the nearest road but the policy was always to recover our own dead for proper burial and although there were then few helicopters in the country one was made available to collect our body. There was no suitable clearing anywhere near the incident and the company had to carry the body for five days before they could find somewhere for a helicopter to land. I decided to fly with the pilot to help with communications and navigation if necessary and eventually we found the clearing and set down. My former company commander, Ian Craig-Adams, came up to the machine as soon as the rotor stopped and his first words were 'I'm sorry but he's gone off a bit.' This was all too obvious to the pilot and me. It was a tiny machine and there was no way the grisly package could be stowed inboard. It had to be wrapped in poncho groundsheets and lashed to the belly of the aircraft between the wheels. It was a relief to take off and escape from the awful stench. We flew back to Butterworth where the Station Commander and our Commanding Officer awaited us at the landing site with a large party of pall-bearers and mourners behind them. As we touched down and the smell hit us again the two commanders decided to salute. This was suitably respectful but they seemed unable to agree upon when to stop saluting. After a minute or two the pilot said 'I don't know about you, mate, but I'm off before I'm sick!' Out he got and walked away across the tarmac. Still the commanders saluted. Eventually I decided to take the initiative, got out of the helicopter and began to untie our package. It was only when one end of it thumped squishily on the tarmac that at last formality ended and soldiers were ushered forward to take over.

An hour after getting back to camp, bathed and changed, we were celebrating the Coronation with champagne and brandy in the sergeants' mess, where the RSM, Griffiths, formerly an Ulster Rifleman, and one or two technicians were British but the great majority Malay. In the midst of this party we learned that Everest had been conquered at last, which added to the gaiety and the necessity for further toasts. The horrors of the morning were soon forgotten and I left a while later to go to a ball at the Runnymede Hotel in Penang. I mention this because it was planned that I should meet there a blind date, one Shirley Webb, the seventeen-year-old daughter of a Malayan civil servant. I arrived to find that she was unwell at home but that her younger sister Brenda would stand in. Helped no doubt by the earlier celebrations with the sergeants I regret to say that I remember little about the evening. I learned later that Brenda had been unimpressed. Soon after this the Webb family moved to Alor Star, the capital of the state of Kedah, and 5 Malay moved into a new barracks, also at Alor Star, beside the airfield that had been one of the Japanese Army's first objectives in December 1941. This coincidence meant that I soon met Shirley, my original blind date, and we have now been happily married for more than forty years.

Well in advance of the battalion's move into its new barracks the Commanding Officer and I set up a tactical headquarters, really a communications centre, at Alor Star because our operations were now concentrated in Perlis and Northern Kedah on the Thai border. Seton Dickson moved into his quarter a couple of miles away and I became the first, and for a month the only, resident of the new officers' mess. One embarrassment was continual attention from enterprising contractors who sought control of food supplies, maintenance, cobbling, hairdressing and all the other lucrative businesses that support a community of 800 men and its families. I was made many direct offers for personal gain and these were easy to decline, but I would also often find packages of food, drink or totally useless trinkets left at the mess entrance with no indication of their origin.

During the next three months of operations there were, for me, two incidents of note. Intelligence was, at last, improving as increasing numbers of CTs surrendered, higher rewards were paid for information, and more of the population hitherto coerced into supplying the terrorists recognised which side was going to win in the end and decided to back the winner. One such item concerned the delivery of food by a Chinese man to a particular point on a lonely road where it would be collected by a small group headed by a leader who was high on the wanted list and had a valuable price on his head. The informer expected to meet the party at a certain time and described exactly where this would be. At that time information as reliable as this for ambush purposes was keenly sought after by the rifle companies, but if something came up for action at short notice it was sometimes given to me and my intelligence section, which comprised experienced Malay soldiers who were also good shots. On this occasion we were given only three days' warning and the police Special Branch advised that any reconnaissance would have to be covert. Consequently, at four o'clock the next morning I was loaded into the boot of a policeman's car and driven thirty miles to be dropped off at a point near the ambush site before dawn. I was to remain in the area until soon after dark in the evening. Apart from possible CTs there was probably no one within five miles of the spot and I had a lonely and creepy day prowling around, checking likely approaches, siting the ambush in detail and being ultra-careful to leave no trace of my presence.

I had no idea from which direction the CTs would approach or, later, depart with their supplies. The ambush party was to be dropped off from a small police truck in much the same way that I had been and was therefore limited to six. With this number we could not cover all possible approaches so the ambush would have to be sprung while the food was being unloaded from the informer's car. I therefore picked a fire position on a small ridge thirty yards away which would give a good view of the pick-up point, and from which we could throw grenades to the most likely withdrawal route. To be further away would make accuracy of shooting less reliable and put the informer's life at greater risk.

After a day to make models and to rehearse in detail we took up our positions according to plan and lay motionless for about nine hours until, two hours before delivery time, we heard the CTs arrive, unpack and start to cook a meal about fifteen yards away from us through the undergrowth but out of sight. Thus we stayed for about an hour and a half when the CT leader took the wise precaution of putting out a sentry. Unfortunately his choice of the vital ground was identical to mine. By luck or by prudent skill I had placed Sergeant

Majid toe to toe behind me to protect my back. He allowed the sentry to come within six feet of him and then had to open fire, seriously wounding the young Chinese terrorist who dropped down a slope into bushes. The rest of the party, still out of sight, beat a hasty retreat, pursued by a fusillade of fire and grenades which shed some blood, but they got clean away. The wounded man was crying out '*Saya mati-lah*' (I'm dead), which raised little sympathy, but by the time we got to him it was true. Half an hour later the informer arrived and we had to tell him of our failure. Quite rightly he became extremely agitated, having suddenly become exposed to serious risk of reprisal and also having lost some of the reward money because we had not killed the leader.

There was an unusual sequel to this little action. Much later, as Shirley and I were being driven from our wedding in Alor Star to the reception, our car was overtaken by a Chinese who looked in and waved. It was the informer, who had waved simply because it was obviously a wedding party. When he saw at whom he was waving his expression changed and he roared off at high speed. I was comforted, though, to know that no murderous reprisal had been taken against him.

The other story from this period is very different. One of our platoons, commanded by Richard Greenfield, a National Service subaltern (and later a journalist with a national newspaper), was patrolling close to the Thai border and had been out of communication for a couple of days. This was not all that unusual with the fairly basic high frequency radios of the day but the border was a sensitive area and we decided to call up an Auster air observation light aircraft and go out to look for them. The aeroplane was piloted by Mike Hickey, a fellow member of my Sandhurst intake. We soon found the platoon, with whom all was well except for their radio, and were flying back at about 1,000 feet when suddenly Mike turned sharply to his left and pointed down. He had spotted a bandit camp and there, in the middle of it, was a bandit looking up at us. This was a perfect target for an airstrike by the Hornet fighters based sixty miles away at Butterworth. Unfortunately there was no way we could communicate directly so we hastened back to Alor Star and telephoned from the air traffic control post there. It was agreed that half an hour later we would meet the Hornets in the area and although we could not talk to them we would mark the target with smoke and they would attack it.

We returned to the area and soon afterwards four Hornets arrived and circled above us among light cirrus clouds. We flew to the camp and dropped our smoke marker in the centre, although at this time we could see no sign of life in it. As soon as we were well clear we waited for the attack. And waited. And waited. The pilots told us later that they had been unsighted by cloud, but we were furious because during the delay, of some fifteen minutes, the wind blew our smoke about 600 yards south of the target, where eventually it was accurately bombed and strafed. A follow-up patrol found the camp and a quantity of stores and food but no sign of the occupants.

This story, too, had an interesting sequel. Nearly a year later Mike Hickey and I were at a party with Frankie Brooke, the Brigadier. He told us that a bandit had just surrendered and amongst other things had recounted his experiences of the day of our airstrike. He claimed to have been the chap looking up at us from the camp and said that he and his companions had guessed that air attack might be imminent. They therefore decamped at speed and ran, unfortunately for them, 600 yards south! The bombs and cannon fire struck among them and two had been killed and three wounded.

5
Malaya – Operation Sword

In mid-1953 intelligence pointed to the CT regimental commander, Toh Kar Lim, having set up his headquarters in the Bongsu Forest Reserve in southern Kedah. This was an area of primary jungle some twenty miles square, surrounded by a perimeter road but otherwise trackless. It was decided that 1st Malayan Infantry Brigade would mount a major operation to clear this area and eliminate the CTs in it. Two battalions, ourselves and 1st Battalion The Manchester Regiment were to be engaged and we were each given a particular area of the forest for which to be responsible.

The Manchesters, commanded by a very entertaining character, Lieutenant-Colonel Neville Close-Brooks, were based in Penang. Their operational record left something to be desired because they were the only battalion to have caused more casualties to their own side through negligent discharges than they had to the enemy. My only contact with them to this point had been as a member of a court martial. The accused was a thoroughly evil National Service soldier in his early twenties who had been forcing younger, nervous privates to give him money either by threatening them with a bicycle chain or telling them that he would direct his gang back in Manchester to hurt their parents. We had no hesitation in awarding the maximum two years' imprisonment but as he was being marched out he stopped, pointed at the members of the court and said convincingly 'You're next.' No doubt to judges and magistrates this is commonplace but this man was so satanically malicious that I determined not to go anywhere near the Manchesters or their home town on a dark night in the future.

5 Malay were to set up a tactical headquarters in a large garage behind the police station in Kulim, the principal town of the area. To prepare for this the Commanding Officer and I, as his intelligence and signals officer, went to discuss the operation with Superintendent Murphy, the flamboyant senior policeman in the District, who, as one might guess from his name, was very much an Irishman. We were to stay the night in Kulim and Murphy had obtained for us the house

of a couple who were back in Britain on long leave. This was a rambling, wooden, colonial-style house and having been given the keys we went to set ourselves up there.

Seton Dixon decided to take a room just inside the front door on the right at the foot of a staircase and I, up the stairs and across a landing, a room that faced the back of the house. It was a split level building and my room was level with the ground at the rear. I dropped my suitcase just inside my room and then went down to attend to Seton's wishes before we went out to the local club for supper with Murphy. When we got back to our house and I went to my room I noticed that my case had been moved to the other side of my bed. This was suspicious, because only we had the keys and there were no staff. An hour or so later I was under my mosquito net reading when there was the distinct sound of someone having jumped down from the window onto the wooden floor. I could see the window, which was open, but no sign of what had made the noise. Then I heard the sound of footsteps making their way across the room, past my bed, through the open door and down the stairs. At this point there was a spine-chilling screech and I leapt out of bed to investigate. The noise had come from a ginger cat which was rigid on the stairs hissing with fright and with its fur standing on end. Seton then rushed out of his room and said that the brushes and things which he had put on his dressing table had been hurled across his room. Sleep for the rest of the night was, at best fitful, but there were no more incidents. We told Murphy this story the next morning and he then told us for the first time that the house had a reputation for such happenings. It had been a Japanese *Kempetai* (not unlike the Gestapo by reputation) headquarters during the war and a sergeant of The Royal Scots had been tortured to death there and was believed to visit from time to time. We moved to another house!

There was a large open garage behind the police station and when operations began we established our headquarters there, and by partitioning it off with canvas marquee walls set up areas for the radios and for talking, eating and sleeping. This was to be home for the next six months as Operation Sword, as it was called, ran its course.

After a few days of patrolling to become familiar with the area, brigade headquarters ordered an operation which we considered to be little short of dotty. Operations on brigade scale were largely experimental at that time and the Brigadier put forward a pet theory. This was based on his assessment of several operations in which intelligence had indicated that CTs might be encamped in a particular area and the tactics had been to surround it with 'stops' and then get one group of those stops to move in and assault. Such tactics, he said, were seldom successful and he thought the wily CTs had found a way of escaping them. He would surprise them. His master plan was to march in two complete battalions side by side, forming a double line about two miles long. The battalions would then turn outwards and set off through the jungle away from each other. The thing went on for three days but no CTs were contacted, which came as no surprise to most of us. Apart from anything else moving through thick jungle in extended line is seldom possible.

Our Commanding Officer decided, I think to find favour with the Brigadier, that he would mount a broadly similar operation and would march our battalion in to form a long straight line, allotting about a mile to each company. The line would then set off through the jungle until it came out some five miles further on. Our three company commanders thought this idea as crazy as the Brigadier's and were strongly opposed to the whole thing. They were to move off at dawn and I went out to spend the night for old times' sake with Ian Craig-Adams and C Company who were getting what sleep they could in some abandoned rubber tappers' lines. I have an ugly but vivid memory of waking in the half light to see the massive frame of Craig-Adams, in a sarong, standing on the little concrete patio of our hut with a bottle of Tiger beer to his lips inserting liquid at one end while simultaneously ejecting it at the other.

I saw off the companies on their mission, accepting the grumbles of the company commanders who were in a state of near mutiny. I later learned that this was increased when they discovered that there was more than the usual *belukar* (thick secondary jungle) to fight their way through before reaching the easier going in primary jungle.

Communications with those in the jungle were by 68T high frequency radio. The technique was to raise a vertical wire aerial as high as possible. This was done by tying a heavy stick to string which was joined to the aerial. The stick was thrown as high as possible over a branch, lowered back to ground level, and the aerial could then be pulled up to the branch. Reception at headquarters was by means of a 62 radio with a huge horizontal H-shaped antenna. Mostly this system worked quite well by voice although it was subject to interference and signallers had to be trained to send and receive by Morse code. In order to economise on air time and not to interfere with movement the routine was to call up the companies and platoons at 0700 hrs and again at 1710 hrs. The headquarters would remain open all day on 'listening watch', so that anyone could call them at any time with urgent messages or news of contacts. Movement at night was rare in the jungle for practical reasons and battalion nets usually closed down from about 1830 hrs when interference became unworkably bad.

On the particular operation that I am describing the evening call to the companies was unusually clear. The commanders replied in quick succession as soon as I called and, while announcing that no contacts had been achieved, gave their positions as being according to the orders they had been given. The Commanding Officer congratulated me on the excellence of the communications and went off happily. I had dark suspicions which were found to have been justified when some time later one of the company commanders told me that the going had been so difficult that they could not possibly get the leading companies as far as they were meant to go. They had therefore agreed on mutiny, stopped all together in one place and were sitting round all using one radio. The operation, hardly surprisingly, got no useful results and thereafter, with one exception, the companies operated in their own areas, patrolling and ambushing, and significant numbers of CTs were killed or surrendered to the battalion.

After one night ambush in which two CTs were killed and another wounded I went out with a party from battalion headquarters to help search for the wounded man. At one stage I waded along a stream which had thick undergrowth on either bank. About a month later a CT surrendered because his wound would not heal. He was brought to the police station where I went to look at him. He was a scruffy and very sick-looking Chinese individual who had been totally apathetic up to that point. However when he saw me his pallid, emaciated features lit up. 'I saw you' he said 'when I was hiding by a stream and you were looking for me. My rifle was pointing at you and I could have shot you, but I knew that if I fired I could not possibly have escaped.'

Our B Company had one singularly successful operation. The company was commanded at the time by Captain Tengku Ahmad, known as Tengku Bab, who later became the Malaysian Chief of Defence Staff. They had pursued a group of CTs to a large jungly copse in a rubber estate, which they surrounded. The eight CTs would not accept calls to surrender and made a run for it. Unfortunately for them they chose the line of escape best covered by fire and were all gunned down. It was common practice at that time to display the bodies of dead terrorists for the public to see, partly to show the people who had been killed, partly to discourage anyone thinking of supporting the terrorists, but mainly to show that terrorism did not pay and would only reach one conclusion. This grisly practice was effective but of doubtful morality and this particular exhibition of eight bodies outside the police station was photographed and reached a British national newspaper under the headline 'The Star Turn – Bandits' Bodies.' Barbara Castle expressed disgust in Parliament and shortly afterwards the practice was rightly vetoed.

I had a bitter disappointment at this time over a potential intelligence coup. The CTs had no radio network but they did have receivers to keep in touch with the outside world. One of our soldiers went to a radio repair shop in Kulim and the Chinese owner whispered to him that he had been passed, through a third party, a radio which he understood came from Toh Kar Lim's headquarters and which he was given one week to repair. As soon as I heard I telephoned the Technical Staff branch at Malaya Command headquarters in Kuala Lumpur and asked if they could fit some sort of bug into the radio which emitted a signal detectable and traceable from the air. If they could do this we would have constant knowledge of Toh Kar Lim's whereabouts for at least as long as the power source lasted. Perhaps it could even be powered through the radio's battery. There could be inestimably valuable operational consequences. Even in 1953 such a device must have been available somewhere. Even if it had to be flown urgently from the United States it would have been well worth the expense. To my intense chagrin they described the effort as 'too difficult in the timescale' and nothing came of it, although we did successfully ambush the party that came to collect the repaired set.

We had four British National Service officers in the battalion and one of these was Derek Wilford, later well known for having commanded the Parachute Regiment battalion on Bloody Sunday in Londonderry in 1972. He was one of those people to whom things happened and it seemed that whenever he went on patrol or set an ambush there would be some sort of CT contact. There was argument about whether this was due to luck or skill but the characteristic was exemplified on Operation Sword. There came a time when we had a fairly accurate fix on Toh Kar Lim's headquarters position and we were keen to mount an operation to attack it. Sadly from our point of view the matter was taken out of our hands and it was decided that it would be an ideal target for the recently developed technique of dropping the SAS into the jungle by parachute in strength. We and the Manchester Regiment were to form a square perimeter with sides about four kilometres long, which is easy on a map but a very different matter in the jungle. I went out on this operation myself and at one time was under heavy, but happily inaccurate, fire from a Manchesters' patrol which was lost and more than two miles from where it thought it was. The SAS drop duly happened but several things went wrong and they suffered accident casualties in their drop. We on the perimeter were then sent in with medics and stretchers to help with the casualties and the CTs melted away. Their camp was found but it had been vacated.

The only success on the operation was scored by Derek Wilford and his platoon. On their way in to their cordon position they stopped for something to eat and while they were there a lone terrorist came into their camp and asked to surrender. Derek told him this would not be acceptable unless he divulged immediately where his camp had been. This he refused to do. At this time Derek's signaller, Corporal Zainal, was throwing up the string to lift his aerial, in order to get through to report the incident. The CT on seeing this was convinced he was about to be hanged and immediately agreed to tell all he knew, which confirmed our information about our target.

It was during Operation Sword that I had the first of my direct contacts with General Templer when he came to visit. He wanted to see some of the troops involved and also some of the villages in the area. I was detailed as his guide and we set off in two scout cars, he in one and I in the other. We were to pass through a 'New Village' and soon after going through the gate I was given orders to halt immediately. Templer was a terrifying figure, well known to have a sharp temper and an acid tongue, and I wondered fearfully what was the problem. The great man leapt out of his car and across a ditch to where three Tamils were swinging their scythes to cut the grass outside a building. I rushed after him just in time to interpret what he had to say to these bemused and very nervous men. 'You are one of the reasons why we are going to beat the terrorists and win this Emergency,' he said. 'The government has set up these New Villages and unless they look clean, smart and efficient they will not be serving the purpose for which they were created. You are doing your bit to keep this village smart and I just wanted to thank and congratulate you.' He then galloped back to his scout car and on we went. The Tamils were totally astonished by this performance but one can guess that within minutes the story, no doubt much embellished, would be all round the village, and another blow was struck for public relations.

Soon after arriving in Malaya I had taken advantage of the interest-free loan offer for buying a car, which had to be new and British according to the terms of the loan. I settled for an MG TD in British racing green, which gave me endless pleasure for the next three years. It was a fun car which I loved driving, but I regret to admit that I seriously crashed it early in its life. There was a girl, Elizabeth Elphinstone, whose fiancé had contracted TB and been sent home for a cure. She was very down and at a dance at the Kedah Club I offered to cheer her up by taking her for a spin in the MG. This was in Alor Star where I had only recently arrived and did not know the geography well. I asked Elizabeth to suggest a route and off we went. 'It's straight along here,' she said, 'you can put your foot down.' The straightness lasted for only half a mile and the road then bent sharp left. I failed to take it and we dropped into the eight-foot deep ditch still travelling at a good pace. But for a wooden bridge at precisely the right place we would have toppled right over and might well have been killed, but we came to a sharp stop with our nose in the water. Elizabeth appeared to be unconscious and I shouted 'Liz, Liz, for Christ's sake wake up!', which, thank heavens, she did, being just winded and badly bruised. I only had a couple of cuts and bruises and we had been extraordinarily lucky. I went next morning to the garage where the remains of my car had been taken and looked ruefully at the considerable damage. 'Nasty mess innit?' said a passing British mechanic. I had to agree. 'Yeah,' he went on, 'couple was killed in that last night.' I was later charged by the police with driving without due care and because Elizabeth just happened to be the daughter of the Chief Police Officer made no defence and paid my fine without complaint.

By the time of Operation Sword Shirley, the girl who should have been my blind date on Coronation Day, and I were deep into courtship. The country was full of young British men serving with the forces, the police or in the many business enterprises and there were not nearly enough girls to go round. Competition was fierce and I was determined not to lose out through being away in Kulim which was ninety miles away. Every Thursday night there was a dance in the Kedah Club in Alor Star and I negotiated with the Commanding Officer that I could be released from the headquarters from after the evening radio call until the 0700 hrs call on Friday morning. This gave me thirteen hours to clean up and dress, drive ninety miles, attend the dance, say goodnight (this could take quite some time, and for the purpose we had our own special spot by a local cemetery), and then drive the ninety miles back to Kulim. Keeping awake on this journey was often a problem. Some of the road was susceptible to ambush and when tiredness forced me to stop for a few minutes I picked the spots to do so with some care. My favourite was in the middle of a long pontoon bridge and I kept a weapon ready on my lap just in case, though fortunately never had cause to use it. Looking back on this time it is abundantly clear that I must have been very seriously in love.

It was near the end of Sword that I proposed and was accepted. I went rather formally to Shirley's father to seek his approval. He had been fully briefed by his wife on what he was to say and this was that Shirley was still only eighteen and in their opinion needed longer in which to make up her mind. It was therefore agreed that she would accompany them on their forthcoming long leave in England. If things were still the same on their return they would agree to a wedding in mid-1955. Love had to be convincingly proved again and during four months' separation we each wrote every day. I numbered mine and the last one was 127.

There was one snag in what was proving to be a wholly satisfactory relationship between us and our plans for the future. The first hurdle for promotion in the Army was a written exam to qualify for elevation to captain. In 1953 I had been summoned to Taiping at twenty-four hours' notice to sit this exam when I did not even know that passing such a test was necessary, let alone its syllabus. It was not particularly difficult if one had spent a little time preparing for it, but this I had not done. It was hardly surprising therefore that I failed one of the three papers (Military Law), and would have to wait another year before I could sit the exam again. I told Shirley that if I failed a second time I would have to think again about getting married. If I fell at the first hurdle I would have to assume that I was in the wrong career and start again elsewhere. I felt I could not visit such uncertainty on a young wife.

About a month before the exam the following year I took a week's leave and went to stay with a friendly police lieutenant in Sonkhla, Thailand with the intention of studying seriously. This, I found, was not too easy in the Thai police social scene, but I managed to work during the daytime and returned to Malaya reasonably confident. The exam was again to be sat in Taiping, about a hundred miles south and I was just leaving the mess in Alor Star when I was called to the telephone. A French girl with whom I had been enamoured before leaving England had learned of my engagement and had flown out to protest. She was staying in Penang and if I did not call on her that day she would come to Alor Star and create a fuss. She was an excitable character and if she said 'fuss' she meant 'fuss'! I therefore diverted to Penang, which was half way to Taiping, and for hours engaged in a fierce argument about whether or not I was embarked upon the right course. So many hours, in fact, that I missed the last ferry and had to catch the first one in the morning. With the MG on its best form I could just make the exam centre in time, but was not really at my most alert for the two three-hour papers that day. I thought, nevertheless, that I had done well enough. It was with considerable shock that on 24 November I received a letter from divisional headquarters to say that I had failed again and would I let them know how I believed this had come about. I began to think about calling off the engagement and to wonder what career I might pursue next.

Two months later, in January, I was sent a copy of Special Army Order No 126 dated 15 November 1954 stating that Temporary Captain J. B. Akehurst had, along with about 500 others, passed the examination for promotion. Later still I heard that I had earned 'Distinguished' marks and that the signal to Malaya Command from the War Office to this effect had been misread. Nowadays one's first thought would probably be to sue the authorities for defamation but my only interest then was that progress towards marriage could return to its blissful course. On 5 January 1955 Shirley came back to Malaya with her father by P&O liner, disembarking at Penang, and there was a rapturous reunion. That evening we became engaged over a Chateaubriand for two at the famed E&O hotel, sealed with a three-diamond ring. Two days later, in Alor Star, washing up reduced the three stones to two and there was a panic-stricken dash to the vendor, Mr Sena in Penang, who kindly accepted responsibility and restored diamond number three.

The way was now clear towards a wedding later in that year but my narrative must now go back to mid-1954 to cover events unconnected with courtship and nuptials.

6
Malaya – Third Year

Shortly before Operation Sword ended we were replaced by 2nd/10th Gurkhas who were kept in Malaya Command reserve for reinforcement or replacement wherever the Command considered necessary. Battalions permanently stationed in Malaya were taken out of operations for two months every other year for retraining and refreshment. In our case we were to include a parade to receive Colours from General Templer, so drill and parade rehearsals tended to take priority over operational training. Sword had been a success and although Toh Kar Lim had not been eliminated he had lost a number of his followers and he was never so effective or dangerous afterwards. He did, however, manage to surprise the experienced and efficient Gurkhas soon after they arrived. It was a common pattern that units new to an area were tested out by the enemy soon after their arrival and the CTs opened fire on 2nd/10th's Headquarters Company camp from a safe distance late one evening. The cooks and bottle washers were immediately called to arms and taken out by the company commander to pursue the bandits, who left an easy trail to follow. The trail led into a well-prepared ambush in a narrow reentrant and the Gurkhas took some casualties, including a bullet in the backside of the company commander himself. They treated Toh Kar Lim with more respect after this incident but over two months extracted full revenge.

In 1998 I was astonished to see Toh Kar Lim himself appearing in an ITV documentary on the Emergency. Plump, sleek, and wearing a smart suit, he came across as pretty pleased with himself – with, I suppose I must concede, some justification, having survived all the long odds that we mounted against him. It was during this interval in 1954 that 1st Battalion The Northamptonshire Regiment passed through Singapore on the troopship *Asturias*, en route for Korea. The war there was over but they were to have a busy though boring time and also to suffer under canvas the full rigours of a Korean winter. The stay in Singapore was to be brief, from 0900 hrs to 1500 hrs only, but Peter Worthy and I thought it well worth driving up to 500 miles each way to see all our friends. It turned out to be a memorable, hectic and, for me, a nerve-racking day.

The Commanding Officer, Lieutenant-Colonel Jimmy Dickson, a talented but not a popular officer, was the first down the gangway when the *Asturias* docked, shouting in his whining voice 'Ah, two of *my* officers come to greet me I see.' We did not explain that he was probably the officer we least came to see, but we soon gathered up our friends and drove them into town to celebrate the reunion and hear all the news. Somehow a number of us finished up in the same restaurant, Prince's, for lunch where much more alcohol was consumed than was good for any of us, particularly those, like me, who were driving. About an hour before the ship was due to sail John Wetherall climbed into my MG, his substantial frame making it look truly a 'Midget', and we set off for the docks. I hardly knew Singapore and got seriously lost. The minutes rushed by and John was already wondering what the penalty would be for missing the boat when we tore along the straight North Bridge Road at a rate of knots. A trishaw chose the wrong moment to appear unheralded from behind a parked car and we just touched its front footboard. The last thing I remember seeing was the rider going upwards off the saddle, but with the threat of being shot for desertion hanging over John Wetherall's head we dared not stop and rushed on, just making the docks before the gangway was raised.

Aware that I had committed a serious offence, I cancelled my plan to stay the night in Singapore and drove out over the Causeway into Johore, eager to put the island as far behind me and as quickly as I could. Just as it was getting dark I came to Ayer Hitam, an uninviting small town with no obvious hotel, and I decided to make for Malacca, some hundred miles ahead. This was probably the most dangerous bandit country in Malaya at that time and there were almost daily terrorist incidents. The policeman at the gate leading out of Ayer Hitam was most reluctant to let me out but pleading some rubbish about operational necessity and showing that I was armed I was eventually allowed to proceed.

After about fifty miles without incident or pause I came to a village called Bumbong Lima, which was enclosed in a high barbed wire fence. The entrance to the village was through a large barbed wire gate on my side of a hump-backed bridge which concealed the village itself from view. There was no sign of life and I hooted my horn and flashed my lights for a few minutes before realising that I would have to make an important decision with some urgency. I was alone in what was probably bandit country, drawing attention to myself, whereas in front of me there could well have been an armed policeman or home guard, too frightened to make himself known, but prepared to shoot anyone who threatened his security. I settled for bandits being more dangerous than home guards or policemen and climbed over the gate, some ten feet high. The bridge had sally-ports every ten yards or so and, with my heart in my mouth, I dashed from port to port feeling very exposed in the bright moonlight. But nothing happened and I walked to the local police station, woke the sleeping occupants, gave them the benefit of my opinions about their alertness and after a few minutes set off for Malacca, which to my surprise and relief I reached safely at about midnight. I decided not to visit Singapore again for as long as possible. It had been quite a day.

Our Colours parade went well. The Malay's natural sense of rhythm makes him very good at foot drill and he is always clean and smart, but we were soon back on operations. I had another short period as intelligence officer before rejoining a rifle company and it was during this period that I had my second personal glimpse of General Templer in action. The chain of command in Malaya for operations was firmly based on a joint approach, which indeed became a pattern for the future in many parts of the world when the armed forces were in support of the police and civil authorities. Each State had a War Executive Committee (SWEC) chaired by the British Adviser and comprised of senior police and special branch officers, army commanders and civil administrators. In each District there was a similar committee appropriate to that level known as a DWEC. It was my duty to accompany the Commanding Officer to a SWEC meeting and to sit behind him. At one such meeting the committee members were arguing endlessly about the problem of getting planters to buy radios. Planters' houses were, of their nature, isolated and all too frequently a target for terrorists, whose first action before attacking would invariably be to cut the telephone lines so that the planter and his family could not call for help. Planters were encouraged in the strongest terms to have radios supplied by the Government and on the police VHF net for their added safety. The catch was that they were required to pay for them and as they were expensive, a number of planters, particularly those not backed by large international companies, decided to take their chances and do without. The problem was to get them all to buy the radios, which was in our interest as well as theirs.

The discussion was at its height when suddenly, unannounced, Templer arrived and said he was in the area and thought he would just call in to see what was going on. As soon as he heard the problem he fixed the assembled company with his unnerving stare and said: 'Gentlemen, it's simple. Get a section of the Malay Regiment here to go out at dead of night to a couple of planters' houses in turn, cut their telephone wires, and fire a few bursts of Bren over them. Then let the buggers sweat till the morning! They'll soon be queuing up for radios.' Turning to the public relations officer he had brought with him he said 'And that's not for the Press either!' A couple of nights later we acted on this advice and it worked. Within a fortnight every planter in Kedah had a radio.

I was now with D Company in Sungei Perahu, a small company camp some thirty miles east of Kedah Peak mountain. The company commander was a light infantryman called Gordon Pople who was easy to get along with. He had been in Malaya before and had some good tactical ideas. Soon after we arrived in our little camp a policeman leaving Malaya offered us his two Alsatian dogs, Prince and Freda. Prince turned out to be too difficult to manage, but Freda was very amenable to training and became a cherished pet. One had to be careful because of Muslim sensibilities to dogs and to this our soldiers were very sensitive. If a dog touches a Muslim his religion demands that he wash a total of twenty-one times, seven times with water, then seven times with sand, and finally seven more times with water. This had been a very sensible precaution in Mohammed's time in the Middle East but some of us found it hard to justify in the modern civilised world.

Prince's departure was precipitated by an incident when Gordon was taking company orders, a military occasion when instant justice is administered for minor offences. He was by his side when the company sergeant-major marched in a miscreant Malay. The stamping of feet by the advancing soldier was too much for Prince, who leapt out with a snarl and nipped one of the threatening legs. That had to be the end of Prince's time with the company and Freda was looked upon with dark suspicion until she proved herself on operations. She was invaluable on night ambushes when she would give advance warning of approach, long before we could hear anything, by a low growl and a stiffening of the hairs on the back of her neck.

There was also one occasion when we were walking along a track and she gave warning of something ahead. I turned her loose and she dashed into the bushes to flush out a terrified tapper whom none of us could possibly have seen. The Malay soldiers were hugely impressed; it might have been a bandit who could have successfully ambushed us. Thereafter Freda was generally accepted, though never touched of course. She was exceptionally adaptable and would, for instance, run any distance to jump in the back of the MG on the command 'Get in!' She had eight puppies shortly before our wedding whose sale helped considerably towards paying for our honeymoon.

We had plenty of excitements in the next few months of jungle bashing. One, for me, had nothing to do with banditry. I was lying in my *basha* (a shelter made with a groundsheet) late at night when I heard the pad of feet and heavy breathing a few inches away. There was also a feral smell. Rigid with fright I lay still and held my breath. To my relief the creature moved away and next morning I was shown the pug marks of a full-grown tiger!

A successful patrolling technique called 'fan-patrolling' had been devised elsewhere in Malaya and we adopted it with enthusiasm. A company would set up a base in the jungle, and from it send out a number of four-man patrols on compass bearings at intervals of about fifteen degrees in the form of a fan. The groups would move out slowly and quietly for a thousand yards depending on the thickness of the vegetation, then turn right for a hundred yards before turning back, again on a compass bearing, to base. We found we could do this twice in a day and it was a very thorough means of searching ground. Should there be a contact all groups would turn inwards and thus create an effective area ambush. On one occasion with us it worked perfectly when one of our little patrols surprised three CTs making a food dump. One of them was shot there and then and the other two ran off, but both went straight into other groups and thus all three were accounted for. In this period we lost one soldier, an Iban tracker brought in from Borneo, killed, but eliminated eleven CTs, which was an above average score for a company.

The most extraordinary jungle experience of my tour was when we were in a company base deep in the jungle. At about eight o'clock at night we heard Chinese singing. We could judge the direction fairly accurately and had a reasonable view of the probable distance because our fan patrols had been out that way and had not located a camp. Sound travelled well in the jungle at night and it was likely to be about 1,200 yards away. Trying to move through the jungle at night towards what was clearly a large group of terrorists was judged impractical because of the impossibility of control and the inevitability of noise. Similarly one could bet that the singing would soon stop, as it did, and we would be groping in the dark. We could try setting off next morning but experience told us that the camp would be well protected by sentries and we would be likely to be seen first, at which the CTs would clear off at high speed. Gordon therefore decided that the best option would be a bombing strike if it could be arranged quickly. Lincoln heavy bombers were based in Singapore and had developed a technique, called 'pattern bombing', of twelve aircraft flying in close formation towards their target and then all releasing their bombloads simultaneously. When the first bombs exploded sympathetic detonation would explode all the others while they were still falling, and instead of being deadened by landing among trees in the soft jungle soil a devastating rain of shrapnel would be sprayed from various heights on anyone below.

The first problem was to get our request to the outside world. As I have already explained the battalion net closed after dark so there would be no joy there. However I managed to coax our 68 set to communicate with a military net in Kuala Lumpur and asked them to telephone our battalion headquarters to get them to open up their radio. This worked and generated a flurry of activity. By midnight a strike had been arranged for 1030 hrs and another company, commanded by Alan Peckham, had been roused and despatched to a point on the nearest road to us, from there to march in at first light to join us. With commendable speed a ground liaison officer had been sent to the area and he arranged that the aircraft would fly over the precise summit of Kedah Peak, and then for so many seconds on a bearing before dropping their bombs. Meanwhile we waited, ready to follow up the strike as quickly as we could.

By 1000 hrs all was ready and we sat in a small clearing from which we could observe the approach of the Lincolns. Bang on time they came, flying straight towards us and we prayed fervently that they had got their timing right. We saw the bombs leave the aircraft and had the feeling that they were coming straight for us, but the GLO's calculations had been exactly right. With a shattering roar the bombs exploded. Almost immediately there was the sound of screaming coming through the trees towards us and we thought at first that it came from fleeing CTs. No such luck. It was hordes of monkeys and other terrified creatures swinging through the trees away from the bombing.

The two companies then set out to see if the air attack had worked. On the way we came across a huge but somnolent python curled up beneath a tree with a shrapnel wound in its neck. The Malays insisted on pausing to capture it. Their method was ingenious. They cut a hole through one end of a long bamboo pole and through this threaded a long creeper with a slip knot at the end of it. They poked the python with the pole, up came its head to see what was going on, and over it went the slip knot, which was immediately pulled tight. With its head trapped firmly at the end of the pole the snake curled itself at once round and round the pole's full length and the Malays were able to move up to chop off its head in safety. We dined on its meat that evening (rather like chicken), and the soldiers turned in a tidy profit by selling the skin.

We searched the bombed area later, which had suffered amazing devastation – hardly anyone beneath it could have survived. We found where the bandits had been, pretty close to the middle of the strike, but no sign of any casualties. Some time later we learned from a surrendered terrorist that the singing marked the end of the biggest ever meeting of CTs in Northern Malaya. They had gathered to discuss future moves, and sixty or more had been in the camp at the time, including all the senior leadership. Luckily for them they had dispersed at 0800 hrs the next morning. But for two and a half hours we might have set up the biggest single slaughter of bandits in the whole campaign.

I am less proud of another incident. I was sitting on a fallen tree cleaning my rifle when a shot rang out and the bullet thudded into the tree inches from my backside. It was a negligent discharge, a rare event with our soldiers, and I had the man put under arrest with a view to disciplinary action when we came out. A few minutes later I left our little base to attend to a call of nature. A suitable hole was usually dug in the camps but, with perhaps false modesty, I preferred to go outside the base for the purpose. I had a Patchett sub-machine gun (very like the more familiar Sterling developed on the lines of the old Sten) and while squatting I noticed that I had not cocked it, which was silly when one was alone fifty yards or so outside the camp. As I went to cock it the little lever slipped from the palm of my sweaty hand and there was a burst of three shots. A hundred soldiers back in the base immediately stood to and I had to make my shamefaced way back past an outer perimeter bristling with weapons and itchy trigger fingers. I decided to let off the previously offending soldier with an admonishment rather than the more severe penalty which his offence would have justified.

On another occasion, when Gordon and I were both in camp at Sungei Perahu, we received a deputation from the nearby village saying that they had set a trap for a mouse deer, but that it had caught a very fierce and very angry black panther. There was no way it could be freed and the villagers had no firearms, so would the intrepid *Tuans* please come and shoot the beast? Perhaps we were intrepid until we drew near the screaming, snarling creature, but intrepidity waned fast. A trap for a mouse deer was unlikely to be all that strong and the prospect of being near an enraged panther when it broke loose was unnerving. After some debate we climbed a very uncomfortable and wobbly tree about thirty yards away from the creature and after waiting some time for it to be still for long enough to present a certain target, Gordon shot it. The villagers were delighted and probably made a lot of money from the pelt; black panthers were quite rare. Some days later they brought us our reward, a long black whisker each. These, we were assured, if crushed and eaten would have truly amazing aphrodisiac and potency effects. These were not tested, at least not by me. Gordon looked a bit sheepish when I asked him about his whisker a few days later.

Our wedding day approached. We wanted it to be in Alor Star in the company of most of our friends but the only Anglican church there was a scruffy Nissen hut. The nearest church of sufficient size was in Penang, which would have been attractive but have seriously reduced the congregation. The British Adviser very kindly offered us the use of his splendid residency, but the Revd Jack Griffiths, who was to officiate, said that for this we would have to obtain the permission of the Bishop of Singapore. We were told that this could be obtained by telephone and an appointment was made for the purpose. Unfortunately I had unexpectedly to go into the jungle on the appointed day but Alan Peckham, to be my best man and now adjutant of the battalion, arranged a three-way conversation with me on the radio, the bishop on the telephone and he, Alan, acting as a middle man between us. The bishop was well known for being difficult and occasionally irascible, so I was a bit nervous about our communications arrangements. All went well until Alan was explaining to the bishop that the Nissen hut was nowhere near big enough for the probable congregation and described it by its local nickname, 'The Tin Tabernacle'. There followed some tricky moments but all was well in the end and the momentous event was planned for 18 May. I caught dengue fever ten days beforehand and this threw the whole thing into doubt, but I recovered quickly enough and was up in three days.

Jack Griffiths had insisted on giving us advice before our wedding but he, too, was indisposed with appendicitis and we had to go to visit him in hospital in Penang. I do not remember receiving any advice, indeed I do not think he offered any; the conversation was confined to briefing him on the arrangements, but it was apparently important to him that we should see the scar left from the removal of the offending appendix. He had a substantial belly and the whole display was singularly unattractive to the embarrassed bride-to-be.

At breakfast on our wedding day Gordon Pople insisted that champagne was important 'to soothe the nerves', and when Alan and I arrived at the residency in good time the kindly British Adviser insisted that brandy would be essential 'to soothe the nerves'. So far as I remember my nerves were duly and well and truly soothed, although there was a tense moment during the service. The room in which it was to be conducted was on the ground floor, but the piano to accompany the hymns was on the floor above where the pianist was out of earshot of the proceedings below. The British Adviser was, quite reasonably, not prepared to move the instrument for fear of knocking it out of tune, so an usher was positioned half way up the stairs with the duty of alerting the pianist when to start playing. The bride arrived looking quite gorgeous and the first hymn, the standard wedding favourite, 'Love Divine, All Loves Excelling', was announced. There followed a pause of perhaps a minute, with no sound from the piano. Eventually Brenda, Shirley's sister and one of the bridesmaids, decided to go it alone with her very fine voice. I, no doubt encouraged by champagne and brandy, joined in less tunefully but with enthusiasm, together with some of the congregation. Unfortunately this famous hymn has two acceptable tunes and it was when we were half way through our first line that the pianist at last struck up – with the other tune! After that I was distracted, when kneeling and supposedly solemn, by Jack Griffiths's appearance. He was in full fig from the ankles up, but below his cassock you could see he was wearing sandals over bare feet with large and rather ugly big toes poking out.

The reception was held in the Kedah Club and eventually we left in the MG. I had snaffled a bottle of champagne (to soothe the nerves) and put it in the back of the car in an icebox. After we had driven a few miles there was a loud bang from behind. The bottle had exploded, shattering itself and most of the icebox, but luckily none of the bits came forward. We drove the 150 miles to Ipoh, where we stayed in the bleak and noisy Station Hotel, before going on the next day to the Cameron Highlands. The long winding road up into the mountains was considered to be in serious danger of being ambushed and all travel had to be in convoy with cars like ours interspersed with armoured vehicles. We stayed in the Cameron Highlands Hotel, which was quite excellent, and enjoyed a wonderful honeymoon.

While we there the battalion moved south to Muar in Johore, and there I rejoined D Company in its little Bukit Serempang camp in the shadow of Mount Ophir, to be occupied a few months afterwards by Frank Kitson (now General Sir Frank, who appears in a later chapter) and to inspire the homily in one of his books on how terrorists should be defeated. We set about getting to know the area wondering why we had been moved to somewhere totally new, leaving another unit to have to learn about the area we had left. We thought, and I still think, this was flawed policy. In the seven weeks I was there we put in a lot of work but achieved no contacts, although there was one operation that caused me some alarm through my own silly fault.

We had been in the jungle for two weeks and I was commanding the company temporarily, the Malay company commander having left for a course. We were based on a plateau about half way up Mount Ophir, a substantial mountain, and had been finding a number of old bandit camps, but no new ones. Late one night we heard the sound of firing in the far distance and next morning we were told to form a 'stop-line' facing the direction of what had been a bandit ambush of a police armoured vehicle. At about 1600 hrs in the afternoon we received a long operation order, the essence of which was that a bombing strike was planned and that we should move about 4,000 yards to take up a new stop-line. I was at some pains to explain that in that country to move 1,000 yards in a whole day would be quite an achievement. It would take at least an hour to get my soldiers in from their positions, leaving less than two hours of daylight. We had a new Commanding Officer, Lieutenant-Colonel Richard Bryers, formerly of the King's Own, who was a thoroughly likeable and efficient officer but who had not yet been in the jungle himself. Looking at his map he decided that I was just being difficult and told me to get on with it. Remonstration was clearly getting me nowhere, so foolishly I decided to disobey without telling anyone. I called the soldiers into base and settled down for the night with the intention of moving in the required direction early the next morning.

On the 0700 hrs morning call, on which I declared myself to be where I had been told to go, I was told that a new appreciation had been made of the bandits' likely movement and that the target for the twelve-Lincoln strike had been changed. I was to turn and face it. Imagine the consternation when I checked the target map reference to discover that not only was it within 200 yards of my actual position but that it was due in at 0900 hrs. I could hardly admit that I was far from where I had already announced myself to be, so seldom can a company have packed up and moved with such speed. When the strike came in, bang on time and target (which we knew to be unoccupied) we were a bare 600 yards away and profoundly impressed by the noise of it. We reached the devastated area with commendable speed and duly reported with suitable regret that the strike appeared to have inflicted no casualties. Three days later I came out of the jungle for the last time, considering privately that I had finished a not unsuccessful tour on a singularly low note.

I now had a couple of weeks to pack up, sell my lovely car (for a song), collect Shirley from Alor Star and move to Singapore to catch the boat home. The secondment terms provided that on completion of a tour one was given a lump sum of money, equal to the air fare to Britain, and with that one could make whatever arrangements one liked. We and the Peckhams had decided to supplement the money and book ourselves on a luxurious Dutch liner, the *Oranje,* which would take only nineteen days to sail back and provide comfort, entertainment and stupendous food – the Dutch, of course, being renowned trenchermen. Normally around twelve stone I had fallen to nine stone four when I emerged from the jungle, but much of it was replaced during the voyage. Even the breakfasts included eight possible courses.

It was a memorable voyage and a suitable end to what had been a marvellous tour. We stopped at Medan, Colombo, Port Suez and Alexandria but at none of them long enough to go ashore. Our first stop of this sort was at Naples and we approached past Stromboli at about seven in the morning. The unique sights of the volcano, and later Capri and the truly beautiful Bay of Naples seemed to justify a

Dry Martini celebration which, followed by a few bibulous hours ashore in Naples, turned out to be unwise. I was bad company for a bit and deservedly felt awful next day. This was soon forgotten when three days later we arrived in Southampton and set off for Deal and the four months' leave which were, again, part of the secondment contract. It was wonderful to be back in England and amongst other things I frequented the Royal Cinque Ports golf club and got my handicap back to where it had been before I joined the Army.

Soon after getting back I learned that I had been Mentioned in Despatches. Probably the most pleasing aspect of this was to get a letter from Derek Houchin, my Commanding Officer in Trieste and now a brigadier, which included the sentence: 'You were right to go to Malaya when you did and I am delighted that you served there with distinction.' This gave me much satisfaction.

For the obvious personal reasons, and for military ones too, I am very glad indeed that I volunteered for the tour. I had matured, embarked upon marriage, and learned much, discovering for the first time the thrill of active operations and an awareness that soldiering could be a very serious business. I cannot remember being fired with any particular career ambitions then, although I think I had become aware that hitherto I had been all too often naive and dilettante. I have always felt that soldiering is a life that must be fun if it is to be successful and have had little sympathy for the over-ambitious, intense and humourless officer, except perhaps when he was doing all his work for me! I like to think that if my profession had ever ceased to be fulfilling and enjoyable I would have left it. I hope I would have had the courage to do so, but happily such a situation never arose.

7
Hong Kong, England and the TA

After three monhs' leave in England I spent two freezing weeks in February 1956 being loaded with facts and exposed to all manner of chemical unpleasantness on a nuclear, biological and chemical warfare course at Winterbourne Gunner on Salisbury Plain Then we boarded the troopship *Empire Fowey* at Southampton, bound for Hong Kong to rejoin the 1st Battalion.

Except for operations such as the recapture of the Falkland Islands in 1982 virtually all troop movement today is by air. Until the late sixties, when numbers to be deployed great distances were sharply reduced by withdrawal from Empire, it was more economical to lease troopships. They varied enormously in size, age, speed, comfort and efficiency, much depending on the operating shipping line. *Empire Fowey* was a large vessel with a good reputation but, with substantial numbers still to be taken to Egypt, Aden, Singapore, Malaya, Hong Kong and Korea, it was fully laden with passengers.

I was allocated a berth in a cabin with three other officers and Shirley another on a different deck with three women. This was not a popular arrangement but unavoidable given the availability of two-berth cabins. Three of us prepared to endure a month of nocturnal separation but one of our number, a flight lieutenant who had married an attractive and sexy Belgian girl a couple of days before embarking, found the arrangement intolerable. Within minutes of our arrival in our cabin he was negotiating with us to allow him privacy in it for two separate hours a day. This was agreed, but for him alone. The rest of us were too embarrassed or shy. Shipboard routine and various inspections played havoc with the airman's plans and there was drama in the Mediterranean when he and his wife were interrupted by the ship's commandant while engaged in naked sport in a shower. The flight lieutenant also drew attention to himself as a golfer. He had recently played golf for Wales and was concerned that a month at sea would play havoc with his swing. He therefore included in his luggage 3,000 balls of which he would daily strike a hundred or so into the sea from a mat in the stern. For those of us for whom the loss of one ball was a serious matter this seemed to be amazing extravagance.

Most people enjoyed travelling by troopship. It had many of the attractions, especially for officers and their families, of the cruises for which tourists happily pay large sums of money, but it also had military benefits. At least two weeks of the journey were in tropical temperatures so soldiers arrived at their destination largely acclimatised and ready for service. There was plenty of time during the voyage for physical jerks, lectures and individual training in new skills likely to be needed where the troops were to serve. Every officer was given responsibility for the training and welfare of a troop deck containing forty or more soldiers of different arms and services, which made demands upon their ingenuity and imagination and certainly kept them from being bored.

After a few months in Korea 1 Northamptons had been posted to Hong Kong where they occupied a barracks at San Wai in the New Territories, near the border with China. The task of patrolling the frontier to prevent illegal immigration had not yet arisen and battalions were only required to man one or two observation posts to detect any unusual events on the Chinese side. Their roles were twofold. First to be prepared to defend the Colony should China decide to pre-empt the ending of the treaty forty years hence, which was thought unlikely, and second to give aid to the civil power if the inhabitants, many of whom lived in poor and crowded conditions, decide to rebel.

Quarters were in short supply and married men were given an allowance with which to seek rented accommodation. Very little was available near San Wai and most of us took something in Kowloon, which involved a daily journey of about twenty miles. Shirley and I were lucky to find a pleasant flat in Austin Road, overlooking the Kowloon Cricket Club ground.

I was briefly to be second-in-command of a rifle company, next to run four one-week nuclear, biological and chemical warfare courses for the Command in Kowloon (conveniently near home), then to be attached to the Mechanical Transport (MT) platoon before attending an MT course in Singapore. Eventually, some six months after arriving, I would be the MT Officer. An extra job during this period was to be Families Officer which, with accommodation all over the place and many young wives finding it hard to cope with the conditions, could be time-consuming and occasionally daunting. Shirley, not yet twenty-one and newly married herself, was a considerable help but had some challenging adventures. A corporal's wife, Lil, well into middle age and past any early attractions she might have had, was desperate to start a family and had been advised by her friends that position during procreation could make all the difference. She insisted on discussing this with Shirley in graphic, intimate detail and inquiring of her whether she thought any possibilities had been omitted. Regrettably none of the advice ever succeeded and Lil was still childless when her husband died many years later.

Life in Hong Kong was fun, with good training, plenty of sport, and a busy social life back with our friends in the regiment. Wonderful shopping opportunities were on the doorstep but for us there was a snag. I cannot now remember quite how it came about but we were seriously short of cash throughout the tour. Pay was poor, local allowances meagre, and overdrafts from local banks virtually unobtainable. My home bank manager was my father, who was stuffily insistent on remaining in credit. Most expenses were settled early in the month, including mess, NAAFI, grocery, garage, club and sports club bills which all arrived with relentless punctuality in the first week of each month. We managed to scrape through somehow but there was one month when after paying all the bills we were left with sixteen dollars (£1) cash for the next thirty days – so we immediately blued that on a visit to the cinema and continued to live on tick.

I enjoyed the six-week MT course in Singapore and returned to Hong Kong full of enthusiasm to get on with the job. I was to take over from John Wetherall but the annual Command Inspection of Vehicles (CIV) was due in two weeks. This inspection, conducted in frightening detail by one Captain Nelson of the REME and his team, was known to be difficult and reputations could be made or broken. It was clear to me from the handover process that there were plenty of horrors for Nelson to get his teeth into. John and I stood before Lieutenant-Colonel Mike Goodale, the new Commanding Officer, to report that our transfer was complete. 'You may take over now,' he said to me, 'but if you do you must accept full responsibility for the CIV.' This was a true test of friendship and loyalty. With a gulp and crossed fingers I agreed to take it on. John had other troubles at the time. He had been pulled up by the civil police driving his aged Vauxhall the wrong way up a one-way street. The policemen alleged that he was under the influence of drink, that his tyres lacked the legal depth of tread and that the steering was dangerously faulty. All this was shortly to be settled in court and the possible consequences were alarming. In the event John defended himself with customary wit and claimed that the faulty steering was to blame for the one-way street offence, and that towering two feet or more above the Chinese constables as he did they could not possibly tell with certainty whether or not he was drunk. Fortunately the magistrates had a sense of humour and John was let off with a fine and having his car put off the road until fully repaired, which it never was.

We worked like mad to prepare for the inspection, which turned out to be every bit as demanding as we had feared. We just got away with it, earning an 'Above Average' grading, but it was touch and go, and some chicanery was necessary. We had some problems with toolkits and with trailers for instance, but contrived, by distracting the inspectors with coffee breaks, red herrings or whatever, to arrange that they inspected the same trailer or toolkit several times over, thinking each one to be different.

In October 1957 we were enjoying a 'guest night' in our mess in San Wai when the festivities were interrupted by an order to prepare immediately for action and deploy to the heights overlooking Kowloon. There had been serious riots both on the island and in Kowloon; a number of people had been killed including the Swiss consul, and many cars and lorries had been burnt. Few of our families had telephones and with little information available to us we were all worried about them. Although we reached our positions soon after midnight we were not allowed to move down into the town until 1630 hrs. As we drove in we could see debris, burnt-out cars and the odd body in the streets. It was a relief to get round and discover that, though many of them were nervous, none of our families had ventured out and all were safe.

Our orders were to enforce a curfew in an area in Kowloon by standing soldiers in lines along the centres of two main roads, Argyll and Boundary Streets, in order to break the city up into manageable areas and prevent civilian movement between them. This was effective but in the high temperatures called for considerable endurance on the part of the men. Our headquarters were in Kowloon Tsai police station and here we saw things which made us angry and ashamed. One of the seriously troubled areas was the old Walled City of Kowloon where the Triads were particularly powerful. The police had a riot squad made up of tall and tough Pakistanis who formed up in the station courtyard looking formidable with their *lathis*, and immaculately turned out. Two hours later they returned from the Walled City with many prisoners. The police were scruffy and tired and it was obvious from their appearance and the state of their captives that they had been involved in fierce physical contact.

The prisoners were made to squat in the courtyard under hot sun for the rest of that day, the night, and most of the next day without food or water. Any movement was punished with a *lathi* blow and no one was permitted to leave to relieve themselves. One at a time they were taken inside for interrogation and the soldiers found a window through which they could see scenes of severe beatings of both men and women and various acts of cruelty. We were all very upset by this and asked the Commanding Officer to intervene. He tried to do so but was rebuffed by the police, who curtained off the window. All of this was debated for some weeks and a senior policeman was invited to address an audience in the battalion on the subject. His line was that firm action to cow rioters into submission was the only language they would understand and, as we could see, the riots were subdued in hours. Allowed to get out of hand the potential numbers were so many that all control would have been lost. We listened politely and followed the argument, but it left a nasty taste in the mouth. In all 56 people had been killed and more than 400 injured.

In December 1956 my father suffered a severe heart attack in the office of the general manager of the Midland Bank where he was receiving a reprimand for having recommended an injudicious loan to a spaghetti factory which went bankrupt. He was critically ill in St Bartholomew's Hospital and for the only time in my service I experienced the efficiency of the highest category of priority travel for compassionate reasons. Within thirty hours I was back in London at his bedside, and twenty-four of them had been in an aeroplane. After ten days he was still unwell but not dying so I went to the War Office department in Berkeley Square and asked to be returned to Hong Kong. I was told that no one was authorised to travel to the Far East unless they had at least one year to serve there. My battalion was due to return to England in three months and I was therefore to proceed to the Regimental Depot in Northampton and there to await their return. Frantic arguments about my job, my wife, my flat, my car were to no avail, so panic initiative was called for. After some very fast footwork around the War Office I luckily ran to earth a useful staff officer in Woolwich. I have no memory of what his responsibilities were but he was my saviour. He authorised a flight by

BOAC to Singapore but for reasons which now escape me could not sanction travel as far as Hong Kong. I jumped at the chance however, assuming that in Singapore they would find it cheaper and more logical to send me on to Hong Kong than to return me to England.

My flight was due to leave on 30 December and early that morning my father had a second and fatal attack. I telephoned my staff officer who said it was now or never. Cruel though it seemed I felt I had to take the only opportunity I would get and left my mother to make funeral arrangements. My parents had, in fact, somewhat acrimoniously separated a year before so the emotional impact for my mother had been thus diminished. We left London that evening and I discovered that the flight was actually going to Hong Kong and that I must leave it in Rangoon to transfer to another flight to Singapore. I got the pilot to send a signal to the War Office asking for authority to continue to Hong Kong but the duty staff officer who received it was a true bureaucrat and directed that I should proceed to the destination which had been authorised and no other. New Year's Eve 1956 was thus spent in a transit hotel in Rangoon drinking one unbelievably expensive beer. Next morning I saw off the flight to Hong Kong and boarded another for Singapore where it took three weeks to get myself on an RAF flight back home. While I was wandering in the grounds of the mess in Singapore an elderly Sikh jumped from the bushes and insisted on reading my palm. He forecast success in life but warned me 'You will inherit nothing from your daddy.' He was right. My father's will reached me a few days later and included the sentence 'Happily my dear son John is in no need of help from me.' This from my bank manager, who well knew the perilous state of my finances, I thought pretty disobliging.

As the end of our tour drew near rumours abounded about our next destination in Britain. Successively the grapevine assured us we were headed for successively Tidworth, Chiseldon and Watchet. Further rumour had it that the Rifle Brigade had demanded Tidworth after a decision had been taken to send us there. They boasted superior senior firepower at the time and, with only a short time to go before embarking on the troopship *Nevasa*, we learned that Watchet in Somerset it was to be.

Nevasa was a newly refurbished ship run marvellously well by British India Line and it was only her second trip to the Far East. She was fast and well appointed. We were the first complete unit to be carried by her and a silver plaque recording that fact was still to be seen in the main lounge when I went aboard nearly twenty years later. I was appointed Ship's Adjutant for the voyage, which had the advantage that I could select a cabin for Shirley and me, and that my duties were mostly easy office ones, rather than supervising a troop-deck. The Suez Canal had been closed by President Nasser shortly before our journey so we had to sail to Southampton by way of Singapore, Colombo, Durban and round the Cape to Las Palmas. At Durban we were greeted by the 'Lady in White,' well known to wartime drafts for standing at the end of the quay as ships came and went, serenading them with her powerful operatic soprano voice.

I had trouble in Durban. We were there for twenty-four hours and had endured rough seas across the Indian Ocean. One of our passengers was a soldier convicted for murder who was being brought home to serve his sentence. For the voyage he was incarcerated in a cell in the bowels of the ship and had had a bad time through seasickness. He asked me if he could go ashore for some exercise in Durban and, feeling sorry for him, I agreed, subject to his being accompanied by two military policemen. Shirley and I went off with others on a spectacular coach tour to the Valley of a Thousand Hills and returned late in the evening to learn that our prisoner had slipped his redcap guards and disappeared. So far as I know he has never been seen again. There had to be a court of inquiry and my decision to allow him ashore was questioned but although the policemen were disciplined I never heard any more about it.

Doniford Camp in Watchet had not been occupied since the war and although only hutted it was comfortable and in quite good repair. The village was delighted to get the custom that our presence brought and could not have been more hospitable. Conveniently there were pubs which divided themselves up as being officers', sergeants', and soldiers'. Although opening hours depended more on the availability of custom than licensing arrangements, and the local 'scrumpy' cider could be lethal to the unsuspecting, we had very little trouble in the area. There was one incident which achieved a centre-page *Daily Mirror* spread under the headline 'Bonk, Bonk, Bonk, Down Go the Walls' which might suffer other interpretations in nineties language but actually referred to some soldiers knocking down a couple of garden walls while making their inebriated way back to camp.

Drinking was not confined to the other ranks. There was a remarkable occasion when the officers attended a Christmas party in the sergeants' mess. Weaving his way back to his room, which lay across a football field, a famous regimental character, Major 'Rocky' Roche, mislaid his upper denture. Discovering the loss next morning his company was fallen in, shoulder-to-shoulder, to move slowly across the pitch, their eyes to the ground, 'to retrieve any unusual object there'. The missing teeth were indeed discovered, but only by being trodden on. The two pieces of his plate, when shown to their owner, evoked a shout of 'Send for the tiffy!' 'Tiffy' was the expression used for the unit armourer, an artificer of the Royal Electrical and Mechanical Engineers. Dental engineering was not a skill in which he was trained but an effective temporary repair was achieved which saw Rocky through Christmas and New Year.

The battalion was part of the Strategic Reserve and had to be at a high state of readiness, but with the brigade headquarters eighty country miles away in Plymouth and district headquarters in Taunton responsible only for administration, we enjoyed a largely independent existence. We were allowed to train on the Quantock Hills, provided we filled in any holes we dug, and the Dartmoor ranges and its huge training and field firing area were little more than an hour away.

I began in Watchet as MT Officer, but it was soon ordained that this job should be given to officers with quartermaster commissions, so, with some sadness, I left and was appointed Weapon Training Officer. With a staff comprising a colour-sergeant and two storemen I was responsible for weapon training standards in the battalion, coaching shooting teams, and the storage of and accounting for all types of ammunition. It was this last duty which gave rise to a spot of bother. All rounds fired on target ranges had to be matched by a high percentage of the brass empty cases recovered and returned to ordnance. On the other hand a very low percentage of case recoveries was required from field firing exercises in the wastes of Dartmoor. After a few weeks the colour-sergeant warned me that we were well short of the numbers of empty cases required. After some thought I decided that the four of us would go to Dartmoor for a couple of days and scour the known exercise areas picking up the discarded cases. This was entirely successful and we then held exactly what we should. Unfortunately this activity gave ideas to the two storemen, who were a couple of scallywags. They spent two or three weekends collecting more cases in the same way and soon afterwards were apprehended by military policemen while offering their finds to a scrap metal dealer in Taunton. They were convicted by court martial and two new storemen had to be appointed.

Our second year in Somerset found us appointed to conduct 'trolley trials'. As the speed, capacity and quantity of aircraft for the movement of both personnel equipment increased, the Army was wrestling with the possible implications. Rapid deployment of light forces to deal with trouble in its earliest stages was likely to be much more effective than the ponderous movement of stronger, heavier formations which, by the time they arrived, might find matters greatly escalated if not already out of hand. The idea we were to test envisaged the battalion moving in three echelons, an assault echelon with no transport, a follow-up group of twenty-five Land-Rovers, and a base echelon. The assault group, essentially a tactical headquarters, three rifle companies and infantry support weapons, needed some means of humping sufficient ammunition, batteries, food, water and other supplies to sustain it for at least forty-eight hours, and also to enable it to move across country. Someone, somewhere had dreamed up the idea of the trolley. This was a strong wire basket, about six feet long, four feet wide and four feet deep, with a pulling handle at each end, mounted on two wheels with pneumatic tyres. A waterproof canvas case could be fitted so that the trolley could be floated if necessary.

Pulling these things was hard work and the battalion became supremely fit as it lugged its heavily laden trolleys across the most difficult terrain the trainers could find. Some imaginative exercises were held, including travelling by train to deal with a supposed internal security problem in the regiment's home town, Northampton. The final fling was an aptly named Exercise Rock and Roll which envisaged embarking in destroyers and floating the trolleys two or three hundred yards ashore to invade Guernsey from the sea. When the exercise ended the battalion was to enjoy a couple of days camping near St Peter Port. To carry the tentage and stores for this camp, and representing the follow-up echelons, four three-ton lorries and six Land-Rovers were to be taken by landing ship tank (LST) from Portsmouth to Guernsey. I was made responsible for this and in due course led my little convoy to a quayside in Portsmouth and embarked.

The whole event went almost without a hitch. It was lucky that the weather was kind. Only one of the trolleys foundered as they made their hazardous way ashore and we all enjoyed our two days as holidaying tourists. The battalion then re-embarked on its destroyers to be taken back to England, and my vehicles and I rejoined our LST. We were put ashore at Marchwood at dawn on a Sunday morning to be greeted by a team from HM Customs. After the usual rummage for drink and cigarettes the head customs man asked me for my import licence for ten vehicles. I tried to explain that we had simply put the vehicles on the ship, exercised in the Channel Isles for a few days, and were now back again. This brought a demand for a copy of the export licence for taking the vehicles abroad. Nothing like this had ever occurred to me or the captain of the LST, nor, presumably, to the exercise planners at Headquarters United Kingdom Land Forces. I was asked who was the most senior officer responsible for the exercise and said that I supposed that it was General Sir George Erskine, the Commander-in-Chief. To my horror the customs officer took me to his office and telephoned the headquarters at Wilton, demanding to speak in person to the C-in-C, and only to the C-in-C. I could not hear what irascible words were being used when he got through but from the way in which the telephone was held away from the official's ear it was clear that he was being treated to a very senior officer's views about being awoken at 0600 hrs on the Sabbath. We were allowed to proceed without further hindrance and I never heard whether there were recriminations later for the exercise planners.

I do not know what the final report on the trolley trials recommended but can guess from the fact that they were never seen being used by units again. I have run across them twice. Once being used in the grounds of the Staff College to collect fallen leaves and once, more surprisingly, in a farmyard in Warwickshire, but the farmer could not remember, perhaps conveniently, where it came from. I feel sure the Royal Marines would have found them handy when 'yomping' across the Falklands in 1982. This was the just the sort of purpose for which they were designed.

There was one period of excitement when we were stood to for an emergency tour in an unknown location but it was cancelled at the last moment. Orders came later for a full tour in Aden, but not including me, because I was appointed to be Adjutant of 5 Northamptons, our Territorial Army battalion, at the end of 1959.

We had enjoyed Watchet, although the tour was marred for us by personal tragedy. Shirley gave birth to a daughter, Caroline, in Minehead Hospital but the baby had serious internal malformation, which we now know to have been caused by cystic fibrosis, and when only a few days old she failed to survive a major operation. If only CF had been diagnosed then we might usefully have been forewarned when our next child, Julian, became ill early in his life, and suitable treatment could have been prescribed much earlier than in the event it was.

The 5th Battalion had its headquarters in Peterborough, where we were allotted a small but brand new quarter (with a brand new garden mostly comprising builders' rubble). Now began one of the busiest periods of my service.

In the early days of National Service the conscripts, when their full-time service was complete, were required to attend compulsory drills and camps with the Territorial Army but this requirement was dropped in 1957 and TA battalions suddenly fell from strengths of 1,000 or more to 200 or less. The advantage was that all of them were volunteers, imbued with the remarkable enthusiasm for service that has become a hallmark of the TA. In addition to training, time and effort had to be devoted to recruiting and the 5th Battalion more than doubled its strength in two years. Its companies were based at Peterborough, Corby, Rushden, Northampton and Huntingdon. Some battalions were commanded by Territorials, in which case they rated a training major in addition to the total regular staff of an adjutant, a quartermaster, a regimental sergeant-major, one senior NCO or warrant officer per company as permanent staff instructor, and two corporal drivers. We had a Regular commanding officer, Lieutenant-Colonel Reggie Denny, a dominating man of tireless energy and fervour who made heavy demands of his adjutant and quartermaster. Each company held two drill nights per week, training of some sort was conducted on at least three weekends per month and there was also an annual camp of two weeks. My own routine was normal office hours during the week with visits to at least two company drill nights, and attendance at something on most weekends. At the same time I was engaged in studying for the Staff College entrance exam for the first few months. I have never been busier.

The hours put in did not do much for family life but the work was testing and mostly enjoyable. Certainly one felt that one was appreciated and made to feel that it was all worthwhile. The volunteers came from all walks of life and there was much to learn about conditions in civilian life, from which one was shielded when with the Regular forces. I came to admire the ardour and dedication of the volunteers, an admiration I have never lost, and the tour was good preparation for later appointments such as Inspector General of the Territorial Army.

One of the major industries in Peterborough was Perkins Diesel Ltd. There came a day in 1958 when its managing director called for his car and was told that it was off the road. 'Well, find me another,' said he. 'There isn't a roadworthy one available' he was told, to his fury. His company secretary, Lieutenant Colonel Monty Pritchard, had recently retired from commanding a TA battalion and when asked for his advice on how to shake up the firm's transport department he suggested that the local TA adjutant, who, he happened to know, had MT experience, might be asked to lunch to explain how the Army managed such matters. I gave a short presentation, at the end of which I was offered three times my curent salary to leave the Army and join the firm as transport manager, giving me twenty-four hours to consider the offer. Broke as usual, the idea did sound tempting to us and Shirley and I debated it at length. Though it was superficially attractive we were deterred by the fact that we were enjoying the Army which offered security and continuity. The obvious disadvantages were that we did not think much of Peterborough as a place to live, and there was always the possibility that a time would again come when no car was available for the managing director. I would then be likely to suffer the same immediate fate that presumably awaited the present transport manager. The decision was not really difficult but something much more important arose from the episode. We decided that attraction to civilian life could be unsettling and distracting. We therefore took the firm decision to stick with the Army come what may. This helped me to be single-minded later when many friends were debating whether or not to stay.

The setting for one weekend exercise, Oundle Outlaw, was of a threat to the United Kingdom of enemy special forces and fifth columnists preliminary to an invasion. 21 Special Air Service Regiment (TA) agreed to provide the enemy and they would all be identifiable by their woollen Balaclava helmets. Through newspaper advertisements and posters we alerted as many civilians as were interested to telephone the police or our headquarters if they saw any of these dastardly villains. The people in the Oundle and Corby area joined in with gusto and we managed to round up a good number of the SAS men, but there was one tragic incident. A man out hunting deer with a rifle mistook one of the camouflaged soldiers for his quarry and fired. As so often happens when it is least cause for congratulation, his marksmanship was unerring and the soldier was killed, which was a very disappointing end to a good exercise.

In June 1959 our son, Julian, was born which, after our our earlier disappointment, gave us much happiness. Tragically, he was afflicted by cystic fibrosis but all seemed well at first and it was two years before the correct diagnosis was made, by which time much damage had been done. During his next eleven years he was rarely fully well and had many spells in hospital. Daily physiotherapy to clear his lungs became very wearing and distressing for all of us, particularly for Shirley and for Julian himself.

The Staff College entrance exam began badly. I had prepared carefully but the first paper, Military Law again, was alarmingly difficult. I could not answer enough questions to obtain a pass mark and almost quit the whole exam in despair. Some months later I was simply amazed to learn that I had passed, and with quite good marks too. It transpired later that the law exam had been recognised as being too difficult and all marks obtained in it had been raised by an agreed percentage. The news was soon followed by selection for the 1961 course at Camberley, which dispersed any lingering doubts there might have been about seeking higher pay out of the Army.

As adjutant I commanded the corps of drums and took a close interest in the battalion band, both of which were trained by Bandmaster 'Chink' Holland, a regimental character who had recently retired from the Regular Army after many years' service culminating in being band-sergeant-major of our first-class Regular band. Thanks to Holland both the band and the drums were of high quality and undertook many engagements. Each of these, Holland claimed, took years off his life as he worried about how many of the volunteers would turn up. Usually they all did but it was a constant concern in the TA because there were no sanctions we could apply for absence, apart from dismissal, which was not something one would want to inflict on a skilled instrumentalist. Some of their duties during the summer months were to 'Beat Retreat' on Saturday or Sunday evenings in the towns and villages around the regimental area. These were always popular and well attended, often resulting in new recruits signing on – unlike a famous occasion in regimental history when, in 1913, the whole 1st Battalion set out on a recruiting march the length and breadth of Northamptonshire. The outcome was: recruits nil, deserters three. Holland earned a well-deserved BEM for his work.

At one of the 'Retreats', in Peterborough market square, I was wandering through the crowd when I came across a man of thirty plus years who was clearly emotionally moved by the performance. On questioning him I discovered that he had recently moved to the area and was thinking of joining the TA again, having previously served with a London parachute battalion. He had transferred from the Army to the RAF in the war and had flown Typhoons until being shot down in Normandy. His back had been broken in the crash, which was behind German lines, but French farmers hid him and looked after him until friendly forces overtook him. His name was 'Ali' Barber and he joined us to serve later as Commanding Officer of the battalion and becoming one of the regiment's most loyal supporters. Despite all sorts of difficulties and personal drawbacks (his delightful first wife Jill died of multiple sclerosis, a second marriage folded, and he was always afflicted with medical problems dating back to his crash, often enduring the surgeon's knife), but he never lost his zest for life. Sadly he is now frustratingly confined to a wheelchair but still manages to defy adversity to infect everyone around him with humour and good cheer.

In this, my first full encounter with Terrritorial Army volunteers, I developed a respect for these enthusiasts who, in Churchill's words, were 'twice a citizen'. Their energy was exhausting, especially during the two weeks of Annual Camp, when, on some godforsaken training area in a remote part of Britain, they would train hard and party hard with total disregard for rest and sleep. At the end of the fortnight, when they should have been in the last stages of collapse and their Regular advisers needed a holiday, they would declare themselves fully refreshed and ready to return to work. The married men needed long-suffering wives to put up with the time they spent on their duties but there was no questioning their dedication to becoming as effective soldiers as possible during the time available.

In January 1961 we moved to Camberley.

8
Introduction to the Staff

The attractions of the Army staff course at Camberley included meeting up with old friends from Sandhurst and early service, and getting to know and understand some sixty fellow students from Commonwealth and foreign countries. Assembling during the first few days brought many reunions and earnest discussions about how to tackle the course, which had a formidable reputation and would largely determine one's Army future. Three of us, Basil Bagnall, Derek Boorman and I, decided that three heads were better than one and therefore to do our work together whenever possible. We would discuss the problems together and read each other's work through to check for silly spelling or typing mistakes before handing it in. This, of course, is a sensible way to tackle real staff work and I commended the system to students later when I was on the Directing Staff, and later still as Commandant. We joked that our group was ideal: Basil, a cavalryman had the ideas, Derek shone on detail, and I could spell. Basil, who left the Army a few years later, not therefore realising his potential like his brother who became Chief of the General Staff, endeared himself to us from the start by having indulged in some effective smuggling. He came from Germany where spirits were very cheap indeed and had filled two four-and-a-half-gallon jerricans each with gin and whisky, bringing them back in the guise of 'spare fuel' for his car. We were much amused by his tale of having been required by customs to pay duty on nine gallons of petrol.

The course was intended to be hard work and students were meant often to be under time pressure, but it was rarely stressful. Provided one did not build up a backlog of work there was time to enjoy the social life and the many sports and games that were available, including an introduction to softball which the four American students organised with missionary zeal. In the first few days every student had to give a lecturette to his division of sixty for fifteen minutes on any subject of his own choosing. Some of us found this an ordeal and felt to be on test, but its real purpose was to help the instructors to identify and remember who the students were. In this it was highly effective and nearly forty years later I can still remember many of the subjects chosen by my peers, some of them interesting and a few very funny. One, in particular, by an officer of the Life Guards with a dramatic stammer told hilariously of the perils of being out alone on a horse ahead of mounted troops in the streets of London. Keeping one's distance is very difficult, the clatter of hooves prevents one from hearing muttered instructions from behind, and if one looks back one's horse tends to veer dangerously to one side. He described this happening to him and thus catching his boot in the sling of a footguardsman holding his rifle at the 'present' who was not prepared under any circumstances to let go. He was therefore dragged slithering on the tarmac for some distance and did not observe the discipline of silence when venting his opinions of mounted officers who could not ride straight. I talked about the problems presented by selecting a subject and the possible damning effects of picking the wrong one. Soon after we left the lecturettes were dropped from the curriculum as being too time-consuming and not valuable instruction.

The early weeks were devoted to learning and practising basic staff work, writing official letters and discovering the format of military papers and orders. The approach to problems was strongly encouraged to take the form of the military 'appreciation', a simple and logical method calling for defining the problem, deciding the aim, considering the factors affecting the achievement of that aim, weighing up the pros and cons of possible courses of action, and finally preparing a plan based on the favoured course. Many of the brighter, questioning officers felt this was forcing their minds into a military straitjacket and thus stifling original thought. I do not agree. It suits me as an effective approach and it also means that when it is used to describe a plan and persuade others to agree with it, everyone trained in this way will find the process easier to follow than personal and possibly convoluted flights of imagination and fancy.

Next in the course came instruction and exercises in basic tactics, essentially the application of sound defensive dispositions, and fire and movement in the attack or withdrawal which have held good during the ages. There was a term on counter-revolutionary warfare followed by one in which everything so far, plus the use of nuclear weapons, was applied to the situation in British Army of the Rhine where 1st British Corps was deployed forward among the NATO forces facing possible attack by the Warsaw Pact. Basically the plan was to defend river lines for as long as possible, but when, inevitably, the rivers were crossed the enemy was to be lured into killing zones where he would be struck by nuclear weapons. A premise was always that because of their massively superior numbers and the ability to choose where to concentrate those numbers, resort to nuclear weapons would eventually become inevitable if the advance was to be stopped. Almost every commander over the forty years that NATO tackled this problem brought new ways to defend but the basic threat remained unchanged throughout as did the conclusion with the use of tactical nuclear weapons. I always had problems with the concept, even when commanding a forward division myself. I mostly kept these doubts to myself, not for fear of speaking out, but because it would question the whole *raison d'être* of NATO deployment. I never believed defence using tactical nuclear weapons could succeed because the Russians had even more of them than NATO forces could muster and would be totally ruthless in using them regardless of destruction of their enemies' cities and civilian casualties. NATO would naturally be constrained by this because its attacks on advancing forces would mostly have to be directed onto friendly territory. I recognised the value of deploying and training for the use of nuclear weapons as an important aspect of deterrence, but if either side ever launched one of them the whole strategy of NATO would immediately have failed.

To be honest I never thought that the Warsaw Pact would wish to attack anyway, although we were always harangued by commanders and their intelligence staffs on the imminent likelihood. I could see no advantage to the Soviet Union in taking on the responsibility for huge new populations whose economies had been destroyed. Although their stance was always aggressive this was really based on the same requirements as NATO's, that is to say defence against a threat, which was the way they saw the Americans and the Alliance. It seemed to me that they would see advantage in allowing the West to remain prosperous, although in the end it was essentially the cost of the arms race that contributed strongly to the collapse of the Communist system.

For me the most enduring lessons of the course were learned on the battlefield tour in Normandy when men who had been there in 1944 at senior and junior levels told us their own stories. These had been well practised over ten years or so but most of us found them riveting. We heard about plans and how they succeeded or they failed, depending perhaps on how good they were (usually the simpler the better), whether the troops were capable of carrying them out and, most of all, what the enemy did to frustrate them. This was the real thing, and we learned about the fortunes (and the fog) of war, how strong or weak individuals could turn the course of an action, together with the importance of morale, administration and supply, and control of air and sea. To hear a company commander describing how we were here, they were there, and what happened brought home to many of us how very different was actual combat from the pretty maps and plans we were learning about in the classrooms or the peaceful English countryside. A favoured expression of the day was: 'That's all very well in practice, Colonel, but does it work in theory?'

There were many interesting lectures on current affairs and the machinery of military organisation and civilian government. Some humour was *de rigueur* in most of these lectures and even now I recall a brilliant talk about local government by the town clerk of Reading. He brought a light touch to everything and described the task of local government as being to look after its citizens from the cradle to the grave or, as he put it, 'from sperm to worm, or from poking to Woking'.

There was no published order of merit on the course but directing staff told us each term how we were doing and the definitive answer came in the nature of the job to which one was posted in October of the course year. I did not think I was doing badly but was frankly astonished when I was appointed to be brigade major of 12 Infantry Brigade Group in BAOR, which was one of the top jobs available to the course. This was certainly gratifying, but daunting too, not having served in Germany or indeed on the staff before. It could accurately be described, provided one did it well, as the first step on the fast-moving escalator of the Army.

Four days after their news a letter came from Colonel P. T. Tower, DSO, MBE, a Gunner, congratulating me and saying that he was to be the brigade commander the following May. He said we should meet and invited me to dine with him at the 'In and Out' the following week. The letter included an apology for the venue, his own much more fashionable club was closed for repairs. My instructor at the time, Lieutenant-Colonel Drew Bethell, another Gunner, warned me that Tower had a formidable reputation for sacking people for the slightest fault, and that he was an ocean racing sailor and a dedicated horseman and polo player. It was with quaking heart, therefore, that I waited on the steps of the club at the appointed hour. Soon an apparition appeared, immaculately dressed but riding a little motor scooter. This apparition dismounted, introduced himself as Philip Tower and led me in for a drink. 'This is most kind of you, sir,' I said, 'but there is something I should like to get out of the way at once. I have been told your reputation and I do not see how I can survive. I have never sailed, horses frighten me and I have never even watched polo. We have nothing in common and it is clear that you will sack me within minutes of our working together. Why not get it over now and we can then enjoy our dinner?' 'My dear boy' he said, 'let's be clear. *I* sail the boats, *I* ride the horses; *you* run 12 Brigade.' And thus it was, and we hardly had a cross word in the two and a half years that I worked for him.

In January 1962 we moved to Osnabrück in North-Rhine Westphalia to join 12 Infantry Brigade Group. Its three infantry battalions included my own, now 2nd East Anglian, the Northamptons having amalgamated with the Royal Lincolns under the 'Duncan Sandys Axe' in 1959, the Lancashire Fusiliers and the Prince of Wales's Own Regiment of Yorkshire. The latter battalion, commanded by Lieutenant-Colonel Billy Armour, was based in Wuppertal, one hundred miles away. Billy was a crafty Commanding Officer who played the distance card with skill. Mail from him to us never took more than forty-eight hours, whereas he claimed that ours to him took at least two weeks, if it arrived at all. He could rarely be raised on the telephone, having an adjutant with the standing instruction to say that the Colonel was out. This same Commanding Officer once asked me, before a large audience, to explain the difference between Greenwich Mean and Central European times and why the RAF worked on one and we worked on another. This may sound easy but as I was nervous and not expecting it, complications suddenly set in.

The armoured regiment was 16th/5th Lancers who, with the other two infantry battalions, were also in Osnabrück, and our gunners 6th Field Regiment who were in Münsterlager 120 miles away. We had our own service units in and around the Osnabrück area.

The brigade commander was Brigadier Pat Man. On the first morning I was ushered in to his office to be greeted. He smoked sixty cigarettes a day and through the haze I could see a small man with a bristly moustache and round steel-framed spectacles who opened the batting by telling me that he had tried to have my posting overruled not only because he thought brigade majors should be older and more experienced but because he was particularly concerned that I had not served in BAOR. I could only say that I would do my best. I also decided, although I had given up smoking three years before, that I would have to start again in self-defence. Pat Man was well known throughout BAOR for the seriousness with which he took nuclear warfare. There were no 'NBC suits' then and for all exercises 12 Brigade alone were required to don steel helmets, drape them with personal camouflage netting and wear gloves at all times. This, known as 'beekeepers' order', was the best protection available at the time and although I cannot question Man's determination to make training as realistic as possible we were a source of mirth to the rest of the Command.

Pat Man had an extraordinary memory for names and made it a feature of his command style. He reckoned to know all the officers in the brigade together with those of most of their wives and many of their children, together with untold numbers of soldiers. We joked that as he was driven to work he would give a lift to some unsuspecting soldier walking along and minding his own business. The soldier probably had not a problem in the world when he got in the car but he always had several when he got out, and these would be conveyed to us on the staff for immediate inquiry or action. I can remember being asked, for instance, to investigate at once why Private X was being sent on a week's course at about the time his wife was expecting a baby. The answer from his unit was that birth dates were seldom precise and if the baby arrived while the soldier was away he would be recalled at once, but this did not satisfy Pat Man and it had to be changed.

I was determined to prove the Brigadier wrong about my inexperience and worked long hard hours for those first few months. There were difficulties and mistakes but nothing serious and I was relieved to survive until Philip Tower's arrival. He had not served in BAOR either, but had fought with distinction in North Africa and at Arnhem.

An interesting early problem which came our way was a fracas between the Cameronians in the next-door brigade at Minden and the local civilians. This resulted in the *Daily Mirror* describing the Scottish soldiers as 'The Poison Dwarfs'. The soldiers naturally took grave exception to this and came close to insurrection. The press descended on Minden in force and many of the reporters behaved disgracefully, for instance bribing men going home to lunch in their quarters to go back and smuggle out plates of food which were then spoiled, reduced and photographed. There came a point at which we had to deploy one of our battalions to fields outside Minden on a Saturday night, ready to go in and sort out the serious trouble that was expected. Happily things quietened down but the publicity had put everyone on their guard. Two days later the provost-sergeant of the Lancashire Fusiliers, with whom we shared a barracks, rang and told me with some pride that a reporter from the *Guardian* had been seen 'snooping' around the gate. The Commanding Officer was away so he was ringing me, the senior officer in camp, to report with pride that he had 'locked the bugger up'.

Horrified by this news I told the disappointed NCO to release the man at once and bring him to my office, where I hastily laid out tea and other refreshments. The reporter, by now aggressive, said that the press pack were in Minden but he thought he would seek originality and look elsewhere for his story. Now, having been locked up, he thought he had one, and guessed that I would not allow him access to the rest of the barracks. Crossing my fingers I said we had nothing to hide and he was welcome to go anywhere he liked and talk to anyone he found provided only that he ended up in my office to warn me of what I might expect from him. When he came back he said I had been fair to him so he would be fair to me and although he could he would write no damaging story. Relieved and grateful I gave him lunch and he kept his word.

Not long afterwards a Cameronian soldier was court martialled and the press complained that they had not been alerted to this, despite it being of national public interest. The Secretary of State, John Profumo, already under parliamentary pressure for being economical with the truth about the Kuwait operation, explained when questioned in the House that a notice, as required by law, had been posted on the barracks gate and the 'the press had missed a trick'. It was 'not his ministry's business', he said, 'to advertise such events.' The media took this as a challenge and went for him. He happened to be visiting our headquarters a few days later and was called to the telephone during lunch. He returned, white with shock, and left at once. Later that day he resigned having been exposed by the press for his part in the 'Keeler Affair'.

In September of that year there was a divisional exercise which was going to be a major test for us. The outline plan was that 12 Brigade should cross two major rivers but then be subjected to an overwhelming armoured attack, although we did not know about that last part until it happened. The river crossings had gone well and I had learned a little about the art of gamesmanship from our sapper squadron commander. He had to construct a bridge against the clock over the River Leine and we needed to know exactly how long it would take. The squadron commander, Major Len Garrett, promised he would complete the job in one hour. It actually took fifty minutes and Len was warmly congratulated on his efficiency. Much later I discovered that official sapper yardsticks decreed that it should actually have taken only forty minutes.

At about 0300 hrs in the morning of the fourth day we began to get reports of armour approaching our forward positions. In the next two hours those positions were overrun and I woke Philip Tower and advised a tactical withdrawal. 'Nonsense,' he said, 'you're panicking. Let us remain calm and serve breakfast at 0700 hrs as usual. And don't forget I shall want my usual hot rolls and a copy of the morning paper.' By 0630 hrs we could hear the approaching tanks, but the Brigadier was not to be diverted. We were in a wood overlooking a narrow valley and as breakfast was served we could see the leading enemy tank squadron below us about 300 yards away. At this point the Brigadier agreed that things were quite serious and promptly took off in his helicopter with the Gunner Commanding Officer, telling us where to bring the headquarters to catch him up. I was very glad this was only an exercise but with a certain amount of gamesmanship of my own managed to infiltrate most of the headquarters back to safety. Our forward troops were furious that the tanks had ignored minefields, umpires and defensive fire and simply motored on regardless. They felt this was cheating but I had the feeling that the Russians would also have 'cheated' and that the attack was quite realistic. Our brigade was largely overrun but, like all exercises at that time, the enemy advance was stopped by a judicious nuclear strike. In my view that was much less realistic.

At the beginning of my tour army aircraft were concentrated in squadrons, but in order to promote the 'brigade group' concept, which proposed that brigades should be capable of operating independently or switching from division to division with ease, it was decided that those brigades which could provide hangarage and a runway could have their Skeeter helicopter and Auster fixed-wing aircraft devolved to their command. News of this was brought to me by Captain Mike Somerton-Rayner, who would command the flight if it came to us. Mike, an adventurer and a bit of a rogue who was not only a good pilot but a skilled engineer, could be very persuasive. Among many aviating exploits he had rebuilt a crashed Auster in Malaya and flown it back to Britain. This aircraft, known as the Yellow Peril, was with him in Germany and, indeed, is still flying today. Mike told me that Headquarters 1st British Corps would be allotting flights in the order in which brigades could provide the necessary facilities. I took it upon myself to ring up at once and say that we were already prepared. What I did not explain was that the hangarage would be provided by relieving the Lancashire Fusiliers of some of their vehicle garages, and that the runway would run diagonally across their football pitch. This was not popular with Lieutenant-Colonel Jim Wilson, a highly charismatic Greenjacket imported to command the battalion and dubbed 'Swinging Jim' by one of the tabloid newspapers. This sobriquet arose from a combination of competence on a guitar and instructing soldiers in his battalion football team to call him by his Christian name when he was on the field of play as their coach. Not only was he a strong personality accustomed to getting his way, but he was hugely keen on football and was, indeed, the football correspondent of the *Sunday Times*. This job complicated some of our training exercises because we had to make sure he could get away early enough on a Friday to cover a Saturday football match. As an aside on Jim, he once called me to his office, took me through the Army List, calculated that there were too many people of my age in my own regiment and that my chances of command were minimal. I should therefore transfer at once to the Lancashire Fusiliers where I could be assured of command. I did not fall for this and was vindicated not only by commanding my own battalion but also seeing the Lancashire Fusiliers disappear in the next tranche of amalgamations.

Somehow Jim was placated, and accepted that occasionally a match would be interrupted for a 'plane to land or take off. Having our own aircraft in days when what was done with them was not scrutinised by accountants in the way they are today was a bonus, and we made full use of it. Our aircraft were incorporated in every possible exercise and greatly facilitated the many reconnaissances that were necessary (and, I confess, some that were not). My own most enterprising foray arose from a need to visit a brigade adventure training centre. Such training was in its military infancy but recognised as both valuable and enjoyable. Adventure training in our brigade, which was suddenly and rightly becoming fashionable, had hitherto been arranged simply by allotting money to those units who could think up the most imaginative way to spend it. Major John Tippen, our GSO3 (Training), thought the money could be more effectively used if spent centrally on various brigade centres, each run by one of our major units, but open to bids from all the arms and services of the brigade. We set up a canoeing centre in Holland, mountaineering in Bavaria, sailing in the Baltic, and scuba diving in the Adriatic near Trieste. The prospect of going back to Trieste again made a staff visit there essential to me and we decided to go by Auster.

The shortest route would have been over Austria, but as a neutral non-member of NATO that country would only allow military aircraft in its airspace 'for humanitarian reasons'. This we could hardly claim, so, with Brian Read, our new Sapper squadron commander and I as passengers, Mike flew us via Saarbrücken, Lyons, Nice (night stop), Genoa, Piacenza and Rivolta. We had an epic adventure of our own and overcame many hazards, including some aggressive French fighters at Saarbrücken and serious bad weather in Italy, but all was well and the diving centre, run by our new armoured regiment, the 9th/12th Lancers, was first class.

Our Station Staff Officer, Major Jack Bickford, a retired officer formerly of the Worcestershire Regiment, who was an entertaining character with a taste for gin and a perfectly delightful wife, now thriving in her nineties, watched a hockey match in which I was playing for the headquarters. Somewhat disparagingly because I was only thirty-three he said afterwards that it would soon be clear to me, if not already so, that hockey was more of a young man's game. He strongly advised that I should take up fly fishing and undertook to teach me the art. After casting practice on the football pitch he took me to the lakes at Sennelager where, after very few throws, I caught my first trout and have been hooked ever since. I am very grateful to Jack, now sadly long dead, for the pleasure that the sport has afforded to me.

The social life in Osnabrück was such that an au pair was necessary for Julian and we advertised for one in two Dutch papers. A number of us sought Dutch girls because it saved punitive German national insurance extras. In emergency they would be looked after by the military services and for less urgent illness they could be driven home in an hour or so. We had a number of replies and chose Topy Das, who was just sixteen and wanted to learn English and German. She stayed with us for three years and became, and still is, a friend of the family. She went to an Italian aristocratic family after leaving us and later became an air hostess with Alitalia, rising to become their senior stewardess. She now runs a boutique in Rome but has never married.

The Army was becoming more alert to the need for physical fitness and the fact that too much drink was being consumed, especially in Germany where it was cheap. The corps commander, Lieutenant-General Sir Charles Jones, nicknamed 'Splosh' after some bridging disaster in his younger days as a sapper (I think), set out to brief everyone in the corps on the dangers of alcohol, especially when driving. He lectured us in the garrison theatre, warning that alcoholism began with orange, became gin and orange, then gin and tonic, on to pink gin, gin and water and finally just gin. He said there should be no drinking at lunchtime and that it was positively rude to expect people to drive more than a short distance to a cocktail party. When he got back to our mess for lunch I found in my pigeonhole an invitation to drinks from his headquarters at Bielefeld forty miles away, and the general himself quickly demolished three pink gins before lunch. Nevertheless I believe his message did have some effect.

Some time after Pat Man left I decided to give up smoking again and the REME warrant officer commanding our light aid detachment (small mobile workshop) bet me that I could not do so for six months. When I won this bet he said that rather than pay up in cash he would be honoured if Shirley and I would be his guests at the annual masonic ladies night dinner. Curious about this organisation I gladly accepted. In the event I was surprised – and, I have to admit, disapproving - when I saw men of all ranks from private to major addressing each other on christian name terms. It seemed to me to be a secret society which cut across the hierarchical system and laid itself open to abuse, though I had no evidence that this was the case in that lodge. During dinner the German head waiter whispered in my ear that he thought I might be the senior officer present and that I should be aware that President Kennedy had been assassinated. I passed this on to the major who was in charge of the entertainment with the suggestion that dancing after dinner should be cancelled and that we should all make our way home. He decided to call a meeting of his committee and returned to announce that they had decided that Kennedy would have wished them to carry on as planned. Shirley and I left quietly, much embarrassed.

Most brigade majors held their jobs for two years but for some reason the system lost track of me and I had a third year. Reasonably professionally competent by now I was thoroughly enjoying the job and particularly a friendship with Brian Read, the sapper squadron commander, whom I designated my key tactical adviser, and our Deputy Assistant Adjutant and Quartermaster General (DQ for short), who was the senior administrative officer on the brigade staff. This was Major John Chapple. John and Brian were quite exceptionally capable and likeable officers and the brigade was running smoothly. Philip Tower trusted us and even if he did not agree with any decisions taken in his absence he never failed to support them on his return.

There were two annual 'trade tests' for brigades and their commanders in BAOR. One was the autumn exercise, which was usually fun, but the other, far more daunting, was the winter study period. Hours would be spent over maps and cloth models debating the best way to solve the insoluble, namely how to win if the Warsaw Pact attacked. These events took two days and were attended by many senior commanders usually including the C-in-C, most of them working out what to say in forthcoming confidential reports. Philip was nervous about this; it was not really his scene and he did not want to cross swords with BAOR pundits who tended to be very fixed in their views. He was also conscious that none of his staff had previous BAOR experience and were sceptical about some of the pet theories. I, therefore, suggested that we move to safer ground. The impact of the Staff College battlefield tour had been such that I felt sure a similar tour of Arnhem would be equally valuable, and much more interesting than tactical theories over a model. Philip had been Brigade Major Royal Artillery in the battle there himself and knew a number of others who would be prepared to come and tell of their experiences. It was not lost on him that Major-General 'Tubby' (later General Sir Mervyn) Butler, the divisional commander, was of the Parachute Regiment, and the C-in-C, General Sir John Hackett, had himself commanded a brigade in the battle. The war stories were enthralling and the tour a great success, which did no harm to anyone's career.

Some months before the end of my tour the Commanding Officer of 1st Battalion, 2nd East Anglian, Lieutenant-Colonel Pat Erskine-Tulloch sent for me and warned me that because of my youth he feared I would not command a company when I returned to the battalion, because there were too many majors senior to me. Perhaps I was overweeningly self-satisfied at that time but I felt that after three years as a brigade major anything less than commanding a company would be unreasonable. Knowing that the Parachute Regiment had a number of vacancies, and foreseeing an active and perhaps exciting time I launched an application to transfer. This caused a furore and I was castigated by Colonel Reggie Denny, now Brigade Colonel The East Anglian Brigade, for conceit and disloyalty. However, after a month of exhausting physical preparation for acceptance by the Paras I was assured that I would command a company in my own battalion after all, and I confess that it was with some relief that I withdrew my application. I am not proud of this episode but it had a happy outcome for me.

I had thoroughly enjoyed my time with 12 Brigade and it had not only taught me about staff work and the mystique of BAOR but had forged many valued and useful relationships. I felt I had been compared with my peers over the previous four years and not found seriously wanting, so it was with a measure of self-confidence and satisfaction that we now prepared for a spell in sunny Cyprus.

9
Company Command and Back to Camberley

Military people, who frequently change the nature and location of their work, are often asked which place or job they enjoyed most. I do not find this easy to answer, having been lucky enough to have taken pleasure in everything I did. Distance lends a rosy tint to one's memory, as one recalls the good things and tends to forget or laugh about the bad things, but none of the jobs I did ended with a minus sign in the enjoyment balance. Other tours may be more taxing or rewarding but for the infantry officer command of a company is probably the best time. An infantry officer's ambition, traditionally, should be to command his own battalion and that is certainly a marvellous thing to do, but it is also where the buck stops. In addition to excitement and fulfilment it brings with it many worries and disappointments, especially when officers or soldiers let the side down in some way. A company is different. It is probably the last time that one knows everyone under one's command well, and pretty well everything about them, and the administrative responsibilities are relatively light.

Company command in a Sovereign Base Area in Cyprus at that time must be hard to beat as a peacetime occupation. The two SBAs were not outposts of colonialism but had practical importance in the waging of the Cold War and possible involvement in Middle Eastern troubles. Akrotiri was a staging base for air operations and Dhekelia the home of vital intelligence radio listening posts with a wide radius of interception northwards and eastwards. In each Area there was a battalion whose role was to protect that Area from internal unrest or external threat. There were many wearing guard duties to be performed but plenty of time over for training and sport, with ideal weather conditions virtually all year round and a wealth of interesting training areas and opportunities. Troubles there have certainly been, with the endless differences between Greek and Turk communities and occasional, usually muted, objection to the occupation of the SBAs, but our tour was untroubled by either of these threats. This was, of course, before the 1974 Turkish invasion and the respective attitudes towards us of the two resident nationalities were interesting. The Greeks, inimical since Enosis days, were in many cases surly and resentful of the British presence, but the Turks, in the minority and feeling threatened and oppressed, courted British friendship as a source of protection in the event of attack by the Greeks. Returning to the island ten years later one saw signs of this situation being exactly reversed, including the reasons for it.

National Service had provided a wide variety of interests, skills and talents (or lack of them) in the make-up of a group of soldiers. From the country's point of view it was an irreplaceable source of manpower when Britain's military responsibilities demanded so much greater strength than today. Few National Servicemen, with distant hindsight, will now say that the experience was a waste of time. Mostly they say that it was an experience which made them fitter, quickly mature and self-reliant, and with a better understanding of good behaviour and sympathy for the needs of other people. There are often calls for a return to some form of service to counter the selfishness, violence and lack of consideration for others that is so widely prevalent in the country in the nineties. This is totally impractical, if only on grounds of expense when the costs of arming, equipping and paying the conscripts is added up. Least support for the idea would come from the Services themselves. They would not wish to be made responsible for the nation's discipline; their role is defence, not social engineering, and it is very frustrating for Regular soldiers that as soon as a group is welded into something worthwhile it departs *en masse* and is immediately replaced by another, new lot to be moulded into shape.

Command of Regular soldiers called for a slightly different style. National Servicemen were, many of them, reluctant soldiers and obedience and respect had to be obtained more forcefully than with volunteers. I am not suggesting that officers and NCOs had to change their methods substantially but it was possible to relax and trust more than before. Because their time in the Army was so short National Servicemen had to be taught to obey without pause or question and many officers, though not the best ones, found it unnecessary to explain and justify their orders in a way that became necessary with Regular soldiers. Modern professionals, taking a close interest in their career, were entitled to full explanations about tactics or procedures and were encouraged to ask questions. Dealing with them in this way built up a mutual trust and respect so that if, *in extremis,* the boss needed to say that there was no time for questions it would be accepted. This may be oversimplifying the case but, statistically, the numbers of soldiers charged with minor offences dropped dramatically when National Service ended. The change of attitude was very apparent to me when I rejoined the battalion that I had left in 1958, nearly seven years before.

When the initial amalgamation of the regiments of Eastern England regiments was ordered, the officers and men were, with good reason, mostly bitter and resistant, particularly those older members who had long service in one of the former regiments. The need to reduce the total number of battalions was hard to gainsay but the senior retired officers, the colonels of the regiments, and many of the longer-serving officers, warrant officers and sergeants found the whole exercise distasteful. The common thought, though rarely spoken, was: 'My regiment should be preserved, that regiment should be disbanded.' Reasons given to back this were based on history, current strength, recruiting potential, current role, state of training, anything really to avoid or postpone the evil day. This discord came to a head when the order to form four battalions from the original seven was decreed. The colonels could not agree on titles, mainly because some of the regiments were in East Anglia, but others (such as Northamptons, Royal Lincolns and Leicesters) were not. They persisted in their recalcitrance until General Templer, the Chief of the Imperial General Staff of the day, lost his rag (which he was prone to do) and directed that there would be one title common to three new battalions, namely 'East Anglian', although they could be separate regiments if they so wished. They did, and it took another five years before the decision was taken, still disputed to this day, to form a 'Large Regiment' entitled The Royal Anglian Regiment, initially with four regular battalions but, after successive cuts, now only two.

The battalion, housed in good barracks in Dhekelia and commanded by Lieutenant-Colonel Dick Chambers, was in good order and happy. I was given B Company, which was up to strength, and I took over from Derek Wilford, now a Regular, whom I had last known as a National Service subaltern in Malaya. The soldiers, mostly from Lincolnshire, Northamptonshire and Leicestershire, were generally well-behaved and well-motivated. The company sergeant-major, McColgan, and the sergeants ran a tight ship and discipline was seldom a problem. There was plenty of sporting prowess in the company and at the annual distribution of battalion internal prizes the company lifted most of them. One, on which McColgan had set his heart, and, I suspect, has never forgiven me for losing, was the drill competition. This was instituted to decide which company should provide the Escort to the Colour on a forthcoming 'trooping' parade. One point separated Michael Barthorp's A Company and B. The words of command for the final test were given by the company commander himself and in our case, to my shame, I gave the order to 'break into quick time' after the slow march past on the wrong foot. This, McColgan claimed, cost us the one point, and sadly I am sure he is right. He allowed me no credit for all the ones I gave correctly.

We had rehearsed for this competition while detached for a month to a small camp near the summit of Mount Olympus guarding the radar station there. There was little else to do and much of our time was occupied in parade ground drill, which, as I have explained elsewhere, is not really my scene, and in education. In order to qualify for their pay soldiers had to pass the 3rd Class Army Certificate of Education. This was a fairly simple test in maths, English and general knowledge and we had too many men who had previously failed or not taken it. The platoon commanders and I took up schoolmastering for a month and managed to get all of our students through, although I have to confess to a measure of teaching solely towards a particular exam and have a twinge of conscience now, as a school governor, when I inveigh against that style as not providing education in the true and broader sense. This is one of the pernicious effects of league tables for schools.

Evenings on Mount Olympus were mostly spent in teaching my three subalterns bridge. At least one of their mothers, Lieutenant Guy Hipkin's, applauded this exercise although to her disappointment it failed to implant in her son any lasting enthusiasm for the game.

There were many exercises and we became well trained in low level tactics although there was no armour to train with and guns and aircraft were few and far between. One of the highlights was a month in Libya when we were introduced to the desert. The North African campaign was one that I had studied for the staff exam and it was a great experience to visit some of the famous places of 1940 to '42, with evocative names such as Tobruk, Derna, Halfaya Pass, Bomba and Mechili, and to learn about some of the techniques and problems at first hand. I loved the desert. It could be too hot, too cold, too flyblown, too dirty or too gritty, but there was a certain romance about it and the very special experience was the sky at night, when the stars seemed to be twice as close as anywhere else in my experience. The maps were quite good and I became deeply interested in navigation by mileometer, sun-compass and the sun by day, and even more so in using the same instruments and the pole star by night. This could be astonishingly accurate and on one night move of the whole company in vehicles we were only 300 yards out after thirty miles.

The GOC Cyprus, Major-General Rodney Burgess, paid us a visit in Libya and because he had recently directed that 50 per cent of our training should be at night, and because B Company happened to be planning live firing by night on the date that he visited, we were a natural target. The following account, written at the time, is taken from the regimental magazine.

> My plan was simple and straightforward, though as will be seen, far from foolproof. I wanted the company to see the cumulative effect of all their weapons firing at once and to achieve this I lined them up about 500 yards from the seashore to oppose an imaginary invasion. The layout may have been tactically unsound but it did mean that everyone could fire at once, including our anti-tank guns on a flank and our mortars behind and to one side so that they would not be firing bombs directly overhead. The idea was that trip-flares set off by pulling on wires from the position would be sited at intervals coming up from the sea. These would represent the enemy advance. At the final flare, 200 yards away, illuminating rounds would be fired by the mortars to show up a line of targets which would then be engaged by everything we had got. There was not enough ammunition for a dress rehearsal but I was confident of a spectacular display.
>
> We dug the positions in the morning and in the afternoon the company pulled back to rest while company headquarters put out the targets and the trip flares. The CSM and I attended to the latter and, to avoid accidents, decided to leave the safety pins in until last light, just before the company moved up to practise night occupation. When the time came the CSM was otherwise engaged so I went forward to remove the pins from the flare pots myself. Everything was ready by 2000 hrs and we

sat and waited for the general's party which was due to arrive at 2100hrs. After half an hour the CSM whispered: 'You did remove *both* pins?' I was too old a soldier to fall for that one and just laughed. With a quarter of an hour to go the CSM said: 'There *are* two pins, you know.' I had only removed one. In pitch darkness in front of a position bristling with itchy trigger fingers we went out to find the flares and remove the other pin. To remove the pin on the spring of a flare you must first replace the one on the pot. Trying in the dark to get a slightly splayed pin in a small hole when you are trembling with suppressed tension and, I confess, suppressed giggles, is not easy, but somehow it got done. We returned at 2100 hrs to find the signaller trying to receive a morse message about the general's time of arrival. He could get everything except the time. Generals are usually late so we relaxed. Suddenly the signaller got it – 2115 hrs. We looked up and there, about five miles across the desert, we could see vehicle lights approaching. The plan was for the general to visit the mortars first and Terry Taylor [later Colonel and, as a civilian later, for some years commander of the United Nations Chemical Weapons Inspection Team in Iraq], the Support Platoon Commander, and I ran as hard as we could go and just made it.

'Good evening sir' we said, trying to look relaxed despite heaving chests and pounding hearts.

After looking at the mortars I led the vehicles back along a track to a slight bend from which we could walk to the main position. Unfortunately it looked different in headlights and I had to guess. Everyone got out and I apologised to the general and his party, which included Dick Chambers and Michael Barthorp, now second-in-command, for making them walk but it would only take ten minutes. We padded off into the desert, I having lost all night vision because of the vehicle lights. After fifteen minutes Michael came up beside me and asked, sardonically, if I was aiming at a star. No, I was not. After twenty minutes Dick Chambers asked if I could see that distant lighthouse. Yes, sir, I could. The problem was that I had not the faintest idea where I was. I saw a low hill and asked the party to wait while I went up 'to get my bearings', and collect my thoughts. I couldn't see a thing but decided to stake my all on a gamble: 'It's all right general, it's just over there' I said with all the confidence I could muster, and aimed due north. The next ten minutes took ten years to pass and I could hear the general beginning to clear his throat ominously when to my amazement and delight a voice rang out: 'Who goes there?' It was a welcome sound; if that sentry had been asleep we might still be walking.

After these adventures I feared the shooting might be an anti-climax, but it went like clockwork and was a most impressive show. With a mighty crash of sound the still desert night was filled with streams of tracer and the red glow of ricochets sailing, seemingly slowly, at all angles. White phosphorous from the mortars painted a superb backcloth to the display.

When the general had inspected the targets, which fortunately were well peppered, I guided the visitors back to their vehicles, where happily I had had the foresight to tell them to leave on their sidelights. The general was pleased and the party drove off. Heaving sighs of relief I set off back to the position. Half an hour later I was still looking for it.

Cyprus was good for us. Julian had a spell of better than usual health, the weather was always good, the spring flowers beautiful and we were back among the friends of the club that is a regiment. Social life was entertaining and one of the great treats was what for years I used to describe as the best Sunday lunch in the world, namely the Harbour Club in Kyrenia, where, overlooking the picturesque little harbour, one could enjoy food and drink of the highest class. We managed to revisit it ten years later but by then in Turkish hands it was not the same at all.

All good things come to an end and more or less at the same time I received a posting order to the directing staff at the Staff College, and B Company was warned for a three-month emergency tour in Aden, where the increasing civil unrest had meant a call for substantial reinforcement. Our particular job was to protect the airfield at Khormaksar where the Station Commander was a future Chief of the Air Staff, Sir Michael Beetham. It was not a very demanding task but there were a few bombs and shootings which provided occasional excitement. The company was quartered on one floor of the Red Sea Hotel at the east end of the Ma'alla Strait, or 'Bomb Alley'. The other floors offered accommodation for civil aircrews in transit, which provided welcome light relief. The company suffered only one casualty during its tour. A private soldier slept on guard and was sentenced to fourteen days' detention. On his way, under escort, to the detention centre the Land-Rover had a grenade thrown at it. One of the fragments clipped the prisoner's ear, shedding much blood but with no serious effects.

I had hoped to complete the Aden tour with the company but the Staff College demanded my presence urgently. I was given a week to leave Aden, pack up our quarter and move back to Camberley. The timetable meant that I served only twenty-seven days in Aden when, to qualify for the new General Service Medal one had to do twenty eight. Medals then were much prized and even harder to come by than today when numerous United Nations operations qualify, so I was disappointed not to add to my lonely one from Malaya. My flight to Cyprus meant a change of aircraft in Bahrein. Imagine, then, my chagrin when the Comet aircraft I was due to catch from Bahrein lost an engine and I had to wait five days there before a replacement was delivered. We got to Camberley a few days late but nobody there seemed the least put out and I was not due to start teaching until the following term.

The Staff College year was divided up into six terms and directing staff could expect to teach their syndicates of ten officers for four or five of those terms. The remainder of their time was spent in preparing the instruction and the exercises, for which they were spread among various teams, Basic Tactics, Staff Duties, Logistics and so on. With my scepticism about nuclear operations Murphy's Law dictated that I should be appointed to the nuclear team. One side of me said that I was hypocritical in professing enthusiasm for something about which I had severe doubts, but the other argued that if I had doubts I should at least study the whole subject thoroughly in order to justify those doubts to myself, if not to others. The theoretical side of nuclear tactics was actually very interesting and the only real disadvantage was that I had to deliver one of the most boring lectures of the year, namely 'nuclear effects'. I had to admit to colleagues that it was boring despite all attempts to enliven it but they got at me in the first year by removing one of the pages of my script and seeing whether anyone noticed. They did not and having, by this stage, lulled myself into near stupor neither did I.

For one of the early lectures of the year Lieutenant-Colonel David Anderson, Royal Highland Fusiliers, and I were asked to operate the slide machines in the projection room at the back of the Alanbrooke Hall, the great lecture theatre. This particular lecture was supported by more than a hundred slides, all neatly packed in four boxes in the correct order and the right way up. Half way through the event there was a crash and I looked over to see that David had knocked over the box of slides next to be shown and they were scattered across the floor. We tossed a coin to determine which of us should go down into the hall and declare a 'short break due to technical problems'. I lost. The presenters were not pleased.

A fellow instructor was Lieutenant-Colonel Harry Dalzell-Payne, Queen's Own Hussars. He was a Sandhurst contemporary and unquestionably the outstanding character of our generation. He had a razor-sharp brain and could not only think on his feet but articulate the result of such thought with powerful and persuasive argument. He was inexhaustible and a burner of his candle at both ends second to none. It seemed he could be fired up with strong drink and fervour at about six in the morning and yet be fresh as paint and looking as if he had slept well two hours later. He and his wife lived next door to us and we were both instructors in the detached division at Minley Manor which was some three miles away from the main college building and had a style of its own. Naturally Harry and I shared transport and took it in turns to drive to work. This led all too often to our returning home hours later than anyone else because Harry liked a drink or two and a chat to round off his day. Probably the worst such experience was after a guest night when at 0530 hrs he and I were sitting in a Little Chef restaurant en route, I almost comatose with tiredness, but Harry engaged in lively political discussion with two lorry drivers. That was the only time Shirley ever had to ring up to ask where I was and whether anything had happened to me.

Harry always lived close to the edge and a common expression about him was that he was destined either for field marshal or court martial. Sadly, although he avoided the latter, he did come unstuck over an allegation that his house staff were involved in the smuggling of some port in a horse box, years later, when he was commanding a division, and he had to leave the Army as a major-general.

The brief Arab/Israeli war in 1967 called for close Staff College attention. Among the student body were one Israeli and ten or so from Arab countries. The Israeli left for home at once, returning ten days later having qualified for a couple of medals. He described waiting at Heathrow with the actor Topol and then sitting uncomfortably in an aircraft stuffed with Centurion tank spares. There was,

COMPANY COMMAND AND BACK TO CAMBERLEY

naturally, intense interest in the war and we, the staff, set up an information board in the main hall on which the latest information was plotted with pins and chinagraph, red for Arabs and blue for Israelis. After two or three days the Arab students demanded a collective audience of the commandant, Major-General 'Tubby' Butler, who wondered what on earth was coming. 'We wish to complain officially,' they said. 'Why on your information board have you marked the maps in blue for Israeli forces and red for the Arabs when the convention is for friendly forces to be marked in blue, and enemy forces in red?' There was no answer to this and with no Israeli now present we turned them into enemy on our map.

One of the map exercises in the year was a very complicated one on the logistic support of a supposed strong invasion force in Burma. I hasten to say that the choice of terrain was practical and in no way political. One of the problems involved complex juggling of road, rail, water and air transport and it was to my syndicate that General Butler chose to pay one of his visits to listen to the instruction. I had divided the syndicate into two groups and invited each to present their solution, trying, as was the general, to follow their calculations in our 'pink'. This was the Staff College answer, or DS solution, named after the colour of the paper on which it was printed and provided to help the instructor. One of my sub-syndicates, headed by Captain Bill Woodburn, a bright Sapper, produced a solution that delivered the supplies quicker and more efficiently than the 'pink'. I could not weave my way through the calculations to work how this was done and when the time came to comment and sum up I had to admit that I was stumped. The general left, inviting me to call on him in his office when we had worked it out. I turned the whole thing over to Woodburn to prepare a suitable answer. This was sent to the Commandant's office and nothing more was heard, but I could have wished that the general's only visit to my syndicate that year might have been when something more in my line was being discussed.

As when I had been a student, the battlefield tour was, for me, a highlight, if not the highlight, of the year. I was put in charge of the Overlord team which comprised six veterans from D Day with fascinating stories to tell of their experiences on that day and the ones that followed. My job was to ensure that the presenter and the students were all in the right place at the right time, and then to point out the ground and to orientate everyone with their maps. The difficult part was marshalling the presenters who, over the years, had become great friends and regarded the whole exercise as an excuse for their biggest continuous four-day party of the year. One of the most remarkable was Colonel Alastair Pearson, holder of four DSOs and commander of a parachute battalion on the extreme left flank of the invasion in the Bois de Bavent. He had divided his battalion up into small patrols and then held off successive divisional attacks by the enemy for days. He had exciting stories to tell and the only problem was to tune in and interpret his deep, gruff voice and thick Glaswegian accent. He liked to stay up drinking and talking all night every night and I had to organise a rota of students to keep him company.

In the second year one of our old hands was unable to come and we had to look for a replacement at short notice. We recruited Lord Lovat, featured in the film *The Longest Day*, who had led his commando to relieve John Howard and his glider-borne soldiers at what is now Pegasus Bridge. He travelled to Normandy in a sailing boat and I met him at Deauville to find him well seasoned with good cheer after a bibulous crossing. When we reached his hotel, Le Chat Botté, and as we walked up the short drive, we could see, sitting on the patio and drinking a green cocktail called a Perroquet, the fierce, hatchet-faced features of Colonel Hans von Lück, who had played a major part in defeating Operation Goodwood, a British corps attack towards Caen later in the campaign. The noble lord took one look at the profile of this distinguished former Wehrmacht officer and said 'My God, a Kraut, how terrifying. I'm not going anywhere near him!' and turned and marched off down the road. We had to move him to another hotel.

In early 1968 I learned that I was to command 2nd Royal Anglian in June. Somehow the *Daily Mirror* heard that I was the youngest commanding officer to be appointed since the war. I have no idea how they came by this story. It was not true anyway; I knew of at least one that was younger than I. The story had two immediate effects. The first was that I was nominated by the Ministry of Defence to star in an officer recruiting newspaper advertisement and spent a whole day being bounced around in a Land-Rover, trying to look operational and having hundreds of photographs taken. This exercise came to nothing; not good-looking enough I suppose. The other effect was a television interview in which I was asked, along with other questions, if it would be difficult for me to command a battalion in which some of the officers would be older than I. The only answer I could think of was that it should not be difficult for me and I profoundly hoped it would not be difficult for them.

The battalion was to be the last regular unit to serve in Suffolk and we moved to join it in Felixstowe.

10
Battalion Command

We were the last occupants of Normandy Barracks, Felixstowe. The barracks are now replaced by the huge dock facilities and the only remaining recognisable building is the old officers' mess, which is now a haven in which HM Customs and Excise officers take their tea-breaks. The battalion was in 19 Infantry Brigade in the Strategic Reserve and its role was to be ready to serve anywhere in the world at short notice. The advantage of this was that training exercises could be varied widely both in their style and in where they were held, which made them all interesting. The disadvantage was what is now called 'overstretch'. I commanded the battalion for twenty-seven months and twenty-three of those were away from our barracks and families. Some of the absences were in British training areas but so far as the family is concerned Otterburn and Sennybridge might as well be in Africa or Asia for all the contact they allow.

I took over from Lieutenant-Colonel Ian Haycraft, formerly of the Royal Norfolks, and although I am sure he gave me lots of good advice the only thing I can now remember was commending to me the newly established battalion pig and duck farm which, he said, would make a fortune, as similar ventures had done for units in Germany. The farm was efficiently and amusingly managed by Captain Richard Dinnin and the pigs and ducks were healthy and fat, but Suffolk farmers were not so permissive as German ones and regularly pulled expensive wool over Dinnin's eyes. Resenting our free accommodation for the pigs they ganged up when they came to Ipswich market. Probably they entertained Richard generously before and after the auction but it took the best part of a year before he discovered that our pigs were fetching half the price of everyone else's. The farm was fun and gave rise to some amusing exchanges of signals about its births and deaths and the naming of new piglets and ducklings when we were away, but it made no money and happily was closed before losses became serious.

Within a month of my taking over we were off back to Cyprus for a month for a reinforcement exercise, based in the barracks which the battalion had left less than a year before. It was a busy month but the only event of any significance was the final attack during the final exercise in which the battalion tried out some novel infiltration tactics, moving quietly through the enemy positions by night and then attacking them from the rear shortly before dawn. This was wholly successful and surprised the umpires and exercise directors as much as it did the players, including, perhaps, ourselves.

As Spain was making threatening noises against Gibraltar and had closed the land frontier, it had been decided in 1967 to reinforce the single garrison battalion on the Rock with as much of a second battalion as could be accommodated there, which was a headquarters, two rifle companies and the battalion support weapons. The families and the remaining rifle company were left in Felixstowe, which was a most unsatisfactory arrangement for a commanding officer, but with Gibraltar's castle in our cap badge and three of our former regiments having featured in the great siege of 1779-83, we seemed an eminently suitable unit to come to the Rock's defence in 1968/69.

Lodgings in Gibraltar were provided by the Royal Air Force, which brought their accommodation close to bursting point. The Station Commander was Group Captain Gordon Burgess who felt that tight discipline and control over his expanded community were essential. He was to be a hard taskmaster and, when I went out to reconnoitre, spent much time bringing home to me every detail of his station standing orders which he wished me to bring to everyone's attention before departure. It was clear that the RAF were determined to dominate every detail of our lives much more formally than our people were accustomed to. A cottage in the town was available to me but to keep an eye on things I chose to live in the officers' mess with the others, and am sure I was right, although I took less than kindly to having my room inspected once a week.

Gibraltar has great historical interest and its people were most hospitable to us, but it is very, very small. We could not, of course, cross the border for training, although for the first few weeks it was possible to cross the bay to Algeciras, take a taxi to Soto Grande, play a fully caddied round of golf on that famous course, quaff *sangria* afterwards and yet return with change from five pounds. On one such trip my passport was stolen and I spent a panic-stricken hour trying to track down the British Consul in Algeciras, no easy matter on a Sunday evening, and eventually running for a mile or so to catch the last ferry.

Sadly the Spanish closed even this escape to us. With tiny training areas, a minute firing range and no obvious threat the problem was to keep the soldiers occupied. We set about this with a will, taking advantage of every possible opportunity, and between our rear party and ourselves achieved a diary note in the *Daily Telegraph* for having members of the battalion serving in seventeen different countries on one memorable day. We hitched many a lift for individuals or small groups on HM ships passing through, including a commando carrier off to an exercise in Sardinia and a submarine bound for Naples. Adventure training was becoming increasingly popular and we had schemes in Portugal, Morocco, the US and Canada. We also provided soldiers for several NATO exercises in Continental Europe and with the prospect looming of further exercises in Kenya and the Far East we had officers and NCOs on jungle training courses in Malaysia and Brunei.

One of the duties of the reinforcement battalion was to mount a formal guard at the closed frontier gate leading into Spain. This became a popular tourist attraction – one could even buy postcards featuring the guard. We took over from the Royal Highland Fusiliers and there was to be a handover parade before loads of spectators. Regimental Sergeant-Major de Bretton Gordon and I were concerned lest we were overly upstaged by the eye-catching Scottish uniforms of the Fusiliers and decided to brighten up our chaps' dull khaki with yellow drummers' dress cords on their shoulders, white gloves, belts and rifle slings, and blue peaked caps with scarlet piping. They looked very smart but there was an amusing sequel. From time to time Gibraltar features the military side to its history on its postage stamps and during our tour they decided to mint four stamps showing uniforms progressively through the ages, beginning with the time of the siege and ending with the present day. Private Weston was taken as a model and in due course the stamps appeared. The Colonel of the Regiment was Lieutenant-General Sir Richard Goodwin who was Military Secretary. He sent a furious letter demanding to know why I had not only adorned the sentry in unauthorised uniform, but had even allowed it to be perpetuated on a very collectable stamp. I said sorry in a letter contained in a first day cover signed by me and happily heard no more about it. As a footnote I should add that when the stamp first appeared there was a request for Private Weston to be interviewed by the local press. I had to delay this event because he was at that time serving seven days' detention for some military misdemeanour.

The senior Army officer on the Rock, entitled Deputy Fortress Commander, was Brigadier Tony Arengo-Jones who directed us to pursue a project during our tour. On the Upper Rock there was an old path about 500 yards long which had fallen into total disrepair and which he felt could be an attractive tourist walk if fully restored. A great deal of rock clearance, levelling and paving were necessary but the work was done in about six months and the path, now shown on all maps as 'Royal Anglian Way', was formally opened by the Governor, Admiral of the Fleet Sir Varyl Begg. From time to time over the years it has suffered from rubbish, weeds and petty vandalism but with various Royal Anglian battalions and companies serving there at intervals there have been frequent facelifts. Since the Army finally left Gibraltar I hope our close allies, The Gibraltar Regiment, are giving a little attention to keeping our 'Way' in good order.

We were in hot but extremely friendly competition in many fields with the garrison battalion, 2nd Battalion The Royal Irish Rangers, commanded by Lieutenant-Colonel Donald MacIntyre and with Captain Roger Wheeler, now General and Chief of the General Staff, as Adjutant: so far as I remember honours were evenly shared but there was one field in which they enjoyed a singular advantage. They had a band, and a good one too, whereas ours had had to stay in England, where, under Bandmaster O'Connell, it often gave concerts in the Felixstowe Spa Pavilion which became hugely popular and, I am told, are still talked about there. Not that this was any comfort to us in Gibraltar. I tried to get the RAF to fly the band out but this could not be done, so I went to the offices in London of British India Shipping Line, where I reminded them that we had a special relationship. We had been the first unit trooped in their ship, the *Nevasa*, on our way back from Hong Kong, a fact recorded, as I have said, on a silver plaque in their central lounge. They were shortly to run educational cruises to the Mediterranean from Southampton and I offered them a free band as far as Gibraltar. They accepted with pleasure. It was not our fault that because of fierce storms in the Bay of Biscay they hardly played a note for the shipping line, but it was wonderful to have them with us for a month. They were kept very busy, including accompanying a local production of *Trial by Jury* (or was it *The Gondoliers*?) and putting on a spectacular concert in St Michael's Cave. The finale there was the '1812' and the accompanying pyrotechnics turned the huge cave into a surreal, massive gas chamber, but there were many plaudits and no casualties.

Our most public use of the band was on St George's Day when it beat 'Retreat' in the middle of town before most of the Rock's inhabitants. For the occasion we obtained from Morocco a red rose to present to each of the official guests. This parade was eulogised in the local press in the strongest jingoistic terms. The band did us proud and by playing very cheaply at the RAF's summer ball they earned passage home by Hercules aircraft, which saved a possibly embarrassing expense. We had only arranged to bring them out and had given little thought to getting them back, other than appealing to the Ministry of Defence on the lines: 'Well, they can't stay there for ever, can they?'

During our tour the Spaniards closed off all access into Spain, which caused a domestic crisis because so many manual workers and servants had come in daily from La Linea. It took some days before replacements could be recruited from Morocco and the battalion played its part in providing workers for the bakery and other essential local services. This, too, won us popular acclaim and when we left in August 1969 the local press were overwhelmingly complimentary about our service on the Rock in difficult times. We were leading the annual competition for the Wilkinson Sword of Peace that year but were pipped at the post by the Parachute Regiment battalion that invaded Anguilla on the famous occasion when the supporting warship almost opened fire in their support, mistaking for opposition gunfire the flashes of press cameras greeting their assault landing

The pleasure and relief of returning to our families and the rest of the battalion was shortlived. Within a couple of weeks we were off to Otterburn in Northumberland for a month. Remote and often bleak though it is, Otterburn is an excellent training area and some very nice and hospitable people live in and around it. We had some splendid training culminating in an exhausting chase for a group of 'terrorists' headed by Captain Niall Mayhew, an unconventional officer who had a flair for devising imaginative exercises. After three days of slogging up and down dales the gang was rounded up and we returned to camp. After debriefing the whole battalion on parade on the camp square we staged a mock execution of Mayhew by firing squad. It was conducted most realistically, with Mayhew and Drum Major Shailes, his henchman, tied to posts, blindfolded and shot at with blanks, then spouting 'blood' and collapsing dramatically. Most of the battalion appreciated the joke, which would have been totally unacceptable today as politically incorrect, but it was too much for one young soldier who was fooled by the blood and promptly fainted. No counselling was necessary however.

Back in Felixstowe I was playing golf on the local course and putting on the 17th green when a breathless club secretary puffed up and said that Chapman Pincher, the influential correspondent of the *Daily Express*, wanted to speak to me on the telephone. This was an alarming prospect and I ran to the clubhouse. 'I have a letter from one of your soldiers.' he said 'He is coloured, along with about thirty other soldiers in your battalion, and you have grouped them all in one platoon which is made to do all the unpleasant chores and dirty jobs in the barracks.' 'I think I know the author,' I replied, 'I fined him yesterday for absence without leave and he didn't like it. I can assure you that our twenty-seven coloured soldiers are spread all through the battalion and as far as I know are content with their lot. I can further assure you that there is no question of racial prejudice in allocating the duties and chores and that this is the first hint of a complaint that I have received.' 'Thank you,' said Pincher, 'there is no story and I shall not use it.' With a sigh of relief I returned to my putt.

I shall return to the matter of political correctness and racism in the final chapter but I must be allowed a brief anecdote about Private Cumberbatch, of West Indian origin. He was applying dark camouflage cream to his very dark features one evening before a night exercise when he came in for some good-natured ribbing from his white peers. 'You go on like that,' he shouted, 'an' Ah'se gonna emmergrate!'

Most of the soldiers in the battalion were alert, enthusiastic, well-behaved and intelligent. One notable exception on all these counts was a lad who attempted to desert. He went to ground in his native Yorkshire and soon found that he needed a job. On applying for one he was asked for a reference. He cannot have given much thought to his nomination – he gave the name and address of the RSM, thus bringing upon himself an unwelcome visit by a military policeman the next day.

We now moved to Colchester, much more closely under the eye of 19 Brigade Headquarters, which was also stationed there. Our move coincided with the arrival of Brigadier (later General Sir George, and Adjutant General) Cooper, a Sapper, to take over from Brigadier Bill Scotter (also later General, and C-in-C BAOR before sadly dying prematurely). In Meanee Barracks, next door to us, were 2nd Battalion The Light Infantry, whose Commanding Officer, Lieutenant-Colonel Peter Sibbald, was determined to be first to be visited by the new Brigadier. He invited him to come along at midday and stay for lunch, but did not say what the programme was to be. The Brigadier arrived in his normal working dress of an army pullover and beret to be greeted by a guard of honour and then escorted to the square to find the whole battalion on parade in its best kit drawn up ready for inspection. This completed, the Brigadier was invited to address the battalion. All this would have been fine had he been forewarned, but, unprepared as he was, Brigadier Cooper, who could be irascible if crossed, was not best pleased. When joshed about this Peter Sibbald claimed that he was just indicating his view that infantry brigades should be commanded by infantrymen, not engineers. If true, this was not a tactful way of going about it. We learned from the experience and the Brigadier's first visit to 2nd Royal Anglian was to a mess dance.

The next item on our agenda was a month in Kenya to prepare for a much bigger enterprise, a brigade group reinforcement of Malaysia with three months of training and exercising. I had not been to East Africa before and the country, its game and its people were wonderful new experiences. It was in the early days of independence and the political situation was uneasy. We were only the second unit to undertake this particular exercise and the white population thought our purpose, though unspoken, was to show that we could come to their rescue if anything went wrong for them. This was not so, but we did little to deny it because we were welcomed with open arms as protectors and shown the most wonderful hospitality wherever we went.

We heard many tales about the difficulties experienced by the Europeans with the new African Government, and of their fears for the future. One example we could see for ourselves. As we drove along the laterite roads we passed farm after farm and could see at once which were owned by white settlers and which by the new African possessors. The first were green with lush grass and showed the effects of careful husbandry; the second were brown and bare because in order to provide for the large families which descended on them many more cattle were kept than the acreage could support.

There was also a story current, although I cannot vouch for its truth, about a store in Nakuru which had been known as the 'Harrods of Africa', run by an Indian, which had huge stock and boasted being able to supply anything one could think of, if not immediately then within a very short time. The Indian had been dispossessed by the Government and the store given to an African, who was quickly 'supported' by a huge family. When three months later a lady shopper commented on the empty shelves everywhere and asked why this should be so, the storekeeper replied that the Government did not provide new stock. The lady asked: 'What about the money you got from the sale of all that stock? Why have you not bought replacement stock with it?' 'Ah,' said the African, 'that is profit.'

On the Staff College course before this tour I had known a Kenyan officer in one of my syndicates and, on my way to our base at Nanyuki, I had looked him up in the defence ministry in Nairobi. He told me that he was shortly moving to Nanyuki to take command of the Kenya African Rifles battalion there. Soon afterwards I had occasion to call on that battalion to discuss arrangements for a possible joint beating of 'Retreat' by our corps of drums and theirs wearing their wonderful colobus monkey headdresses. With some difficulty I made my way through to the office of the Commanding Officer, a huge, dramatically scarred man reminiscent of Idi Amin. By way of casual conversation I told him that I had recently met his successor who, I understood, was coming to take over in two weeks' time. The African rose to his feet in the most menacing way and roared: 'He no take over from me, dis *mah* battalion!' I did not argue, but noticed that when our parade came off three weeks later he was still in command.

The layout for the exercise was for the headquarters to be centrally located at Nanyuki at the foot of Mount Kenya and for the three company groups to occupy bases up to 100 miles distant. The companies were to move around every week with an interval for each at Lake Naivasha for a break and a chance to see and learn about the bird life there. Two bases were in the forest on the lower slopes of Mount Kenya and the other in the bush with virtually unrestricted rights for field firing. The layout was basically a large square and we arranged for battalion tactical headquarters to move cross-country between them. This was a remarkable experience in the best traditions of the expensive safari, with unparalleled opportunities to see game in its natural habitat and endless challenges to get our vehicles across rivers and rugged country. Another adventurous pursuit was for as many of the battalion as possible to climb Mount Kenya as far as possible, which meant to point Lenana at 16,350 feet, for which each man received a certificate recording his achievement.

Princess Alice, Duchess of Gloucester, became Colonel-in-Chief of the Northamptonshire Regiment in 1937 and, though quiet and shy, had endeared herself exceptionally to everyone. After the various amalgamations Princess Alice continued as a Deputy Colonel-in-Chief with special interest in the 2nd Battalion. Visiting us shortly before the Kenya exercise the Duchess gave us a personal mission. In the late thirties a lake had been discovered, for the first time, at 11,700 feet on the north-eastern upper slopes of Mount Kenya. The Mountain Club of East Africa decided to name the lake Alice, after Alice Montagu-Douglas-Scott, a frequent and popular visitor to East Africa, as a gift for her wedding to the Duke of Gloucester which had taken place in 1935. So far as Princess Alice knew no one had visited the lake for years and she thought it would be nice if her regiment sent a party to check on it. A patrol of eight under Captains Gowing and Pond and Lieutenant Hazan managed to get to the lake, found it to be in good order, and placed a plaque on a rocky promontory above to record the event and the reason for it. A telegram confirming this was sent to Her Royal Highness.

Despite rigorous training and exposure to many hazards of topography and fauna we returned to England without having taken any casualties, although one soldier, Lance-Corporal Hardy, had had to be taken to a Nairobi hospital to have his appendix removed. We visited him soon after the operation and found him the only European in a huge ward which was crammed full of patients on wooden pallets for beds. There was nothing we could do for him other than supplementing his diet and making jolly conversation but we certainly did not envy him. He suffered no ill effects and recovered remarkably quickly, spurred, no doubt, by the urge to escape from that ward.

I had to return to England during the exercise, at two days' notice, to be interviewed at the Ministry of Defence for a Defence Fellowship. I had been directed by Brigadier Cooper to apply for one, which meant a year's study on a subject of my own choice at a university. Having no idea what subject to choose I sought the assistance of Dr Wayper at Churchill College, Cambridge. He recommended study into the so-called Transatlantic 'special relationship' and gave me material to read up. There was not a lot of spare time to devote to this and when, having flown through the night, I confronted the selection panel, I was neither at my best nor well prepared. The panel thought my subject too broad for a year's work and awarded the fellowship, rightly, to a much more intellectually inclined and qualified officer, Brigadier (later General Sir Hugh) Beach. I returned to Kenya on the same day with a feeling more of relief than disappointment.

Soon after our return I had a serious problem. Whenever I have been asked for advice by officers shortly to take up unit command I have offered three suggestions. One, be scrupulously thorough with your financial responsibilities and take nothing to do with cash on trust; two, allow subordinates freedom to get on with their jobs and do not interfere unnecessarily; and three, develop a special relationship with your regimental sergeant-major. The good RSM will have his ear to the ground and can be a valuable source of information, even, if the relationship is right, to the extent of indicating what the lower ranks think of their commanders. This is not encouraging disloyalty, it is getting early warning when things are not going right. I had such a relationship with de Bretton Gordon but when he left to be commissioned he was replaced by a very different sort of man. This one was of the old school who believed that sergeants should be hard-drinking, hard-swearing, macho individuals, all of which he was himself, which was quite out of tune with the intelligent young NCOs who were then coming into the sergeants' mess. After a couple of warnings with no apparent effect I decided that he must go. Military rules at the time demanded that a protracted sequence of formal warnings should be followed but, after agonising over it and taking advice from some officers, I called him in and told him I could work with him no longer. I would break the rules and send him home to await a decision by higher authority, and thus force a choice between him and me, which was effectively no choice. I was suitably admonished but the RSM left. Sadly he died of a brain tumour not very long afterwards. This had been a difficult episode but I am sure the right action was taken and there were few in the sergeants' mess who disagreed with it.

These were times of progressive withdrawal from imperial and various overseas commitments. Final departure from permanent stations in the Middle and the Far East was just around the corner but the Government, as advised by Denis Healey, the Defence Minister, wanted to show its allies and former dependants that it could still quickly deploy forces to their support if necessary. To prove this theory Exercise Bersatu Padu (freely translatable as 'Solidarity') was the rapid deployment of a brigade group to Malaysia for three months, during which time it would show its effectiveness and how quickly it could adapt to local conditions.

In March 1970 we flew to Singapore. I had the dubious privilege of being in the aircraft containing most of the British journalists covering the exercise and got little sleep, being peppered with questions for most of the journey. One of the reporters, Harvey Elliott, had been reading up on local conditions and discovered that there was a high incidence of venereal disease and wanted to know what I was going to do about it. Many possible answers occurred to me, especially one to the effect that my mind was on higher things, but I curbed my tongue and gave an official view.

On landing at Changi in Singapore we were greeted by General Sir Peter Hunt, the C-in-C, and I was taken to a VIP room to await completion of unloading. This was my first visit to the area since 1955 and I was surprised as I looked for references to the exercise in the local papers by the whole of the *Straits Times* front page being taken up with an aerial photograph of the smoking ruins of the Cameron Highlands Hotel, where we had honeymooned fifteen years before. I hoped it was not an ill omen of some sort.

The press was to be treated to a demonstration of how quickly we could prepare for operations by coming out to our base at Kota Tinggi, the Jungle Warfare Centre, and seeing the battalion ready for action. This was stage-managed so that six hours after landing and having driven the best part of fifty miles, two companies emerged in fighting order and open formation from a clump of jungle to advance towards the assembled journalists. As theatre it was impressive and earned us good publicity, although it did not fool Gordon Lee, the very experienced defence correspondent of *The Economist*. He whispered in my ear about acclimatisation and jungle skills. We became friends and he was kind enough to write in complimentary terms about 'that excellent battalion'.

Bersatu Padu was an exciting exercise which caught everyone's imagination and is often discussed by participants to this day. There was one small incident in which I was able to make use of the Malay that I had learned on my earlier tour. We had been given the task of seeking out some Royal Marine 'terrorists', which, with all the cover offered by the jungle, was no easy task. We knew their general area and I was able to take to a helicopter and land near local peasant labourers and ask them in their own language if they had seen any soldiers wearing the distinctive uniforms identifying them as our enemy. This was successful. They had holed up in a small copse to which I was able to direct our companies from the air. They surrounded it and obtained the required surrender.

Unusually there had been a drought for some weeks and one of our companies, commanded by Major Michael Aris, which was looking for a band of Marines, were surprised by the enemy coming to them under a flag of truce to ask for water, so that they could continue to operate. Michael was only prepared to offer water in exchange for surrender and sought my agreement to this line, which I gave. The Marines were very upset about this and complained to the exercise controller, but they left empty-handed and survived somehow.

The final phase of the exercise was a move up to Trengganu, followed by search operations culminating in a brigade attack. It all went well and everyone involved was pleased. I will not describe the detail but refer only to two unconnected things. The first was an opportunity to see the arrival of breeding turtles on a nearby sandy shore to lay their eggs. It was an amazing, almost surreal thing to see these huge, black beasts emerge in the dusk like prehistoric creatures, leaving the sea for the first time for years to struggle their way up the sand to a point above the tide line. There they would excavate a hole in which to lay up to 100 white eggs like ping-pong balls. Nothing would deter them from this natural requirement. Talking, inspecting closely, even riding on their backs would not interrupt their progress. What saddened us beyond measure was that the eggs were regarded as a delicacy, especially in Thailand, where they fetched good prices. Consequently Malay children would catch the eggs in buckets as they were being laid, thus negating perhaps a decade's progress towards continuation of the species.

The second, very different, memory is of listening all night in our tactical headquarters near the shore to the results of the British General Election. It was a close-run thing, Edward Heath and the Conservatives eventually running out with a majority of thirty-one. Many bets were made in Trengganu as we listened and, like a fool, I started smoking again.

A fortnight after our return we were the first unit to be visited by the Heath Government's new Secretary of State for Defence, Lord Carrington, who after going around the battalion took lunch in our mess. We all found him a most attractive personality who had great charm, who listened and who talked with knowledge and common sense. We were sure that he was going to be a minister in whom we could have confidence.

Soon it was time for me to go. I had been very lucky, as so often in my career, in my immediate boss and in everyone around me. The differences in infantry battalions since I had been a subaltern were marked. The senior NCOs at both times were Regulars and shared the basic characteristics of the soldiers of the Eastern England regiments, namely reliability, steadiness, and taking their work seriously. Those of 1950 had mostly been through the war and were given to much reminiscence. Many had served in India in peacetime and found coming to terms with post-war attitudes confusing. The war had been a great social leveller but officers still enjoyed a respect which came from their rank and education and not so much from having earned it. By 1970 members of the sergeants' mess were generally younger and better educated, partly because of the training they were given in the Army to cope with ever more complex weapons and equipment. This trend has continued apace during the last quarter-century and today's soldier has to be quick, intelligent and very professional. Officers had to earn their spurs and soldiers expected them to be capable in every aspect of infantry soldiering if they were to win full respect.

Previously the soldiers themselves had been conscripted, now they were all volunteers. I have touched on the effects of this in an earlier chapter but although literacy in the academic sense was lower than we might have wished, the broadening effects of universal television were becoming generally apparent. They were career soldiers and mostly tended to be more ambitious and keen to advance professionally. Discipline rarely had to be enforced overtly, the atmosphere generally could be more relaxed and there seemed to be more laughter. Commanding Officer's orders, once a long daily queue, probably happened only once or twice a month and there were many more people coming for career matters or interviews than there were miscreants. Morale was pretty high in both cases but it was different.

It had been a full and busy tour, described in the regimental magazine as 'happy and eventful', with many travels and adventures. The losers had been our families, who had seen so little of us, and I felt particularly sorry for Shirley, who had to cope not only with Julian's developing illness, which demanded constant and often harrowing attention, but also, with many others, to organise diversions and provide a shoulder to cry on for many of the other wives who were left to fend for themselves. Few commanding officers' wives get as deeply involved these days. Our wives considered that it went with the job and many were the unsung heroines. For countless good works they received no reward other, perhaps, than occasional satisfaction and inadequate thanks and recognition from the authorities, and, sometimes, their husbands. Nevertheless it was a sad day for both of us when I made my last addresses to the various messes before being towed out of barracks on a Land-Rover in the traditional style. In my talks I had told everyone that despite gathering troubles in Northern Ireland they were destined for Münster in Germany and would not be called upon for yet another period of unaccompaniment. I was glad not to be there to be called to account for this optimistic prediction when, a week later, my successor, Lieutenant-Colonel Dick Gerrard-Wright, was summoned to brigade headquarters to be warned for a four-month emergency tour in Belfast in a month's time. I am happy to report, however, that they conducted themselves in Belfast with praiseworthy effectiveness.

11
More Colleges

In August 1970 we moved to a newly built quarter in Whetstone, North London. As I looked disconsolately at the garden, which contained more rubble than soil, a head appeared over the garden fence and inquired, almost in one sentence, whether he and his wife could do anything to help and whether I played golf. I asked for local advice and received it, but the head, which introduced itself as being that of Brigadier Jack Bridge, the Director of Army Postal and Courier Services, was more interested in my reply about golf. He, too, had recently arrived and was a golf fanatic. As soon as he learned that I played, though sorely out of practice, he insisted I joined him every Sunday morning, and most Saturdays too, at Stanmore Golf Club. Though reluctant at first I soon rediscovered my enthusiasm for the game and, apart from an interlude while serving in Oman where no course was available, I have been closely involved ever since. My *curriculum vitae* has consistently given golf as 'a game at which I wished my skill matched my enthusiasm', but it has given me reasonable exercise, much pleasure and many friends. Without the happy chance of moving next door to the Bridges I might not have become so involved. Presidency of the Army Officers' Golf Society, chairmanship of the Army Golf Association, captaincy of the generals' teams against admirals and air marshals, and against the Variety Club Golfing Society, and membership of the Senior Golfers' Society, and many engagements over the years may all date back to that head over the fence.

My appointment was as Junior Directing Staff (Army) at the Imperial Defence College in Seaford House, a historic building in Belgrave Square. Here a year's course set out to give some seventy-six senior officers and officials of around brigadier or equivalent seniority, from Britain and fifteen or more Commonwealth and other countries, 'the opportunity to study national and international strategy and security, international relations as a whole, and those aspects of public policy which are related to defence and security'.

The management of the course was vested in a commandant, and an admiral, a major-general, an air vice-marshal and a diplomat of equivalent status who each had a staff of one officer at lieutenant-colonel level. Together with these latter four was a Junior Directing Staff (Coordination) who was *primus inter pares* among the juniors and worked directly to the Commandant. The sailor among us was Sandy Woodward, a submariner later to become nationally well known in the Falklands campaign. The administration of the college was in the hands of a retired officer with a small staff of civil servants.

Until 1969 the IDC course had the reputation of being interesting but very laid back, with lectures and discussions but with no very clear structure and little hard work. Denis Healey determined to revitalise the course and make it give better value for money. To this end he appointed as commandant an academic instead of the customary four-star service officer. His choice was the Hon. Alastair Buchan, son of John Buchan, who set to work with a will, creating a course structure which largely survives to this day. He also introduced formal seminars to follow every lecture, an exercise in crisis management, and, horror of horrors for those who had joined expecting an idle time, the requirement for each member to prepare a thesis. This did not make him popular but there is little doubt that he achieved the purpose for which he was appointed. We considered a high honour, probably a knighthood, to reward the enormous amount of study and hard work he devoted to the course, would be almost automatic, but I understand that neither the Foreign Office nor the Ministry of Defence was prepared to forgo one of its precious quota of such awards and he got nothing, which we, on his staff, thought was shabby treatment. He was a workaholic and a most interesting man whose next appointment was to a chair in International Relations at Cambridge. On the day of Edward Heath's referendum about going into Europe he took two of us to lunch at the Garrick, where I asked him whether he would be voting for or against. Alastair, who had far more detailed knowledge and understanding of the matter than most people in the country, told us that he was really unsure. He planned to vote in favour, but only because he had a gut feeling that it would be to our disadvantage to be excluded; he could think of no convincing and logical justification for either course. The conversation has given me a permanent mistrust of referenda. So few people understand the questions, let alone know the answers.

The job of the directing staff was to meet in committee under the

Commandant to decide the sequence of study and then to select and invite the best lecturer on any given subject that they could find, and in the seniors' case, to chair subsequent seminars. The net for lecturers was worldwide and, with only travel expenses and a very modest fee to offer, a good deal of flattery and persuasion was involved to get them to come to London. We were helped by Alastair Buchan's own wide circle of acquaintances and by the high reputation enjoyed by the IDC, although during my first year there Denis Healey decided that the title was no longer appropriate and changed it to Royal College of Defence Studies.

In my first year I worked for Major-General Vernon Erskine-Crum, an Olympian figure of powerful personality and intellect who, I understood, was very highly thought of and destined for high places in the service. Rumour had it that the Army had appointed him to the college specifically to keep an eye on the new Commandant to prevent any academic excesses or flights of fancy. Certainly I saw some of this in action. Alastair Buchan paid very close attention to Erskine-Crum's views and seldom dissented from his recommendations which, in committee, were always impeccably timed. I held Erskine-Crum in deep respect. He could be impatient and quick to anger and I was, frankly, nervous of him, but in the few months that I worked for him I learned a lot.

There was one particularly tense interlude in our working relationship during the college's visit to the North Atlantic Treaty Organisation and Supreme Headquarters Allied Powers Europe in Brussels and Mons respectively. Having visited NATO and enjoyed the gastronomic delights of Brussels to the full, the course was accommodated in a single high-rise hotel in which there was only one lift. Everyone was told to be on the buses for the forty-mile journey to Mons next morning by 0830 hrs. With breakfast on the seventh floor, and accommodation much higher than that, much more time was needed than most individuals had allowed. There were two buses and it was my job to check that everyone was on them before departure. By 0835 hrs at least twenty had not made it and Erskine-Crum was getting restless and tapping his foot on the pavement, asking me every sixty seconds or so whether everyone was aboard. At this point men in the front bus saw particular friends they wanted to join in the rear bus and vice versa and began to move from bus to bus, making the counting of heads virtually impossible. By 0845 hrs the major-general was getting very angry indeed and I was not sure whether the party was complete, but in deference to his temper I decided to take a chance and declare that all were present. Three hours later during a presentation at SHAPE at which Erskine-Crum was seated in the front row and I at the rear, an apparition, with bits of sticking plaster festooning the results of a hurried shave, appeared beside me. This was Colonel Tonne Huitfeldt, from Norway, who said that a combination of a very late night and inadequate provision of lifts had caused him to miss the buses and he had come by taxi. He must, he said, go at once to apologise to the major-general. I grabbed his arm, sat him down, and forbade him to do any such thing. He was much amused by this story when I reminded him of it twenty-seven years later and we were both generals.

The tours were highlights of the course but fraught for the junior directing staff whose job it was to arrange them in detail. There was a near diplomatic incident in Berlin soon after the Brussels affair. A senior Indian officer was asked by military policemen to open his briefcase for a routine security inspection. The officer was not going to have a mere corporal look in his briefcase at any price, thus causing those of us around him to speculate furiously upon what it might contain, especially after a night on the town in Berlin. I halted procedures before a possible punch-up and asked for a pause while I fetched the major-general. The matter was resolved by the Indian agreeing to open the briefcase for the major-general himself to inspect, but Erskine-Crum never told us whether it contained anything that might interest us. Erskine-Crum left the college at the end of the year and in 1971 was appointed General Officer Commanding Northern Ireland at a time when the Province was going through a particularly difficult time. Sadly after only two months there he died of a heart attack, which was, in my view and that of many others, a severe loss to the Army.

It was during the visit to Berlin that I finally gave up smoking, and I commend my method to anyone thinking of packing it in. I told many people that I would give up on a certain day, which I knew to be the one following some heavy entertainment in the Berlin Officers' Club. At that function I deliberately drank much more than usual and the resulting hangover made tobacco singularly unattracive. I could not have smoked that day even if I had wanted to, and if I had there would also have been serious loss of face for lack of will power. I have not touched tobacco in any form since.

Erskine-Crum's place was taken by Major-General Richard

Clutterbuck, who was heavily engaged in writing a book on terrorism, a subject on which he later became an expert and a well-known university lecturer. He was entertaining to work for but I often wondered why he would send me off to various libraries and sources to research statistics on international terrorism at times in the year when terrorism was not part of the curriculum. All became clear when I read the results of my labours in his book and I was slightly miffed when given no credit in the foreword.

In 1971 I became the JDS (Coordination) and it was Alastair Buchan's second and final year. His successor was to be General Sir Mervyn Butler and the procedure was that for two months before he took over he and I would be set up in an office in Lansdowne Square, away from the college, to plan the 1972 course. 'Tubby' Butler was at that time Commander-in-Chief United Kingdom Land Forces and very busy. He knew me well and, apart from a weekly visit for an hour in the office and a pub lunch, left me to get on with it. This was not particularly testing because Alastair Buchan had set a clear and successful pattern and General Tubby had no wish to change it significantly. We did not know it at the time but he was beginning to suffer from a disease similar to Alzheimer's, which eventually killed him two years later. He was commandant for only eight months and there were several cases of erratic behaviour, the worst being an affront to a German diplomat of noble birth. General Tubby was arguing heatedly in the bar with some British cronies about the necessity for parachute troops in modern warfare. The diplomat tried to venture an opinion but was told that as 'just a German civvie' he could not possibly understand and his opinion was worth nothing. It was not easy to prevent this from becoming the subject of an official complaint.

General Tubby had always been a character. He played on his Irish descent and on having toured professionally with the famous Dublin Abbey Theatre group presenting *Playboy of the Western World*, before coming to England to join the Army. Hard-drinking, hard-swearing, he was a soldier's general and fully acted the part; a sort of tough leprechaun who revelled in his membership of the Parachute Regiment and loved to be in the company of fellow members of that regiment. Until he became ill, and one of the symptoms was to become irresponsibly inebriated on very small quantities of alcohol, he was rumbustious company and universally popular. I did not realise that he was not well when he certainly tested my loyalty during a visit to a conference of NATO college commandants in Rome. During our free time there he was determined to sample the nightlife and I was prepared to escort him. I was equally determined to visit St Peter's, however, and persuaded him to come with me. As we left a baking St Peter's Square and went inside, the sudden coolness and the immensity of the building was overpowering I was almost overwhelmed by its holiness and atmosphere of peace when this terrible little general beside me nudged me as a pair of jeans walked by us, and said: 'Look at that girl's bum!' Later, much later, that evening we spent some time in a nightclub off the Via Veneto and ran up a substantial bill for champagne before the general told me that he had little cash and no credit card. I was in the same position and it says much for his personality and power of persuasion that he managed to cajole the manager into allowing us out into the night without paying and without penalty.

Eventually, after a confrontation during a party at a foreign embassy, the Chief of Defence Staff, Field Marshal Sir Michael Carver, directed that he be sent on leave and that his place should be taken, temporarily, by Rear-Admiral (later Admiral Sir Anthony) Morton, who was the senior sailor on the directing staff. Tony Morton still had his own job to do and leant quite heavily on me and the Secretary, Brigadier Francis Gore, to conduct the day-to-day business of the Commandant, which I revelled in.

Every year the college divided, as it still does, into seven or eight groups to visit various areas of the world and these tours were eagerly anticipated and invariably enjoyed. I timed my service at the college badly, arriving while a tour was in progress and leaving just before the one two years later, having sweated for weeks on making the very complicated arrangements for two of the parties. I was able to go on one only, to Singapore, Indonesia, Australia and New Zealand. The tours were well established and enjoyed a high reputation; we could get interviews with very senior people and privileged access to centres of beauty and culture. We learned a good deal and shared our experiences and opinions with the remainder of the college with presentations soon after our return.

Each group had a leader, ours being Brigadier Desmond Mangham, and a lieutenant-colonel or equivalent as 'shepherd', which could occasionally be stressful. Among this international group of senior officers would be some who were exceptionally conscious of the rights and privileges to which they considered that their rank entitled them.

Singapore passed without incident and we were all impressed with its evident dynamism and the rigid control of its society. The litter rules, for instance, were draconian but effective. It was all very different from my memory of it.

In Indonesia we stayed first in Djakarta, an extraordinary city of contrasts. We rated a cavalcade escorted by police from the airport to our hotel, which was flattering, but we were alarmed by the way in which any traffic threatening our smooth passage was directed to halt by the side of the road. If a motorcycle policeman thought his directions were not being followed instantly the unfortunate miscreant would be given a sharp reminder in the form of a heavy pistol butt smashed onto his car bonnet, leaving a deep dent. The centre of the city, with its high-rise buildings and profusion of neon signs, gave an impression of wealth, but going out for some exercise in the evening I did not have to walk far to leave the bright lights behind and reach dark and squalid slums. These impressions gave rise to cynicism when official briefings bragged of 'successful democracy and a burgeoning economy pointing to fair opportunities for everyone'. Cultural visits, especially to rural Jogjakarta, were much more enjoyable.

We were due to fly on to Perth on the once-weekly Cathay Pacific flight, but on going ahead to the airport to check our booking, which had been confirmed, I learned to my horror that the flight was overbooked and four of our party could not travel. They would have to wait a week or spend two days returning to Singapore and getting a flight from there. Fortunately there was time for panic-stricken negotiations resulting in the airline squeezing four more first-class seats into the existing compartment. The leg-room was disappointing, especially for Desmond Mangham who was well over six feet tall, but the service and catering beyond praise. There was one difficult moment when a senior officer from a Commonwealth country, whose brains we knew to be well south of his waistline, caused outrage by groping one of the delectable hostesses as she leaned forward to serve a drink. Not for the first or last time our leader had to intervene with abject apology.

It was my first visit to Australia and we went to Perth, Sydney, Canberra and Dubbo, a small town on the edge of the outback. Everyone we met was outstandingly hospitable. Our broad 'snapshot' impression was of a huge but underpopulated country still packed with natural resources, but with severe labour problems. We visited a major steelworks at Port Kembla, not far from Sidney, and saw nothing but a total strike. Some of our hosts blamed poor labour relations on 'the English disease' and claimed that all of the difficulties were the product of recent 'Pommy' immigrants who, they claimed, were besotted with trade union malpractices and only professional at whingeing. We were not able to judge the truth of these claims but it was clear that there was little central government action to improve matters.

In the Dubbo area we visited a huge mixed arable and cattle farm where the owner, our host, gave us not only a fascinating insight into his methods and problems (which he clearly overcame) but also a buffet lunch of gargantuan barbecued steaks in his garage during which he hardly drew breath. He was one of the funniest men I have ever met, packed with countless well-rehearsed stories but ready with immediate witty reactions to almost any remark. The only one I can remember now was his instant response to a question about the national lottery. 'Lottery!', he said, 'lottery! I'm the sort of fella that even if I won half a woman in a lottery it would be the half that eats!'

There were two officers from the United States in the party who were determined to extract every possible ounce of education and enjoyment from the trip. They asked me to carry a bottle of Crown bourbon with me for their use at all times and referred to me as 'The Keeper of the Crown'. Late one night they insisted on visiting the notorious 'Southern Cross' area whose sleazy reputation was well known to them as an 'R and R' area for fellow countrymen serving in Vietnam. As we came to one bar a tumble of brawling bodies spilled out onto the pavement before us and we all saw a knife drawn and thrust into one of the combatants. The Americans wanted to stay and watch the outcome, but I managed to hustle them away, foreseeing difficult complications if we were rounded up as witnesses. We learned from the papers next morning that there had indeed been a fatality in the 'Cross' area the night before and I felt we were very well out of it.

In New Zealand we were lucky enough to visit an agricultural college in Christchurch, followed by two or three days free in Queenstown, South Island, with a look at Mount Cook on the way. This was followed by progress through briefings in the capital, Wellington, and on to various points in North Island, including Lake Taupo, where we caught fish, and Rotorua, where we were given presentations on Maori matters and a 'Poi' dancing display, and walked among the bubbling, quaking hot springs. The trip ended at Auckland.

The overall impression was of a country of wide variety and spectacular beauty with a culture and style half a century behind the rest of the civilised world, which gave it a special charm. Sheep were much in evidence, as were vigorously expressed views on Commonwealth Preference, or rather the lack of it, and the potential disloyalty and ingratitude of Britain joining the European Common Market. There was little heavy traffic and one policeman explained that the country's dreadful record of traffic accidents was caused by a universal assumption that nothing was likely to be approaching around the corner or over the hill.

To a fly fisherman and golfer New Zealand seemed to be a paradise. I do wish it were nearer. It is the country which I would most like to revisit, but it is so very far away and I do not enjoy long flights.

I was most grateful on our return to be presented by the rest of the tour group with a memento engraved 'From The Flock'. These tours were by no means easy to organise and may seem to the outsider to have been an expensive waste of time and money. In my view nothing could be further from the truth. The course set out to expand the horizons of senior officers of the future, most of whom would work in international environments. Learning directly from the top people in the countries we visited about their situation, their priorities, their ambitions and their attitudes to other friends and potential foes was not only fascinating, it was education of the highest class.

It was disappointing to make all the preparations for two tours in 1972 and not to be able to go on either, but my next job offered compensations. It was to command the Junior Division of the Staff College at Warminster, which meant an escape from London and commuting, promotion to colonel, and a very nice house close to the office. In effect I was moving from junior staff at the most senior officers' course to senior staff at the most junior officers' staff course. I was to be the third commandant since the course had been established and I completely believed in its value and was of the opinion that it was the best course to be set up by the Army since the war. Up to the time of its establishment there were no provisions in the Army for all officers to learn about arms and services other than their own until going to the Staff College itself, which only trained about one third of any generation. Lip service had been paid at Sandhurst but that was at divisional level. This course received all officers of captain's rank from every arm and service and offered basic instruction in staff work for one month, followed by a second month of basic tactics, followed in turn by a 'Practical Fortnight' which got all the arms officers, i.e. armoured corps, artillery, engineers, infantry and signallers, out onto the Salisbury Plain training area for exercises in the various phases of war using all the men, weapons, vehicles and equipment of the resident 'demonstration' units .

The Junior Division came under the command of the Staff College at Camberley and the commandant and deputy commandant visited from time to time, but we enjoyed almost complete autonomy and independence, which all officers appreciate if they can get it. Our hosts, the School of Infantry, found our demands tiresome from time to time but relations were generally excellent.

I soon made two changes to the practical training. The first was to let officers of the administrative services take part. They felt they should be included in order to learn something about the people and events they were organised to supply and support. Secondly it seemed to me that it would be logical to practise the tactics as soon as they were learned in theory. Both of these ideas were put into immediate effect and although it meant that command appointments were spread more thinly I think that most people thought the changes were appropriate, not only to involve everyone on the course but to spread out the use of demonstration troops over a longer period, giving them more time to effect repairs and make preparations. We therefore had an excellent ten-week course four times a year with 110 students on each one. We did not want it to suffer the distraction of competition, and although a report was sent to their commanding officers, students were not graded or put into an order of merit: they either passed or they failed, and we made sure that there were virtually no failures.

The staff comprised a lieutenant-colonel, John Oborne when I arrived, succeeded later by Bill Winder, fifteen majors as instructors, most of them fresh from the Staff College course, and two administrative officers, one of whom was Alan Peckham who had been our best man in Malaya. Alan was there because I wanted him and he was keen to come. When I asked the Military Secretary's branch to post him in they looked up the job description and said that not being staff-trained he was not qualified for the job. I waited an hour and then rang to say that the job description had been changed. Slightly to my surprise this was accepted and Alan soon joined us. He stayed for fifteen years, was always popular with staff and students alike, did the job well and thoroughly enjoyed it. He and his wife, Finola, still live in Warminster.

Our quarter was next door to that of the Commandant of the School of Infantry, Brigadier Frank Kitson. He had recently left Northern Ireland, where he had been one of the enforcers of the unpopular internment policy, and he was regarded as being at considerable risk from the IRA. His house was fitted with elaborate alarm systems, constantly being set off by gusts of wind or passing sparrows, usually in the small hours, and we became accustomed to these diversions. At times of heightened tension a sentry box was placed close to the Kitsons' front door and there came a bitter winter's night when the sentry's discomfort was alleviated by the provision of a paraffin stove. Unfortunately the sentry brought this into the sentry box and then set off to patrol the garden. At two in the morning the first thing we heard was a crackle of small arms fire. Rushing to the window we could see the box blazing away merrily. The crackling noises were the result of the sentry having left live ammunition in his box, which the blaze was setting off. The duty fire picquet soon arrived with a Land-Rover, on the front of which was a fire extinguisher. At this point Frank came out in his dressing gown and bravely ignoring the bullets whizzing around drove his car out of the garage, which was threatened by the flames. He then grabbed the extinguisher, inverted it, banged it on the ground in the approved manner and stared as a jet of fluid at most six inches long trickled uselessly to the ground. It was a richly enjoyable scene.

There are dozens of Kitson stories about this most unusual officer who could be wonderful company if in the mood or unhelpfully brusque if he was not. My favourite at Warminster came not from Frank himself but from Chiggy, his younger daughter. Chiggy was taken to the pantomime *Dick Whittington* at the Bristol Hippodrome and there came a point when the youngest children were invited to join the cast on the stage. Chiggy led the stampede and on arrival was asked by the star if she had a cat at home. On confirming that indeed she had she was asked its name. 'Jomo' she chirruped. 'Why Jomo?' asked the star, 'Because my daddy [who had been active in the Mau-Mau campaign in Kenya] says he's big, he's black and he's bloody difficult!' This brought the house down.

Many of the officers of the supporting corps and services delighted in the opportunities to 'go to war' tactically in the practical exercises. One of them, Captain Bob Birrell of the Royal Corps of Transport, a rally and motoring fanatic and later to serve with us in Oman, foresaw the possible answer to a long-held ambition. For as long as he could remember he had wanted to command a tank and we duly appointed him to do so on our 'advance to contact' exercise. This began in the dark at the western end of the Plain and everyone was lined up ready for the off just before dawn. At the order to advance Bob commanded his tank for about fifty yards until it fell nose down into a deep hole, where it stayed, stuck, for the rest of the day. Bob was still proud of having achieved his ambition.

We loved Warminster and the job was fine, but the tour included a very unhappy event as Julian's cystic fibrosis took its final course. After spells of illness and increasingly frequent stays in the Royal United Hospital in Bath he eventually, in February 1973 aged thirteen, died after a long agonising period in a coma, during which the end was clearly inevitable and one felt so utterly helpless to do anything about it as his breathing became ever slower and more laboured. CF is a dreadful disease for everyone involved. The lungs become clogged with mucus, which has to be moved by back-patting physiotherapy and coughing at least twice a day, and they become a breeding ground for infection which grows increasingly resistant to antibiotic treatment. Julian was a bright, intelligent child who understood from quite early on what lay in store for him. He endured his sufferings with immense courage, although this was often tested when yet another stay in hospital was necessary, and when injections were needed in his painfully thin arms or legs. He was braver than one might expect when ill or in hospital, and cheerful, lively good company when he was well. It took much longer positively to identify his disease than it should, but, once diagnosed, treatment by Army Medical Services and a number of civilian hospitals and consultants, especially University College Hospital, London, was as good as we could hope for. The chances of parents with the particular mix of genes having a healthy child were quoted to us as one in four. Two chances would have CF like Julian, and one would be death in infancy. Although Julian had given us much joy, as well as the pain, we decided not to gamble on another attempt. One useful legacy from the ordeal, perhaps, has been to give Shirley and me a better understanding and sympathy when other parents suffer the loss of children. As I write it seems that medical victory over CF may at last be in sight. Earlier diagnosis and more effective treatment are already here.

At Christmas 1973 I was astounded to be asked by telephone if I would agree, if selected, to command the Dhofar Brigade at war in Oman. I knew there was a possibility of brigade command in 1974, but had certainly not expected this plum. The reason for seeking my agreement was simply that no officer could be posted on secondment to another country without having volunteered to go. Although the prospect was certainly daunting, I had no difficulty in deciding to accept and did so there and then. Three months later I left the Junior Division and embarked upon a ten-week Arabic course at Beaconsfield. I was sad to leave Warminster after less than two years because not only was it run in an agreeable place among congenial people but the course seemed to be thoroughly good value for the Army.

My confidential report was written by the Deputy Commandant at the Staff College, Brigadier Tim Morony, a charming Old Etonian of exceptional wit, who died long before his allotted span was up. He had a special way with reports, and I shall be quoting from some of them in a later chapter, but his final comment on me read: 'It is one of the characteristics of the excellent officer that he should appear able to do his job with one hand tied behind his back. With John, however, I have sometimes heard a whisper of "Look, no hands!" He is truly an excellent officer.' I have always wondered about this remark; one knows the likely fate of those who ride their bicycles with no hands and with the prospect of fighting a war before me I pondered whether this was an auspicious start.

12
The Dhofar War

Although I find it hard to pick the most enjoyable tour in my service the two years in Oman were unquestionably the most exciting. When I give this answer to questioners today most of them wonder what I am talking about. The war in the Sultanate of Oman was not a 'British' war and the governments of the day did not want to draw attention to the help they were providing to the Sultans to defend their country against Communist insurrection. The policies then were post-imperialist and withdrawal from Empire was nearing completion. Britain certainly had vital interests in the Middle East but, after the less than proud withdrawal from Aden in November 1967, was not prepared to risk the political unpopularity, both internationally and at home, of deploying substantial forces back to the Gulf or the Arabian peninsula. Many British politicians feared not only the political backlash but also the danger of getting involved in an open-ended commitment. The more far- and clear-sighted among them could, however, see the serious consequences that would inevitably follow the establishment of a Communist regime in Oman which, with its strategic position at the entrance to the Gulf, could hold oil supplies to the West to ransom. This might easily be followed by a 'domino effect' up the southern shores of the Gulf.

Oman in the sixties was ruled by Sultan Said bin Taimur, who was forced, by poverty and the proximity of wealthy neighbours, to adopt severely repressive policies. Canute-like he tried to hold back the tide of oil-rich development and modernisation pursued by the prosperous Gulf states and to prevent his countrymen from learning and envying the new lifestyles of their Arab brothers nearby. Movement in and out of the country was closely controlled, development, education and modern medicine were denied to the people. There was no television and transistor radios were forbidden. Punishments for irreligious behaviour and many minor offences were draconian.

This situation could not last and the fiercely independent people of Dhofar rebelled. At first, in the early sixties, this did not amount to much, but when the British withdrew from Aden the Chinese, followed later by the Russians, provided a base in South Yemen, with weapons, training and money to build the rebel forces in Oman into a serious fighting force. By terrorism, extravagant promises and bribery the people of Dhofar were forced or subverted into giving their support to the rebels, with whose published aims, of achieving autonomy, development, education and medical services, they were mostly in general sympathy anyway. The rebellion became so widespread that the meagre and poorly equipped security forces became unable to control it.

At this stage, in 1970, there were two events of considerable significance. The first was a near bloodless coup by Qaboos to oust his father as Sultan. There were suspicions, never officially confirmed, that there was connivance, if not actual help, by the Foreign Office and certainly British officers were involved, but there was almost immediate transformation. Oman's own oil revenues were beginning to come on stream and Sultan Qaboos could afford to expand and equip his forces and begin true advance and development on every front. The second event was a detailed reconnaissance by Lieutenant-Colonel Johnny Watts of the SAS to advise the British Government and the Sultan on the most effective way to pursue the campaign and recommend what help the United Kingdom might quietly offer. Watts produced a comprehensive report, the burden of which was that much could be done to dominate the rebels step by step and essentially to win back the support of the people. British involvement should be to continue to provide officers and senior NCOs, on secondment to headquarters and units, to reinforce the many British and Commonwealth contract officers already there. There should also be an SAS squadron continuously present through alternating four-month tours, gunners and an RAF Regiment squadron for the local defence of the Dhofar capital, Salalah, and a squadron of Royal Engineers during the fine-weather months, mostly for opening roads and tracks to give better access for the security forces. The SAS would operate in small patrols living with the tribesmen to train them in self-defence and show them what the Sultan could offer if only their areas were secure. Gradually they would, through the families, persuade the rebels that support for the Sultan offered a better deal and they would be well advised to change sides.

The Oman coastline is nearly 1,000 miles long, from the Musandam peninsula, jutting into the entrance to the Gulf, in the north to the South Yemen border in the south. Muscat, the capital, is in the north, separated by 600 miles of sparsely inhabited desert from the southern province, Dhofar, which is about the size of Wales. Dhofar's geography is extraordinary and needs to be seen to be believed. Every year, from June to September, a monsoon cloud bubbles up from the Indian Ocean shrouding a coastal strip up to twenty miles deep in thick, wet mist which drops up to thirty inches of rain. This narrow strip, only a mile or two deep in places, has been eroded over the centuries to form partly jagged mountainous country, the *jebel*, with deep *wadis* with thick tropical vegetation, and partly open grassland not unlike Salisbury Plain. In September, after the monsoon, it is green with lush growth, but even when it dries up in the hot, sun-baked, ensuing months the low trees and thick bushes provide plenty of cover for guerrillas to mount surprise attacks and quickly disappear. In this terrain small groups can be effective out of all proportion to their numbers and the Dhofari tribesmen, with long guerrilla traditions, knew exactly how to make the best use of their land. They were fiercely brave, tactically skilful, and could move at astonishing speed. They had no vehicles, aircraft or artillery but were well equipped with mortars, rocket launchers and small arms. Numbering some 5,000 at their peak and well supported with food, information and early warning from their families and fellow tribespeople, they were a formidable enemy.

From early 1970 to 1973 the outcome of the war hung in the balance and the enemy had some important successes, but gradually, as his forces increased and support came from the Shah of Iran with helicopters and a full Iranian battle group, the scales tilted towards the Sultan. Salalah was secure, a trickle of tribesmen, with SAS encouragement, were changing sides. An important base close to the South Yemeni border, which eventually became the tactical key to the end of the war, had been captured in 1972. This was Sarfait, a barren, rocky area atop a 4,000-foot cliff which dropped in three stages, with narrow plateaux at each stage, to the sea. Inland from Sarfait was open country which the Sultan's Air Force could dominate and prevent significant enemy movement. Below it there was vegetation giving cover for movement by camel trains. The problem was that Sarfait was isolated by a deep chasm and could not be reached by land. All supplies, including water, had to be delivered by aircraft and a finite number of these determined the size of the force that could be maintained on the position. This force, approximately one battalion, was not sufficiently strong to break through the ring of mines laid by the enemy and cut the supply line below. The enemy was also likely to be able to reinforce the area more quickly than the Sultan's forces.

An operation might have been possible but there was another limitation. The Omani battalions were manned by tribesmen from Northern Oman and they did not readily identify with the objectives of the campaign, considering themselves more as mercenaries in a foreign land than as patriots. Many of them were excellent and brave soldiers, but for many others their heart was not truly in it. Things were fine when they were going well but a serious reverse or heavy casualties could be disastrous. Minor mutinies were not infrequent and it was feared that heavy casualties might provoke a major one. The base was secure, but it was hemmed in and a severe drain on administrative resources. When I arrived in August 1974 it had been there for two years and an attempt to break out of it the following spring ran into difficulties in a minefield and failed.

Headquarters Dhofar Brigade were in Salalah and enjoyed considerable independence from Headquarters Sultan's Armed Forces in Muscat, although the major-generals commanding paid frequent visits. Under command of the brigade was an international force of all three services some 10,000 strong, whose fighting heart was provided by two Omani infantry battalions and two Baluch infantry battalions manned by mercenary soldiers from Baluchistan. There were four Omani battalions, two of which would be in Dhofar at any one time on nine-month tours, while the remaining two would be in their permanent bases in the north recruiting and training. All were commanded by British officers and most of the company commanders were British, although 'Omanisation' was now proceeding apace. Omani ground forces also included a gunner regiment, an armoured car squadron, a number of specialist minor units and full supporting services. Jordan provided an engineer squadron in addition to the British one already mentioned and, later, King Hussein sent in his best unit, a Special Forces battalion. There was also the Imperial Iranian Battle Group.

The Iranian Army was largely American-trained for open warfare with heavy use of firepower. They were quite unable to adapt to the subtleties of guerrilla warfare and were arrogantly loth to take advice. They were nominally under command but any order that they did not like was referred back to the Shah in person for confirmation. The battle group did successfully open a road from Salalah into the interior but because they were so inept and vulnerable on mobile operations they were assigned to man static posts along this road to keep it open and free from enemy interference. Heavy firing could be heard from these posts every night but no casualties were ever suffered by the enemy who generally kept their distance.

Every morning there was a meeting at brigade headquarters to hear reports and issue new instructions. At every one of these the Iranians claimed to have mounted night ambushes as instructed. From radio intercept we had good intelligence of where and when enemy parties would cross the road but they were never intercepted. I decided to see for myself why this might be. I arrived at one of the Iranian posts just before dusk just as, with many shouted commands, a platoon was fallen in for night ambush duty. Singing at the tops of their voices they marched off down the road in threes to their ambush area, where they fell out and sat around smoking for three hours. At a further shouted command they fell in on the road and marched back towards their heavily defended post. A hundred yards from it we came under withering friendly fire and leapt for cover. After a few minutes communications were established and we were allowed back in. No wonder night ambushes achieved no success. I remonstrated with the Commanding Officer and he agreed readily with all my suggestions but I am sure they were never put into effect.

Dhofar Brigade also had its own air force under command. All air operations were in support of ground forces in one way or another, there was no external air threat and our aircraft were forbidden to cross the border, so there was little point in command being retained by Headquarters Sultan's Air Force in Muscat, as RAF doctrine would require. When, later, a force of Hunters was created from planes donated by King Hussein they were used to bomb gun positions and the rebel base across the border in South Yemen. Quite correctly these operations were commanded from the north. We were provided with eight Strikemasters, a version of the Jet Provost armed for ground attack with guns and rockets, four Skyvan transports, two Defender light passenger and communications aircraft, and a number of Agusta Bell 205 (the American Huey) helicopters which were heavily used for moving troops and stores and for casualty evacuation.

Finally, to prevent sea supply to the enemy, ships of the Omani Navy, mostly fast patrol boats, were placed under command when south of a certain latitudinal line. No sea supply was ever achieved by the enemy; it would have made an important difference to the campaign had they found it possible.

As rebels surrendered, those – and they were in the majority – who were prepared to take up arms against their former comrades were organised by the SAS into tribal *Firqat*. They were well paid though avaricious, unreliable and unruly, but they knew the land and the people and were essential to the progress of operations, as will be seen.

We flew out in August 1974 noting, as we flew over Cyprus, the white trails of Turkish landing craft conducting their invasion in the Kyrenia area, and we (rightly) feared for the fate of the Harbour Club there. On arrival in Muscat at midnight we were met by Major-General Creasey, the Commander Sultan's Armed Forces and his wife Annette. The next morning he gave me a crisp briefing and clear direction for the task before me. Essentially this came down to keeping Sarfait and Salalah secure, and dominating and pacifying the eastern area in order to free sufficient forces for mobile aggressive operations in the west to clear the country to its borders. We then flew to Salalah, landing in the monsoon drizzle. As I went about the business of taking over, Shirley was taken to Spinneys, the only grocery store. No supplies could be delivered during the monsoon and the shelves were almost bare, reducing to tears the ambitious hostess who faced the prospect of frequent visitors over the next few weeks.

In 1974 when Oman was opened up to the media after some years of exclusion we were visited by a team of journalists including, for BBC Television, Peter Snow. He is a very engaging and strong character who usually gets what he wants from those he interviews. The group's visit began in Muscat where they were briefed by Tim Creasey. One of the questions was 'How many casualties have there been in the war?' 'That's classified' said Tim, and while the journalists were flying south to Dhofar he sent a message directing me not to give casualty figures. I confess I could see no good reason for this but naturally intended to comply with the order when Peter Snow duly asked the question. In response to my saying it was classified Peter said: 'You give us two alternatives. We can report that there are no casualties and that the war is the figment of publicity-seekers' imagination, or we can say that casualties are disastrously heavy.' As neither was the case I decided to tell him what the figures were but asked him not to reveal his source. In the event the figures were not used at all by any of the group. Being frank with journalists over sensitive matters is a chance one may decide to take, and I, usually, have taken it. I have only been let down once, as I shall describe later. The exchange with Peter Snow resulted fifteen years later in my being asked to take part in the 'Newsnight' coverage of the Gulf War.

Officers are taught that every military operation must have an aim: 'to capture or hold a position', or 'to destroy the enemy' for instance. I did not think either of these was appropriate to the situation but recognised that if civil contractors could have safe access to an area the development promised by the Sultan could at once proceed and the original reason for the rebellion could be dissipated. I therefore chose as our aim: 'to secure Dhofar for civil development'.

When the monsoon ended we were able to begin operations in earnest. While waiting at a *jebel* for a broken helicopter to be repaired I had enjoyed a long conversation with a senior SAS NCO who was on his third tour in the country. He sparked off the design for battle that we were to pursue for the next nine months. He told me that the *Firqat* leaders were desperate to get back into their tribal areas, which had very clearly defined boundaries, lead their tribes and pursue their natural existence as cattlemen. If we could retake their areas in enemy-dominated country and somehow provide water for their cattle, they would be prepared to defend them against interference. We put this to the *Firqat* leaders and they were most enthusiastic. The pattern of operations therefore became:

1 Get a *Firqat* leader to identify a defensible location in his area.
2 Mount a battalion level attack to secure that area.
3 Build an access track to the area and an airstrip if possible.
4 Move a drill up the track.
5 Drill a water hole deep down to the plentiful aquifers.
6 Build water storage tanks and cattle troughs.
7 Build the basis of a village, with mosque, shop, school and clinic.
8 Leave the *Firqat* to defend themselves with the threat that if any enemy appeared in their area the water would be immediately cut off. (This was never necessary.)

The enemy quickly realised what we were up to and some of the operations to secure the areas were fierce, but they were always successful and by the next monsoon in June 1975 the eastern area was secure. Meanwhile Iran had reinforced their battle group to brigade strength and they were no longer under my command. They were given the task of building a line from the edge of the monsoon-affected area half way between Salalah and the border and hold it in such a way that no enemy camel convoys could cross it. Although they suffered many casualties and the job took much longer than expected, they eventually succeeded. The situation was now ripe for a major operation after the monsoon to seal the border and reduce the enemy to ever-diminishing groups lacking supplies, money and support.

While the monsoon mists persisted a major operation involving air assault by two battalions was planned. As a diversion the battalion at Sarfait, the Muscat Regiment commanded by Lieutenant-Colonel (later Brigadier) Ian Christie, King's Own Scottish Borderers, were to conduct a diversionary operation from their mountain fastness at Sarfait down towards the sea. This was conducted with great gallantry and skill during two nights and the second dawn found them in control of the first plateau some 1,500 feet below the position. From the cliff above Ian and I looked down on this success and Ian felt that if I could reinforce him quickly he could go on down to the sea and thus cut off the only enemy supply route. I fully agreed with this ambitious idea and quickly obtained approval from the new Commander Sultan's Armed Forces. Major-General Ken Perkins, who also launched Hunter bombing attacks across the border to silence the heavy artillery there.

The operation was a complete success. It had taken the enemy by surprise and the line was built and sealed before he could react in strength. The rest of the war was occupied with reinforcing our positions and 'mopping up'. The enemy lost heart and all but a few surrendered, leaving only small groups here and there who could be a nuisance but not much more.

On 18 November 1975, the Sultan's birthday and Oman's National Day, the Sultan invited many guests to the opening of a new television centre in Salalah. Following the ceremony there was a tea party and reception in the palace to which I was invited (General Perkins was in England at the time). I was quietly following the 'Brits hold back' policy, which obtained on such occasions, and sipping tea in the background. Suddenly an aide called me forward to sit beside His Majesty, to the evident disapproval of many of the guests. The Sultan asked me how the war was going. 'Well, Your Majesty,' I said, mentally crossing my fingers, 'I reckon you have won it!' I went on to say that I was confident that Dhofar was now secure for civil development and that my aim, therefore, was achieved. I considered that only a minor internal security problem remained and we could safely contain it. About ten days later the Sultan announced that his war had ended in total victory.

THE DHOFAR WAR

I have summarised here the operations during my time in Oman. For further details, should the reader be interested, they are contained in my earlier book *We Won A War*, published by Michael Russell in 1982. Although it is now long out of print most British libraries hold, or can obtain, a copy.

A sequel, no doubt to punish me for my impetuous answer to the Sultan, occurred on Christmas Day. Shirley and I and several others were helicoptering around the *jebel* visiting all the Christians we could find, however small their parties, to deliver mail, beer and mince pies. On the last leg of this journey the pilot asked if he could fly out 'low and fast' instead of following the usual procedure of spiralling up to a safe height before setting off across unsecured ground. I agreed and as we flew across a *wadi* I looked down from the co-pilot's seat to see a man with a rifle emerging from a hut. This he pointed at us from the hip and fired a burst of about thirty rounds. Eight of these hit the helicopter, which was very good shooting. One bullet came up between my knees which made me jump, but others hit the oil cooler and the tail rotor drive shaft which caused all sorts of lights to flash and the pilot to send out a 'Mayday' call. We were able to fly on for a couple of miles and flop over a cliff edge to land safely on the seashore and within minutes a pair of protective Strikemasters were overhead and soon after a rescue helicopter arrived. This said much for the alertness of the standby pilots on Christmas afternoon.

My death, wounding and capture were variously reported in over 100 newspapers around the world but we had been very lucky. Half of the tail rotor drive shaft had been shot through and there was no apparent reason why it had not sheared through, which would have been very nasty.

As my time drew to a close I was invited by Admiral Sir Henry Leach, Vice-Chief of the Defence Staff, during a visit to us, to consider a request from Oman that I should remain there, possibly with promotion. In effect this meant deciding whether to cast my lot, probably permanently, with Oman, or whether to soldier on with the forces of the Crown, and take my chance on promotion. Flattering and financially tempting though the offer was, I foresaw reduced interest now the war was over and a gradual loss of influence and involvement as, increasingly and quite rightly, Omanis themselves took charge of their rapidly developing country and its armed services. Omanisation, as it was called, was already under way. It was not really a difficult decision and, happily, turned out to be the right one. I found when I returned to the British peacetime Army that having been in command gave me useful credentials and certainly helped towards further advancement, although it also meant being careful when discussing warfare. Experience is respected but there is a serious danger that one comes to think of oneself as infallible on operational matters. In fact, of course, one is just as likely to be wrong, or right, as most others.

When we were campaigning it was important to understand the cause. Superficially we were fighting for an autocratic country which was not in any way democratic. His Majesty, when questioned by Western visitors imbued with the importance of democracy, would simply answer 'My country is not yet ready for it.' There a few occasions when decisions taken by the Sultan alone gave us pause for thought about the future and the possibility of absolute power corrupting, but we were generally satisfied that Qaboos's rule was benign, good for his country, and unarguably better than the Communist alternatives. Now, nearly a quarter of a century later, those of us who were involved are proud to have played a part in the early stages. The rule continues to be benign and the development in the whole country is staggering. Qaboos continues to be a friend of Britain, with whom there is important trade, and is also influential in Gulf affairs and the Arab League. The oil reserves are finite but substantial steps have been taken to diversify the economy.

Another popular question from Westerners was to ask whether the Omani people resented the Sultan's evident display of extravagance in what was not yet a truly wealthy country when so much of its GDP had to be devoted to defence. Luxurious palaces were being built and the Sultan had a vast fleet of expensive cars which were often to be seen in endless cavalcades. The answer was that very few did object. They would interpret a modest lifestyle as a sign of weakness and failure.

It is well known that Sultan Qaboos was a cadet at Sandhurst and the Academy still holds nostalgia for him. Back in the late seventies he paid a visit there and the Commandant, Major-General Robert Ford greeted him on arrival and presented some Omani cadets. Qaboos said that what he really wanted was to see the room where he had stayed as a cadet. Having seen it he asked to go down to the lake, where he sat on one of the benches in silence. There was a long pause, which Robert Ford had the good sense not to interrupt, at the end of which the Sultan described how his country owed much to Sandhurst. He said he had arrived there as a nervous, self-effacing young man with a tendency to laziness. Sandhurst it was that had shaken him up, given him self-confidence and a sense of purpose, all of which he had gone on to devote to his country. He then said he would like to show his gratitude and asked if there was anything the Commandant wanted. Robert, not knowing the scale of the gift that was contemplated, muttered something about a sports prize, but Qaboos interrupted and said he was thinking of something more substantial than that. 'How substantial?' asked Robert. 'Say a million pounds' came the reply. Robert, when he had recovered, said he would have to think about that but an indoor pool and sports hall were high on his dream sheet. The Oman Hall was duly built and opened by the Sultan. It is a wonderful asset to the Academy.

Shortly after the war ended, in early 1976, the Sultan came to my office in Salalah for a routine briefing, at the end of which he said he would like to reward his forces for winning the war and asked if I had any suggestions as to how this might be done. I said that I thought a 'victory' medal would be very well received. His Majesty said that this would be done but that he had something more tangible in mind. Like money. I said that I thought this presented insuperable problems. The war had been in progress for more than a decade and had been fought by many people of varying ranks and nationalities. It would be impossible to find them all, and how should amounts received vary with rank? And rank at what time? And what about dependants of casualties? And what about former terrorists who had changed sides? I was generally unhelpful, but next morning an ADC from the Sultan came into my office with a suitcase which he placed on my desk and then opened. It contained one million ryals (about £1.5m) in cash. 'His Majesty wishes you to reward the forces,' he said.

My two senior staff officers and I went into a huddle trying to decide what to do. Sending the cash back was not an option, one did not disobey the Commander-in-Chief's instructions if one wanted to stay in Oman. Eventually we decided to share the money equally between everyone who was serving on the last day of the war and entitled to the Omani Dhofar campaign medal. Everyone thus qualified, and no one else, received about £75 in cash. This decision was severely open to question and representation so we kept back 10,000 ryals against possible future claims to arbitrate on which we appointed ourselves both judge and jury. In the event, to our surprise, there were only two claims, one of which we upheld and the other we turned down. At that time there was no provision, other than personal munificence from the Sultan, for dependants of Omani fatal casualties, or for disabled casualties, to receive cash awards or pensions. The reserve cash was therefore used to set up a fund for this purpose. After *jundee*, the Arabic word for soldier, we called it the 'Jundfund'. This caught the imagination of the Sultan himself, of many businesses which benefited from the war being won, and a number of other organisations, including the SAS, who laid on a very lucrative sponsored half-marathon run. I understand that the fund became substantially wealthy and was the source of valuable hardship relief.

Another event involving a large sum of money happened when His Majesty challenged my headquarters to a shooting match. There were to be eight a side and each contestant would fire several different weapons. Qaboos himself and I would take part. When arranging this I asked an ADC whether His Majesty would like any arrangements made for the award of prizes. Once again he came to my office, this time with ryals worth about £12,000. Having bought a few cups and medals and provided cash prizes for everyone there was still a lot of money left over. The butts were manned by some thirty Baluch soldiers who each received at least a month's pay for their morning's work. They must have thought the world had gone mad.

At about this time the Foreign Secretary, James Callaghan visited Oman and came down to Salalah. During lunch he talked with the Sultan about his interest in farming and Qaboos insisted he prolong his stay slightly and come to inspect the pedigree Jersey herd on the royal farm. These cows were very special, even to the extent of being able to listen to classical music in their byre, but for Callaghan's visit they were in the farmyard. The Sultan and he admired them, leaning on a five-bar gate figuratively sucking a straw. I was standing just behind them and was highly entertained to hear our Foreign Secretary say 'You know, Your Majesty, you ought to try keeping pigs.' The Sultan, thinking of the Muslim abhorrence of pigs, paused for a moment and then replied very quietly 'I don't think my people would quite understand that.'

I have two more stories to tell about Oman which were not in my personal experience although one of them is well authenticated, and they have both afforded me much amusement.

As the war neared its end and the Sultan was beginning to open up the country to take its proper place among Arab nations, he knew that one of the indicators of status was the state visit. By way of dress rehearsal for more significant visitors he decided to invite President Hamdi of North Yemen and much effort was invested in the formalities. Little North Yemeni flags adorned every possible post and wall along the routes the motorcade would take and the *pièce de résistance* was to be a grand luncheon in the desert near Nizwa, to which dozens of tribal elders would be invited. His Majesty declared that luncheon would be served in a marquee. The royal protocol department calculated the size of the marquee that would be required and telephoned around the world to find one big enough. They discovered that Courage's in Britain had just what they needed. The problem was that the firm only had one man who knew how to erect this monster and he was well past normal retirement age. 'Never mind,' they said, 'our aircraft will arrive in two days' time to collect the tentage and the skilled elderly gentleman.' This happened and everything was transported to the selected site, where the poor old man, with plenty of soldiers to help him but soldiers whose only language was Arabic, was thrust into a temperature of 130F and told to get on with it. Somehow he succeeded, as did engineers who built a retiring room with full washing and showering facilities for the two leaders. Paths were marked out from where the royal helicopter would land to the retiring room and from there to the marquee. Just before the royal party's arrival daffodils were unpacked from cool boxes and stuck in the sand bordering the paths, where they lasted about five minutes before being burnt to a frazzle.

The luncheon was grand indeed and dozens of the tribesmen sat cross-legged before a giant mat on which were laid out all manner of delicacies. Whole goats and chickens surmounted piles of steaming, fragrant rice, with countless bowls of vegetables and sweetmeats in support. All was going well until the Sultan, seated on a *chaise longue* with his guest, suddenly drew a handkerchief and dabbed his brow. The huge marquee had canvas walls which kept out any zephyr there might have been, so in the extreme heat what came next was a perfectly reasonable thing to do. As one man the tribesmen leapt to their feet, turned about, drew their sharp *khunjas*, advanced on the canvas walls and ripped them from top to bottom. Whether Courage's were ever able to restore their precious marquee, or indeed its proud erector, is not recorded.

Another, less well-authenticated story is of a National Day spectacular at Muscat at which a spectacular parade of the armed forces was to be followed by a lavish fireworks display of hitherto unknown grandeur. The contract for the display was let to a German firm and the climax to their splendid show was to be a bomb fired from a huge mortar centre stage which, when high in the air, would explode to release showers of stars surrounding a large photograph of His Majesty suspended from a parachute. I am not sure whether it was at a rehearsal, or on the night, but at one performance the bomb exploded successfully and released its parachuted portrait, but it was of President Hamdi of North Yemen! I am sure the German firm left unpaid, indeed they would have been lucky to escape with their lives.

Our time in Oman had been a wonderful experience, offering wide variety. There were times of heady success, but also of tragedy and failure. An awareness that one's decisions are likely to cost men's lives, and the poorer the decision the greater the number of lives that will be lost, concentrates the mind wonderfully. Moving among dead and wounded soldiers who lie there because of things you set them to do is a sobering experience. There were plenty of incidents when things went awry but generally there was a most refreshing atmosphere of commitment and mutual trust, especially between pilots and the soldiers they supported. There were many entertaining aspects too. Oman is a country of spectacular beauty and moving on and over it is unforgettable. Everyone involved in the war fought hard, but they also played hard; there were good parties and many moments of pure farce. We were lucky to have been there at that time and because we were well paid and had only food and drink to spend money on, Shirley and I were out of the red for the first time ever.

We have only been back to Oman once. In 1977 the Sultan very kindly invited us to attend his National Day and sent his personal aircraft to pick us up from Heathrow, together with about a dozen others, including Julian Amery MP whose exchange of letters with the old Sultan when Under-Secretary of State at the Foreign Office in 1957 had opened the way to close cooperation on defence matters. John Asprey of the eponymous jewellers was another guest, as was Mary Fletcher, the widow of my predecessor as brigade commander who had died of cancer the year before. We flew in luxury to Salalah where development in the fifteen months since we had left was already apparent. Not only had the runway been reinforced and lengthened to take our Boeing 707 but there was now a new hotel, the

Holiday Inn. This had been taken over by the Sultan for the exclusive use of his guests and we were invited to order whatever we wanted during our three-day stay.

In the next two days we were taken round by our successors, Brigadier Charles and Mary Huxtable, to see the remarkable changes and advances since we had left, and on one evening there was a colourful parade, flawlessly executed in a grand newly-built stadium. On the third day there was to be a firepower demonstration as the centrepiece of the National Day celebrations. King Hussein was to be the principal guest. Before I had left we had organised such a demonstration mainly to impress the Dhofaris with the irresistible power available to the Sultan and it had gone well. I had been lucky then. The weather had been perfect. Today there was a howling gale and we huddled in our seats with the local green and black dice-patterned and tasselled *shemaghs* wrapped around our heads to protect us from flying particles of sand and grit. The Sultan and the King were in a grand royal box bedecked with national flags and the display began with the deployment of troops, mortars and guns by helicopter, showing how quickly and accurately they could come into action. The next phase was the delivery of artillery ammunition by parachute from Skyvan aircraft. This lumbering workhorse, which looks something like a London bus with stubby wings, delivers pallets pushed out of its rear doors. Unfortunately the pilots had miscalculated the effect of the gale on the heavy parachuted loads, which were meant to land about 100 yards in front of the spectators. The wind took hold of them and one missed the royal box by inches before crashing onto one of the limousines waiting behind, seriously damaging it.

13
Brigadier Staff

Leave in the Army is, or was, always described as being a privilege and never an entitlement, except when completing a tour of secondment, when there is a right to a calculated number of days before beginning a new appointment. After Oman I think our entitlement was about sixty days, but arriving back on a Wednesday I was greeted by a telephone call from Lieutenant-General Sir Patrick Howard-Dobson, the Military Secretary, who told me that Brigadier Jack Fletcher, my immediate predecessor in Dhofar and now Deputy Military Secretary (A) was dying of cancer and had not been able to work for some weeks. I already knew this was to be my next job and that it was an important one, but not that it needed to be filled immediately. I was warned to start in the Stanmore office the following Monday. There was to be no argument about this and because it was a most desirable job I did not offer any, but rushed off to buy a car and we moved quickly into a quarter in Bushey.

DMS(A) was responsible for the career management of officers of colonel's rank and above, helped by a colonel and a major and a number of civil servants. Another brigadier, Mike Tomlinson, now dead, and later Dick Vincent with a similar staff dealt with lieutenant-colonels and below. I was told on joining that I need not bother myself with competition for my next promotion because, barring accidents, it was assured. Such worries, I was told, would be distracting and tempt manipulation of careers in one's own favour.

The Army's system for promotions and appointments was efficient and scrupulously fair but not everyone saw it that way. Officers' own views about their talents and capabilities did not always coincide with the Army's view and because the latter was MS's responsibility there were many who regarded MS's system as a black art. There were too many accusations of nepotism, favoured regiments, luck in timing, incompetent reporting officers, anything really that would allow a disappointed officer to blame an outside agency, not himself. Pat Howard-Dobson determined that the customers should be better informed about how the system worked and dispatched his two brigadiers to all parts of the British Army's globe to brief officers in detail. My own travels took me to the United States and Canada, Gibraltar, Hong Kong, Belize, Norway, and often to Germany and Holland. We worked hard to make our lectures both informative and entertaining.

I also gave some lectures to commercial concerns, such as Marks and Spencer, who had heard of the success of the Army's methods and were keen to overhaul their own arrangements.

The basis of the system was the annual confidential report, or CR, initiated by an officer's immediate superior and given to him to see. A criticism of this was that it inhibited the frankness of many who had not the strength of character to report honestly what they thought, and this was certainly to some extent true. On the other hand to have one's report written secretly would not encourage trust or enable an officer to assess his own progress objectively. More senior commanders in the chain could write unseen comments but if they raised any new criticisms they had to show them to the officer and it was a duty of MS to ensure that this was done. Reports were assembled in a book and this was the tool used by selection boards of at least five, and often more, senior officers to grade officers for promotion and make all appointments. It was a feature of the system that no promotion or posting could be effected without a selection board's seal of approval.

The procedure was generally fair. As one looked back through CRs over a few years, it was remarkable how clear and consistent an assessment would emerge, and how often certain adjectives were repeated by a wide range of different reporting officers.

Promotion and appointment had to be preceded by the personnel officer keeping in constant touch with every client officer and thus being aware of the family situation (including health and children's education), personal preferences and any compassionate reasons for special treatment. The two colonels who worked for me, Guy Watkins and John Stibbon, were both outstandingly good at carrying out this duty conscientiously. Guy retired early as a major-general and went off to run the horse racing in Hong Kong, while John became a general and Master General of the Ordnance before, on retirement, becoming Chief Royal Engineer.

In order to brighten the lectures on a potentially dull subject I collected a selection of actual remarks gleaned from many years-worth of reports. There are dozens of them, but these are my favourites, and bear in mind that they are genuine extracts, several of them from reports written by Tim Morony:

'It is sad for this officer that the winning post is moving up the course at the same speed as himself.'

'This officer will certainly be a major-general unless he meets someone of comparable drive going in the opposite direction.'

'X is a perfectionist. He is the most earnest, conscientious and dedicated officer it has ever been my misfortune to meet.'

'I would be delighted to have him in any number of positions.'

'He suffers fools gladly and has always given sound advice to myself and my staff.'

'Because I am a bachelor his charming wife Jane has carried out all the duties normally performed by the CO's wife. I have been wonderfully served.'

'He is safer with a primed grenade than with a pen.'

'He is no Einstein, but then Einstein would have been a very bad soldier.'

'Can express a sentence in two paragraphs any time.'

'Never makes the same mistake twice but seems to me to have made all of them once.'

'It cannot be pure coincidence that whenever I go to lunch he is jogging past the gate wearing a tracksuit.'

'He is no Napoleon and he knows it. The knowledge doesn't bother him at all.'

'He is an officer with many virtues. He is certainly intelligent with a high sense of responsibility. He is devoted to his duty and has a capacity for hard work. He has a very even temperament and is the soul of tact. He is sensitive in his assessments and has a balanced outlook. I would recommend him for a bishopric anywhere in the world now. However, if his fairy godmother asked me what she could do for him I would only wish her to administer some physic which would introduce some iron into his soul.'

Generally speaking the lectures were quite well received, although there were two that were more difficult than usual. One was to the officers of a Greenjacket battalion in Gibraltar. Here there were two problems. One was that it was my first lecture and most of them knew more about MS procedures than I did. The other was that it was given in an echoing hall with a wooden floor and the audience sat on tubular steel chairs which were distractingly noisy if any one shuffled them. And they did.

The other unusual one was in Belize where, although my talk was mainly for the more senior officers, the CO asked me to talk to the captain commanding a company and his three subalterns. I agreed, only to find that it meant helicoptering into a jungle clearing and speaking sitting on a log. As my lecture depended quite heavily on supporting slides and there was neither a projector nor electricity, I fear it left something to be desired.

Early in our time in Bushey we took a week's holiday in Killarney. I believe it was not strictly legal at the time but I travelled under an assumed name and did not indicate my profession at any stage in making the booking. One of my aims was to play on Royal Killarney golf course and on paying my fee and asking if there was anyone who would play with me I was told that an Englishman had just gone to the first tee and would probably like a game. At the tee was a little fellow who introduced himself as Denis. He was not much over five feet tall with red hair that looked as if it had been permed and had a very effeminate air, although he was accompanied by his attractive but non-playing wife. Slightly disdainfully I asked him if he would like to play, which he accepted. I then asked his handicap, expecting 36 or so. 'Eight' he said 'at Seaford.' He played well and as we went round I asked him what he did, this time expecting 'hairdresser', or something of the sort. Another surprise: 'Blacksmith' he said. We arranged to play again on the following day and by this time I felt able to tell him that I was in the Army. 'Oh, I was in the Army,' he said. I suppose I might have guessed by now that Denis was not at all what he appeared, but I had certainly not expected 'Military Police'.

On another day we had just driven around the Ring of Kerry and stopped for a Guinness and sandwich lunch in a small town. I had the clubs with me and asked at the bar where the nearest course was, to be told that it was 'just up the lane'. We went up the said lane but there was no sign of anything resembling golf so I went to a house to inquire. An elderly lady said that the golf course was just through a gate opposite her house and but that it was only nine holes and the green fee would be one shilling. Thanking her and setting off through the gate we could see no tee, no fairway and nothing to indicate where a green might be. I went back to the house to be told that I could pick my own spot to tee off, 'But,' said I, 'where is the flag to show where the green is?' The lady had the answer to that one too.

'We have no flags now,' she said 'they were always getting stolen.' 'So how shall I know where it is?' I asked. 'Oh, you'll find it when you get there' she said. I never did find even the first hole, let alone any other.

One of my responsibilities was the Army Medal Office and administering, but not making, the rules for the wearing of medals. General Sir Timothy Creasey, formerly my commander in Oman and now Colonel of my Regiment, was selected to be the General Officer Commanding Northern Ireland, a job not without its dangers. While in Oman he had been awarded a Jordanian order by King Hussain but the rules said that you could only wear medals awarded by the country to which you were seconded, so he could not wear this order. Tim challenged me to get special dispensation on the grounds that although seconded to Oman he had had Jordanian troops under his command during the war and that should make a difference. Less formally he told me that he had thirteen medal ribbons and he was blowed (at least that was the gist of what he said) if he was going to go to a dangerous place with unlucky thirteen up. I made this a long-term project because the organisation that decides such matters is totally dominated by precedent and turned down Tim's first request flat. Eventually, after months of argument, mostly on the lines that every precedent has to be created before it can become a precedent, the bureaucrats gave in, just in time for Tim to take his fourteen ribbons to Belfast.

The selection of senior medical officers for promotion or appointment was the duty of Number 1 Medical Selection Board and during my time the Army Board became suspicious that the doctors, whose training and experience seldom includes detailed personnel administration, were operating on a combination of nepotism and Buggins's turn rather than fairly assessed talent. In order to satisfy the Board that this was not so, I was detailed to attend the medical board's gradings and subsequent deliberations, simply to see that fair play ruled. The doctors rather resented this and soon found a way round it. Their board members came from many different places and a dinner was instituted the night before every meeting, to which, naturally, I was not invited, and at which tactics to subvert any objections I might raise were thrashed out so as to present a united front on every item. In fact I was content that although a touch unconventional their methods were usually fair enough.

This was the nearest I ever came to working in the Ministry of

Defence and I consider myself lucky to have avoided Whitehall, which I fear is not really my scene. DMS(A) was ensconced at Stanmore but it was a thoroughly rewarding job. Unlike many MOD appointments it seldom dealt with money or theory, but concerned real people, many of them senior to me, who would rightly get angry and distressed if they felt they were not getting a fair deal. I often had to give officers bad news about their prospects and although this was less than enjoyable I was impressed to find so many people who were courageous and pragmatic about their disappointments. There was pleasure, of course, in giving good news, and it was fascinating and a privilege to sit in on the discussions at the very highest level about the most senior appointments. An old adage declares that 'Bread is the staff of life, and life on the staff is one long loaf.' This is certainly not my experience of it.

There were many travels, happily with no loss of luggage or serious delays, and only one alarm. Coming in to land at Colombo on a British Airways flight we flew into torrents of rain. An attractive lady sitting next to me and I were looking out of the window when we suddenly saw that we were flying no more than fifty feet up and almost level with the tops of palm trees but there was no sign of airport or runway lights. There is no question that we were within seconds of joining air crash statistics and my companion grasped my hand in fear. I really thought our last hour had come when the pilot opened full throttle and climbed back up. After a few seconds we saw the runway below us and we went round a second time to land on it safely, but the first approach must have been a very near thing. I later learned that Colombo then had a very bad reputation and pilots hated it in bad weather, when it was apparently easy to try to land some distance before the runway.

In August 1979 the promise given to me on arrival was fulfilled and I was sent to command 4th Armoured Division in BAOR, whose headquarters were in Herford.

14
Divisional Command

When staff officers or company commanders take over there is usually a week or so set aside for handover one to another. In the case of more senior commanders the handover is normally conducted by the staff and the outgoer has left before his successor arrives. The two usually contrive to meet some days before to talk mostly about personalities. In the case of taking over 4th Armoured Division my predecessor Major-General (later Lieutenant-General Sir) Richard Vickers thought it would be a good idea, especially as I had not served in BAOR for fourteen years, to visit him during a corps command post exercise. There would be time to talk and I could see the headquarters deployed.

My ADC, Captain Tim Wilkes, and driver Corporal Baldwin, who had joined the headquarters a week or two beforehand, met me at Hannover airport and led me to a staff car. Tim and I were chatting when Baldwin turned to tell us that the car would not start and needed a push, so my first action as commander designate was to help push the car. After we had been running for a few minutes Baldwin again had to interrupt our conversation by asking: 'Excuse me, sir, where are we going?' to which Tim answered 'Div HQ in the field.' 'Yes, sir,' said Baldwin, 'where's that?' 'I've got a map reference,' said Tim 'where are we now?' 'I don't know' said Baldwin. This was eventually sorted out and Tim learned a lot in his first few minutes, and became an excellent ADC. Baldwin stayed with us, except for one short tour away, for the rest of my service. He was a Cornishman who took delight in passing on and exaggerating bad news if there was any, but he was a first-class driver who knew exactly when to talk and when to keep quiet, which is an important quality in a staff car driver. But our adventures on that day were not over.

We were accommodated in a small German hotel and booked in during the afternoon. That evening I was summoned to dine with the corps commander, Lieutenant-General Sir Peter Leng, at his headquarters. After a comprehensive briefing on what was expected of me and a long, long dinner in the forward headquarters mess it was past midnight when we got back to our hotel and no amount of knocking, ringing and shouting could raise the owner or his staff. I had no intention of spending the night in the car so I climbed up some trellis work to get in through a first-floor window. It was at this point that the owner appeared in a voluminous nightshirt and with volubly expressed opinions of the British Army. Eventually he was calmed and we had a beer together before going gratefully to bed. I learned some colloquial German that night.

A few days later we moved into Taurus House, the divisional commander's residence, a fine and unusual building which had been requisitioned immediately after the war's end. It had been designed by a Swiss architect for a manufacturer of margarine whose nearby factory had originally provided warmth for the house from its piped effluent. The architect's very personal style was to have no angular corners, which made for interesting rooms, especially the central sitting room with its domed ceiling. There were unusual accoustics in this room and, like St Paul's, there were certain spots where sound followed the ceiling and one could overhear a conversation from thirty feet away on the other side of chattering people. It was a fine and comfortable place to live and there was an attractive garden cared for by an elderly Jugoslav refugee from the war. He worked hard but preferred growing vegetables to flowers. Mrs Vickers described him to us as *'blümen* murder', but, though amusing, this was less than fair comment.

4th Armoured Division commanded two armoured brigades, one at Minden, the other at Detmold. The General Deployment Plan (GDP) to be put into effect in the event or likelihood of a Warsaw Pact attack placed it well forward and quite close to the border with East Germany. With my sceptical views about the use of tactical nuclear weapons it was perhaps ironic that in the event of Armageddon I might be the first to need to call for them.

I had another personal problem with the GDP. One of the Soviet Forces' strengths was their artillery and with our deployment so close to the border they could employ this with potentially devastating effect before even leaving their own territory. Add to this my conviction that there were so many opportunities for their efficient espionage system to obtain details of our planned deployment that it was very likely to be compromised, thus pinpointing our every position. I always had it in my own mind to alter our positions from the published ones if the balloon went up, staying within our published boundaries but perhaps not the best positions tactically. This would unquestionably land me in serious trouble with the corps commander but in the light of all his other troubles at such a time I doubted if it would be remembered as important and I hoped it might save many lives in the opening stages of war. Furthermore my conviction that such an attack would never come sustained me in making this somewhat subversive plan. I should perhaps add that although I could never see myself calling for tactical nuclear weapon support and thus, perhaps, initiating the end of the world, I had no problem with the principle of nuclear deterrence. It had been effective for more than thirty years and I saw no reason why it should cease to be so.

I also had little trouble with the message to motivate the division for its role. Although I believed an attack to be unlikely I felt able to tell anyone with conviction and honesty that the reason why attack was unlikely was simply that the effectiveness and efficiency of the NATO defence forces were sufficient reason to make such an attack unattractive. If that efficiency and strength were seen to diminish or disintegrate the situation might then become dangerously different.

On my first day in the office there were on my desk a number of kind messages wishing me good fortune in the job. Calling in my personal assistant, a corporal in the Royal Army Ordnance Corps, I began to dictate my replies. 'Hang on, sir,' said the corporal, and it became apparent that although a good typist he had no shorthand or audio-typing skills. Marvelling at how my predecessor had done all his written work by drafting in longhand, I told the corporal I was sorry but I could not work in that way and called in the excellent Chief of Staff, Colonel Patrick Brooking, to tell him that a competent shorthand typist must be found. No nominations came forward for a few days and I was beginning to get worried when Patrick came in looking pleased with himself to announce that Mrs Sonia Scott, the wife of a major in the Royal Tank Regiment in the garrison, was keen on the job. She had been a headmistress of a school and also PA to a managing director and had all the skills I sought. This proved to be right and Sonia was not only an excellent PA, but also someone who contributed greatly to a cheerful and happy atmosphere in the office for the next two years. It was a wonderful new experience to have someone working for me personally who only needed to be told the gist of most of the correspondence and could then compose it herself. This may be common in civilian organisations but it is rare in the Services.

For reasons of public opposition and environmental damage it has become increasingly difficult to arrange exercises in Germany with anything approaching realism since the early eighties, but then we were allowed reasonable freedom of action, although there were continually increasing constraints, especially when it came to exercise damage, and many were the stories to which this gave rise. The training areas themselves were under continuous environmental pressure but were in any case only big enough for unit level deployments. Under a system called the '443', after the number of the form on which one applied for clearance, we could exercise over huge swathes of German countryside and, generally speaking, most of the population were then reasonably sympathetic. They could see that it was in the interests of their own defence against the feared Russians. Many farmers were positively enthusiastic and invited tanks onto their land because payments for damage were generous and I heard one farmer claim that it paid for his annual holiday in the Caribbean.

A farmer was seen by a fellow divisional commander, Major-General Martin Farndale, flying by in a helicopter, to be standing on the edge of a field heavily scored with tank tracks and looking very agitated. Bravely Martin set down nearby and asked the farmer what was the matter. The farmer said he had been with the Wehrmacht on the Eastern front and was very experienced in armoured warfare. It was quite obvious, he shouted, to anyone with the slightest tactical sense, that the tank squadron in the situation he had just observed should have attacked round the left flank, not the right. 'Your army is useless.'

Damage was not only paid for. Every exercise was supported by a team of sappers whose duty was to repair damage immediately whenever this was possible. One farmer was less than pleased when after digging by hand a deep drainage hole in his field all morning, and then repairing exhausted to a well-earned lunch, he returned to find that his hole had been filled in by the damage team.

We ran several of our own exercises but the big one in my time was Exercise Spearpoint 80 organised by 1st British Corps. This was an affair demanding months of planning. 4th Armoured Division, with a German Panzer brigade under command, were designated Orange Forces and had the job of simulating a Warsaw Pact attack. We entered fully into the spirit of the thing and after very detailed reconnaissance and some rehearsals were able to mount an impressive opening assault, which gave pause for two thoughts. The first was that, given detailed knowledge of the ground, good dry weather and complete surprise, a Soviet attack would be very hard to stop, but the other was that if any one of those conditions was absent they would find it very difficult indeed and soon bog down in treacherously soft ground and be faced with the many streams, rivers and minefields which were major tank obstacles.

Just after the last rehearsal for this exercise, which we conducted in miniature on a training area near Hamburg, we decided that a visit to Hamburg and its infamous *Reeperbahn* would be an amusing diversion for the more senior officers before setting off for the exercise proper. Suitably shocked, appalled even, by what we saw there, the most embarrassing moment came when two uniformed soldiers of the Duke of Wellington's Regiment, sent there to ensure that no men of that regiment behaved badly, recognised me and saluted smartly. Few officers, I suspect, have been saluted in the *Reeperbahn*.

There was another not dissimilar incident at the end of the exercise. We were told by our Army Air Corps pilots that not far from our headquarters' final position there was an excellent hostelry in the middle of nowhere, which, they said, would be ideal for a celebratory drink. Six senior members of the divisional staff set off for this place and found it at about half past ten at night to be in complete darkness. Nothing daunted we went to the front door and rang the bell. After a minute or two, and several more presses on the bell, there was a clicking of locks and banging of bolts and an apparition with rollers in its hair and night cream on its face looked out at us. We asked if we could come in. 'You want to drink, or f--k?' asked the apparition. Hastily we said that a drink was all we sought and we were invited in, but did not stay long.

One of the brigade commanders at the beginning of my command was Brigadier Bernard Gordon-Lennox, a Grenadier Guardsman of high and inflexible disciplinary principles to whom everything was priority one. To this characteristic he devoted his very great energy and drive. There were many tales about this remarkable officer, from which I select three.

The Services Kinema Corporation distributed for showing in BAOR the film *Emmanuelle* which was classified 'X' and enjoyed a reputation of being naughty, although by today's standards it was very tame. Bernard, hearing of its reputation, suspected that it would be unsuitable for viewing in Detmold and, demanding a preview in the morning to confirm this, took a staff officer with him to check. A few minutes were quite enough and the film was banned. The SKC manager was outraged and within minutes the world exploded and the telephone went mad. Senior officers and civil servants from Corps, Headquarters BAOR and the Ministry of Defence vied with each other to threaten dire international action and ask how dare an Army officer presume to know better than the British Board of Film Censors. Eventually the matter was settled by Bernard, who would not himself give way, agreeing to accept a direct and written order from higher authority.

Another incident followed a heavy snowstorm which was disrupting traffic all over North Germany. Bernard was concerned about its effect on Detmold and late at night telephoned the Royal Engineers Regiment at Hameln, thirty-five miles away, which came under his administrative command. He directed that a combat engineer tractor be dispatched at once to clear the roads within and approaching his Detmold barracks. The Sapper driver set off at around midnight and arrived at the barracks, having fought his way all night through appalling conditions, just before Bernard's arrival the next morning. The Sapper reported to the guardroom where nothing was known about him and he was told to wait on the verandah outside while inquiries were made. Wearing a scruffy greatcoat, unwashed and unshaven, the exhausted Sapper lit a fag and was leaning against the wall puffing away when Bernard drove in. Leaping from his car and without inquiring the background he described the sapper as a disgrace to the British Army and ordered the guard commander to lock him up at once under close arrest.

Bernard later became commander-in-chief in Berlin and from a visit to one of his units the following conversation with a soldier, whose name was displayed on a label on his chest, was reported to me:

Gordon-Lennox: 'That's a fairly interesting name – how do you pronounce it?'

Trooper Kuczinski: 'Kuczinski sir.'

Gordon-Lennox: 'Very good. Well, it's jolly nice to have you in Berlin to fulfil the very important role allotted to your squadron. Now that's a very interesting name you have there, how do you pronounce it?'

Kuczinski: 'Kuscinski sir.'

Gordon-Lennox: 'Good. Now you must make sure that you make full use of the unrivalled opportunities that the city offers – there is an awful lot you can do and see. I must say, that's a most unusual name. How on earth do you pronounce it?'

Kuczinski (somewhat desperately): 'Smith, sir.'

I have told these stories about Bernard Gordon-Lennox but I would not wish to leave the wrong impression. Bernard was an extremely efficient and dedicated brigade commander to whom duty took precedence over everything else. He worked hard and had tireless energy which he devoted to his job. Lest he be thought an unfeeling martinet I should add that he and his wife were kind, generous, unselfish and thoughtful hosts and nothing was ever too much trouble for them.

The Royal Welch Fusiliers were in the division, stationed at Lemgo. Their Commanding Officer, Peter Reece, was a cheerful and energetic extrovert who later won a rare DSO when he took the battalion to Northern Ireland. The battalion's big day was 1 March, St David's Day, when the officers' highlight was a mess dinner with various rituals, including the entry of the drum major leading the regimental goat around the table, many speeches, harp playing, and a requirement for uninitiated officers and guests to eat a raw leek. In 1980, happily for the guests, the leek presented to us was not much bigger than a spring onion, but there were other hazards. The corps commander, Peter Leng, and I were invited for dinner at 1930 for 2000 hrs. Unfortunately, just before the guests arrived there was a power failure in the officers' mess. All food had to be taken to the main barracks half a mile away, cooked there, and then brought back, hopefully warm, to the table. The diners were invited to drink and talk quietly among themselves until dinner could be served, which turned out to be just before midnight, by which time we were not only hungry but more than a little merry. None of the ritual was curtailed and we did not escape from the table until 0400 hrs, by which time St David could feel himself well and truly celebrated.

It was with the Royal Welch Fusiliers that I went to BATUS, the British Army Training Unit Suffield, provided by Canada near Calgary. Shirley was able to hitch a lift as Fusilier Akehurst on the battalion's transport aircraft. We made this the beginning of a splendid leave, on which we took a train over the Rockies to Vancouver and then flew round the United States, calling in at San Francisco, San Antonio (of the Alamo fame), New Orleans, Williamsburg and Washington DC. We were also able to take in the Calgary Stampede, seeing the skills of the cowboy displays, and being particularly impressed by 'calf-cutting' in which a horse and rider communicate with each other in the most extraordinary way to extract a particular calf from a herd.

The exercises in Canada were the only ones available to the British Army where all types of live ammunition could be fired in field conditions and they were held over a huge expanse of prairie. The ground had sufficient undulation to test minor tactics but not a tree or building anywhere, which made it impossible to simulate the conditions of the north German plain, where our operational task lay. Nevertheless the use of live ammunition added a valuable touch of realism to the training which the soldiers thoroughly enjoyed. Safety had to be strict, of course, and it was Murphy's Law that while walking behind an infantry attack three Abbot 105 millimetre shells fell short and only a few yards from me. Naturally the divisional commander should not be seen to flinch and this was an occasion when my experience in Oman really did come in handy and sang-froid was shown.

One of a divisional commander's duties was to conduct some of the annual inspections of units and one that I undertook was that of the Army Air Corps regiment in Detmold. It was normal for the inspecting officer to arrange minor exercises on which soldiers' individual professional prowess might be tested and for this one we arranged a circuit on which fitness, weapon training, NBC protection, first aid and other skills would be checked. The scenario for first aid was a vehicle accident and doctors made up some very realistic injuries for soldiers to deal with. One of them involved an injured man vomiting and in order to simulate this convincingly the casualty withheld a mouthful of porridge which he duly spewed over the soldier who came to his aid. With a shout of 'You dirty bastard!' the first-aider punched the casualty on the nose, thus gaining no marks for his test.

Two sporting events with which I was completely unfamiliar were the divisional ski meeting at Ishgl in Austria and the divisional passage race in the Baltic. Both turned out to be quite exciting. I had tried learning to ski twenty years before but the knee injury incurred while playing cricket in Trieste precluded progress. However, I wanted to experience something on the *piste* while attending the divisional meeting. The organisers therefore arranged for two experienced Austrian mountain rescuers to strap me into their *blotwagen*, a sort of stretcher on skis, and then whizz me down the fastest slope. This, though perhaps mildly humiliating, was exhilarating and I got a clear impression, if I needed it, of the thrill of the slopes.

In our first year Shirley and I were invited to start the divisional passage race, four days of sailing with night stops on Danish islands beginning and ending at Kiel. As this duty meant nothing more than being sailed to the start and then sounding a sort of foghorn before departing, it was not exactly challenging, but I could see that the race itself could be fun as well as testing. I therefore created a team from our house staff for the following year and engaged the services of an experienced skipper on the headquarters staff, Captain Peter Newell of the Royal Artillery. Despite our inexperience we managed to win the race although we had taken one or two navigational gambles which only narrowly came off. When we were sprinting for the finish against a team of doctors, our line took us close to the lighthouse at the entrance to Kiel harbour. A groyne, not marked on the chart and below the surface of the water, stretches out some twenty yards from the lighthouse. Our keel hit it with an alarming and crockery-scattering smack but our progress was not interrupted and the Royal Engineers who maintained the boats were mercifully kind about repairing the dent, which was about the size of a pudding basin. I treasure my prize of a sailor's clasp knife.

When our time in Herford ended we had to submit our two Cairn terriers, Dinah and Zoë, to kennels for quarantine. We strongly support any moves towards ending this requirement, which is not only very expensive but also stressful for pets and owners alike. We think that inoculation, properly carried out and recorded, is sufficient protection and hope that the day when this is legislated for is not too far off. The only argument for keeping quarantine that carries any weight with us is the vested interest of the vets and kennel owners whose living standards depend on it and who would face hardship if it were suddenly stopped. We see no reason why it should not be phased out over two or three years, and expect that it will be. We were particularly aggravated when we lost the discount for a shared kennel when our two Cairns, who had usually got on well together, had to be separated when the younger Zoë began to bully poor inoffensive Dinah and severely bit her ear.

To take my leave of Lieutenant-General Sir Nigel Bagnall, the Corps Commander, I asked for a formal interview and put on my Sunday best for the purpose, somewhat to the surprise and I believe a degree of apprehension on the part of this singularly unpompous officer who always preferred informality. There was, of course, nothing to be apprehensive about, but I did want to make a point. I said that I left 4th Division with regret because I would have liked another year of BAOR experience. I did not feel that serving only one earlier tour in the theatre had affected the division much, although I was not wholly conversant with some of the nuances familiar to those who had spent most of their service there. I thought morale and motivation in the division were generally high and that it was as well trained as was possible in the circumstances. I thought it at least the equal of its peers. On the other hand I could not claim it to be as ready for war as everyone required and some even believed. There was a severe shortage of training areas and they and the '443' areas were subject to strict environmental pressures and restrictions. Ammunition availability was, in my view, nowhere near adequate and it was virtually impossible within the rules to incorporate genuine realism in exercises. Above all there was the constant drain of sending units to serve emergency tours in Northern Ireland so that brigades were rarely complete for their training. By the time a unit had prepared for Ulster, served its six months there and taken its leave afterwards, the best part of a year had passed. It also took time to tune back into the mechanised warfare skills of BAOR. Northern Ireland was very good experience for soldiers and junior officers and NCOs but units could never operate there as a whole and the machinery of command and battle procedure became rusty.

Nigel was fairly non-committal at the time but I fear that he took my outpouring as being too negative. Nevertheless I have never changed my view that British forces in West Germany would have had a hard time of it in the early stages if war had come suddenly.

The Ministry of Defence offered an interest-free loan towards buying a house if officers were still serving at the age of fifty. The loan was repayable from the terminal grant they received on retiring. In 1980 I decided that we must get a foot in the housing market and, to this end, having agreed that we would like to return to the Warminster area I began to write to house agents there. We chose Warminster because there were friends there and it had good access to London but had the tempo of a country town, which we liked. There was lovely countryside around and good fishing and golf nearby. I think it was in April that I announced, having studied the programme ahead that 6, 7 and 8 December would be devoted to house buying. From the agents' sheaves of paper we would select a few that we could look at from the outside on day 1. From this survey a smaller number would be looked at in detail on day 2, and day 3 would be for final checks and the making of an offer. With tales of families looking for houses for months, even years, it was not surprising that my plan was thought to be idiotic, but I determined to buy *a* house, even if it was not *the* house. About a fortnight before the expedition Peter Reece of the Royal Welch Fusiliers telephoned to ask us to lunch on 6 December. I explained that I would be in England house-hunting. He said that the Queen, their Colonel-in-Chief, was visiting and he thought this might influence my decision. 6 December was cold and snowy but the event went well. The Queen was delightfully informal and was clearly enjoying her colonelcy.

We rushed home, changed, and set off for Calais. Soon the earlier light snow turned to a blizzard and we struggled to reach the Channel port, eventually catching a ferry at about midnight. With only two days now for house purchase we had raced round looking at the outside, or the area in which they were situated, of some twenty houses before ten o'clock. Then we went to the first agent to ask for visiting powers and keys, although we had seen little to enthuse about. As the agent left to make some calls and collect keys he turned and said: 'I suppose you wouldn't be interested in this. It came in this morning and seems to be just what you want.' We went there first. It was ideal, both in size and location. The present occupant, the widow of a former vicar who had died nearly forty years before, did not want to move but could not afford to stay. She was green-fingered and the garden, which was of manageable size, was the love of her life and in very good order. We made an offer, which was accepted, and went back to Germany feeling very pleased with ourselves. Things are rarely that simple and a protracted period of further negotiations followed as the lady's family pressed her to stick out for more money. Even after exchanging contracts she suddenly threatened to pull out altogether and the legal advice was that, although the law was clearly on my side, her possession plus the fact that she was a frail old lady would win court sympathy over a general. At last we settled on a fair price and we have had the house ever since. Not many people, approaching their three score years and ten, have only ever looked at one house with a view to buy.

We used our house for holidays and weekends for the next decade but did not live there full time until I finally retired, because fine houses went with all my subsequent appointments. Now we exchanged Taurus House, Herford, for Staff College House, back in Camberley for the fourth time in my service.

15
Staff College Yet Again

It was good to be back among the familiar surroundings at Camberley. Staff College House was a comfortable residence, although after many amendments over the years since it started life in the mid-nineteenth century as two semi-detached houses, its interior layout had become slightly potty. Stairs and corridors led nowhere and only two bedrooms had their own bathroom. It was set in lovely grounds and had a fine garden although there was no way of denying access to deer, which made many plants, especially roses, impossible to grow. I spent much money on rose bushes, having been assured that lion's hair and dung would keep the deer off, but it didn't and they soon perished.

The college enjoyed great independence and I took pleasure in accidentally overhearing an argument between the Adjutant-General and the Vice-Chief of the General Staff as to which of them commanded me. In effect, provided good relations were maintained with both of them and with the Director of Army Training, it did not really matter who commanded. We had virtually first pick of all young majors aspiring to command and of lieutenant-colonels who had already commanded successfully. We therefore had a very high-powered team. Essentially their job was to keep in close touch with all doctrine and trends, turn that into instructional material, and then to teach it to a course of 180 students. The student body comprised 120 British officers, including representatives from the Royal Navy and Royal Air Force, and 60 from Commonwealth and foreign countries, mostly, but not exclusively, close allies. The British officers had qualified by examination and were intended to be the best of their generation, of which they represented about one third. Entry was regarded as a passport to higher things and, indeed, most senior officers have been staff trained, although there was a positive effort to ensure that good men who missed out were not left permanently at a disadvantage. I often used to tell students that they were lucky to be there and that no selection system could be flawless. Some were there who should not have been and there were others outside who should.

They were being given an advantage but it was up to them to make good use of it. It was part of the instructional plan to put them under pressure, but never to an intolerable degree and if they could not keep up they should not be there.

The Commandant's job was really not difficult, although quite busy. There were lecturers to be introduced and summed up, many reports to write, occasional guidance to be given, visitors to be entertained, many visits away from the college, much instruction to attend – to get to know how it was going and learn something about the instructors and the instructed – and, finally, many examples of good and bad written work to peruse and comment upon. The very first example of the latter which was sent up to me was, frankly, dreadful. The Commandant was the only person allowed to use green ink and his comments were likely to be passed around among the students, perhaps even quoted in books in years to come. With pen poised I was impressed with a need for *gravitas* as I looked at this work, covered in rude comments in red ink by the directing staff and acid remarks in blue ink by the divisional colonel. I could think of nothing useful to add, but thought 'Seen' would be totally inadequate and simply wrote: 'Keep taking the tablets.' Happily that student's work improved later.

Early in 1982 the college was agog as the Falklands campaign unfolded. The day after his return we managed to get the ousted governor, Rex Hunt, to address us, which he did most movingly, and meanwhile Shirley was trying to soothe an understandably distressed Mrs Hunt with all the sympathy and understanding she could muster. We were all thrilled when the decision was taken to recapture the islands and held our breath like everyone else as the fortunes of war swayed this way and that. Apart from our close professional interest in what was going on there were a number of telephone calls from industrial and business organisations. They were mostly concerned, not with the fighting, but with how such an immense task force had been assembled so quickly and efficiently. They were hugely impressed with the staff work which had gone into the preparations and wanted to know, therefore, how we trained staff officers. So we basked in reflected glory.

I used to accompany teams who went to give presentations to other establishments and one of the annual commitments was to visit the Royal Naval Staff Course at Greenwich. The lights were lowered in the lecture theatre and after a brief introduction from me one of our instructors opened the presentation. It was common practice to begin with a joke of some sort and sprinkle one or two others on the way. It helped to keep people awake. On this occasion our lieutenant-colonel (now a major-general) started with a funny but very crude story to his all-male audience. When I came on to sum up an hour or so later I began by apologising to the ladies in the theatre. This was actually not true, there were none, but it was a successful leg-pull which achieved a very red face.

Another popular visit was by the whole college to various Royal Air Force stations and, being the boss, I could take first pick. In the light of my enthusiasm for golf, RAF Leuchars, within a stone's throw of St Andrews, seemed a natural choice. The Station Commander was Group Captain Mike Graydon, who kindly looked after me personally. This gave me three treats: one, to get to know Mike, with whom I was to work closely later; two, to have two and a half hours piloting a Chipmunk supervised by an instructor I had known in Dhofar, and learning something about aerobatics which had not been possible in the Defender in which I had gone solo in Oman; and three, a visit to the Royal and Ancient clubhouse in the evening and a round on the Old Course next morning. These last two were made possible because by custom the Station Commander at Leuchars was made an *ex officio* member. As we sat in the famous main bar sipping the traditional drink, surrounded by hallowed golf memorabilia of every description, there were only two other men there. They seemed as if they might have been *in situ* for some time; their voices were raised and we could not help overhearing their conversation which was about who was to be the next Secretary of the Royal and Ancient. Apparently it had come down to a choice between Michael Bonallack, the distinguished amateur golfer, and a major-general who was no mean sportsman and an experienced and professional administrator. I was fascinated by this because I was a referee for the major-general. He did not get the job and Bonallack has been hugely successful, but I am sure that my man could have done the job well.

Apart from the military value two memories stand out from a visit to the United States. We went to an Artillery School at El Paso and marvelled at the scale of the operation there and the vastness of the available firing area. The staff officer, Major Donald Ross, who accompanied us (for Shirley came too on this trip) went on the station jogging run early in the morning. I chickened out. During his run, which was headed by the major-general commanding the post, he saw a soldier coming from the canteen to be confronted by the sight of the post commander jogging towards him with two or three hundred men and women in train. Trying to cope simultaneously with a cigarette and a large carton of Coca Cola as well as his mess tins and cutlery, he could not decide which of his handfuls to discard in order to be able to salute. He eventually dropped the lot with a loud clatter and saluted with an anguished look on his face.

Speaking of the high numbers of women at most American posts, there is a story, claimed to be true, of a British Sapper captain visiting Fort Something who was guided to his bachelor officer quarters and shown where the ablution facilities were. Going to these facilities he ran into a muscular lady coming out with a towel round her neck. He apologised for having come to the wrong place but the lady assured him that the facilities were unisex. 'Don't you find that a bit difficult sometimes?' asked the captain naively, 'Doesn't it mean a lot of hassle for the ladies?' 'Oh no,' came the reply, 'we get laid a lot, but there ain't no hassle!'

Another unisex experience came my way later in my service. I was visiting a NATO minesweeper squadron off Lisbon and had to transfer from a German boat to a Danish one. The Danes sent a rubber outboard bouncing across the waves, crewed by a sailor on the outboard at the back and another in the bows holding a rope. It was really quite choppy but somehow my MA and I got into this craft and reached our destination soaked with spray. A little later, while I was talking to the captain, the sailor from the bows of the rubber boat came onto the bridge, lit a cigarette, and looked out to sea. She was a most attractive blonde. I asked the captain if there were other ladies on board and he replied that there were not. I then asked if having just one pretty girl in the crew presented any problems. 'No problems,' he said, 'but sometimes I wish the men wouldn't kiss her every time they pass her in a corridor.'

Later in the American visit, while at Fort Benning, Shirley and I had an adventure of our own. It is rare in the States for visitors to stay in officers' houses and we were accommodated in a compact detached house called a 'VIP Quarter.' These are very comfortable and equipped with every possible requirement. On this occasion we had been travelling all day and Shirley's first move was to take a leisurely bath. While this was going on I looked around the house to see what goodies were provided. One of these was a huge television set and on it was a handheld instrument which I assumed to be the remote control. As I pressed the button on it there was an immediate sounding of sirens and soon, looking out to see what was going on, I found we were surrounded by a platoon of armed men looking alternately inwards and outwards. Their commander, a lieutenant, came to the door and demanded to know who I was. I pointed to a signboard which said: 'Welcome Major-General John Akehurst', but this was not enough. My 'ID' was demanded and fortunately I had it on me. The officer then asked me where my wife was. I explained that she was in the bath, but this only got the response that for all the officer knew she could be being held there by terrorists as a hostage. He was not to be satisfied until he had come upstairs and inquired through the bathroom door whether all was well. The soldiers were then fallen out and the officer explained to me the difference between the panic button and the TV remote control. It was quite funny, but one had to admire the speed of reaction and the thoroughness with which the job was done, particularly in a country where violence may be common but terrorism is virtually unknown.

It was during another visit, to Fort Bragg this time, that we were invited to be part of the annual charity work for the local museum in Columbus, Georgia. The British officer who was looking after us had some wealthy friends who were members of a group assembling enough cash to keep the museum going for another year. The first event was the super-rich dismissing their staff and giving a dinner, cooked and served by themselves, to the merely rich, who had paid substantial sums for a place at the table. We were kindly invited as (fortunately) non-paying guests, and treated on arrival to some pretty awful mint juleps mixed by our host, who, I guess, poured his own drinks but once a year. Dinner followed, which might have been good if the hostess had not been carried away by a conversation about how dreadful it was that a black family was rumoured to be moving in to number thirty-something in the road in which their own number was just short of 3000. This so horrified the lady that she forgot our steaks and 'well done' would have been a euphemism.

After dinner we were taken to a 'silent auction' where wonderful items of jewellery, china, carpets, furniture and various professional services had been presented for sale. Anyone there, except us of course, could have funded the museum for years out of back-pocket petty cash, but they really entered into the spirit of the thing and huge and increasing sums of money were entered onto sheets of paper beside each sale item. Two of the most successful and lucrative lots on sale were a 'root canal' donated by a local dentist, and a vasectomy by a doctor. The latter scored most highly because all these wealthy people were writing down other men's names beside their bids. These men (or their wives) would then rush to pledge more money for yet someone else. The doctor's offer made thousands of dollars.

Another lot was a hot-air balloon flight. I told my American host that I wished I could bid for such a thing and he fixed that I should go up with a friend of his at 0500 hrs the next morning. We bumped across a field for our sluggish take-off, but soon we were airborne and experiencing the thrill of drifting low over the forests. The silence was constantly interrupted by the frequent roar of the 'burn' and the incessant radio chatter of the pilot with our ground crew back-up truck. Balloons have neither brakes nor steering, and they react slowly to burns, at least this one did. Our pilot decided to put down in a field of cotton and headed down to it rather more quickly than intended. We crashed through the branches of a tree trying to respond equally to shouts of 'Keep your arms inside the basket, they might get broken,' and 'For God's sake don't fall out, we shall go up too quickly', but somehow we came to earth without injury and struggled to get our collapsed balloon out to the edge of the cotton field where our truck team awaited us.

Another trip was to Egypt and again Shirley came too. This was a reciprocal arrangement because we had looked after Egyptian visitors the year before. While in Cairo Shirley contracted a sore throat and a hotel doctor had to be summoned. This young man looked like Omar Sharif and Shirley was tempted to keep him busy for all sorts of invented ailments and said he could treat her for anything any time.

I was provided with an escort officer who had been at Camberley the year before. When we went by car to the Naval Staff College at Alexandria I told him that generals could be late with impunity but must *never* arrive early. In this he failed and, ten minutes early, we drew up before a square two-storey house. Through its many windows we could see officers rushing in all directions putting on belts and hats as they ran. Then, around a corner, came a military band led by a small bandmaster, with a lined face speaking of long experience, but now looking very agitated and nervous. His musicians assembled and he signalled them to begin an overture of welcome. As I waited I speculated on whether this might be 'Rule Britannia', 'General Salute', a national anthem, a regimental march, or even 'Jerusalem'. I did not expect 'Colonel Bogey'. The rendering was poor, but recognisable enough to bring the words of the coarse parody into mind. The bandmaster, clearly expecting the worst for having been late, seemed delighted when I went over and congratulated him, showing off some Arabic that still stayed with me.

During that visit we were taken to Karnak and Luxor where we were given privileged visits to all the tourist delights in and around those places. We were flown up the Nile by civil aircraft and Shirley was made nervous by the behaviour of our escort officer's wife who kept her eyes closed throughout the flight, clutched her Muslim equivalent of the St Christopher badge, and recited the Koran to herself without a break. We managed to avoid the perils of 'gyppy tummy' throughout the visit but unfortunately, on final departure, our Air Egypt aircraft broke down at the end of the runway and in the long pause which followed we were given soft drinks which undid all our precautions. I suffered the effects for some weeks afterwards.

We also went to Sweden, where study of their neutral stance backed by strong defensive arrangements was intensely interesting. I had been asked before we left if there was any leisure activity that I would like to pursue and I replied that if any salmon fishing were possible I should very much like that. So one afternoon we were driven some sixty miles from Stockholm, loaded into a little boat, and driven at high speed across a lake. I was eagerly awaiting sight of a likely salmon river when we pulled in to tie up alongside what looked like a large wooden raft. This turned out to be part of a salmon farm and my host lifted a trapdoor to show me dozens of excited, swirling salmon in a very small space. Baiting a hook with a pellet he invited me to dangle it through the door. Pulling out a salmon a few seconds later I was deemed to have been provided with my objective and off we went back to Stockholm. I did not even get to keep the wretched salmon.

I was invited during both my years to lecture the Nigerian Staff College, at which British officers helped as instructors, on counter-revolutionary warfare. I had not been to West Africa before and what follows is an amalgam of the two visits. On arrival at Kaduna I was met by a Nigerian escort officer who shepherded me to a light military aircraft in which we took off in deteriorating weather towards Kano. I sat in the second pilot's seat and, knowing a little about it, took great interest in the navigation and supporting use of radio. The latter was intermittent and I should not have bothered about the former. The pilot dodged around storms and threatening clouds, apparently without recording the direction or duration of these diversions, and it came as no surprise when he called up stations on the ground to ask if anyone could find him on their radar and tell him where he was. Happily, eventually, someone could and we made our destination safely.

After staying the night with Colonel Trevor Hammond, the senior British officer, and his wife and getting an introduction to the frequent water and power cuts, which were a way of life, my host left early to set up my lecture, saying that a driver would collect me in an hour or so. It would not take long to reach the college, and allow time for setting up my slides and a rehearsal. Just as this driver arrived there was a mighty explosion not far away and it soon became clear that a petrol tanker had been involved in a collision and the main road we were due to take was now impassable. In limited English the driver said he could find his way to the college by minor tracks and we set off into the bush. The only thing that saved us from motoring for ever was the pall of black smoke from the stricken tanker which gave us some sense of direction. The driver clearly had none. Eventually we arrived, not long before the lecture was due to begin. It was to be a full hour's worth of talking, based mainly on dozens of slides to help with any possible language difficulty. I had been going for about ten minutes when the power failed and I was left in a pitch-black room with an audience of about a hundred black faces and no light to read a script or power to show my slides. This was one of the more difficult addresses I have given. It did not seem to have gone too badly and eventually the power came back on and I rushed through my slides before taking questions. One of the points I had made was that almost all revolutionary wars, especially in Africa, had a basis in some sort of tribalism, whether that be in the literal sense or in equivalent national, ethnic or religious senses. This struck an unhappy chord and I had to argue a number of examples against heated questioners before the Nigerian commandant declared an armistice. I have a photograph of this session in which I look much like the accused at a court martial.

My return from my second visit involved being driven to Kaduna to catch a local aircraft to Lagos, where the first direct 'jumbo jet' flight to London was to carry me home. The drive in the dark was hair-raising. There was one straight, two-lane, single carriageway road littered with the wrecks of former accidents, and at one stage I saw three sets of lights speeding towards us, occupying the whole road. My driver simply sheered off into the verge which, fortunately, was flat and open at that point and we bumped to a halt as the three vehicles sped past, still in line abreast. On arrival at Lagos I was guided to a very hot, crowded and scruffy lounge to await boarding instructions. The airport was simply not geared to handle jumbo traffic and when the flight was called 400-odd passengers surged to the single metal-detecting security arch. With a mass of hot, pressing humanity I fought my way to the arch, only to be greeted by an official asking for my airport tax voucher. Having flown in and being in transit I had not anticipated this. 'Where do I pay the tax?' I asked. 'Outside,' said the official. The thought of fighting my way back through the heaving mass filled me with despair. Although I had promised myself to eschew any form of bribery I fished out a ten pound note which disappeared into the official's robe as if he were a conjurer and I was through, gasping with relief.

An unusual visit to the Staff College came in the shape of the military attaché from the Chinese embassy, who wrote to say his name was Mr Feng and he was interested in how we organised our field exercises. He was met at the main entrance and brought to my office, where we took coffee and had a stilted conversation for a few minutes. He was noticeably uncomfortable about something and I asked him if anything was the matter. 'Not really,' said he, 'except that I was told I would be meeting the general who is commandant.' I explained that he was already enjoying this good fortune, to which he responded: 'But you cannot be general, you are too young!' Having been a general for some four years by this time I was naturally flattered, but it took some time and the summoning of a colonel as witness to persuade him that I was indeed the Commandant. Age carries authority in China, elderly generals are much respected. Mr Feng then got down to business and we talked about various sorts of exercise. Finally he asked: 'Tell me, general, how often does the British Army hold two-sided live-firing exercises?' I answered that we had one which began in 1914 and another in 1939 but not all that many others, but he was surprised and said that in China they had many. I asked what level of casualties was considered acceptable, to which he replied that anything over five per cent would need to be explained but would probably not call for disciplinary action.

Once every year or so the Queen has honoured the Staff College with a visit and I was lucky enough to be there when Her Majesty came in 1982. The programme was a simple one, involving attending a discussion, planting a tree, taking lunch in the main dining room and finally touring an exhibition given each year by foreign and Commonwealth students showing off their countries and their wares, later to be recorded in a painting by Terence Cuneo. We took much trouble over souvenir programmes, menus and the like but a week before the event we received a signal from the Duke of Edinburgh, who was in Australia, to say that he had seen the proposed programme and he would like to come too. After a brief panic we arranged a new programme, separating the royal couple until lunch, and we managed to get new brochures printed in time.

At lunch the Queen impressed me by asking if a picture which had a glass face and could only be seen at an angle was a particular military epic by Lady Butler. I could hardly see the thing because of the reflection on the glass but she was absolutely right. Before lunch, when we had a few moments to spare, I had taken Her Majesty to show her a major painting on our first floor of a Sikh officer in full dress uniform beside the Tomb of the Unknown Soldier looking down at a small bouquet of flowers thereon. We did not know who had painted it, what it represented, or how the college had come by it; but the Queen did, in great detail. The bouquet was apparently a gesture on her mother's wedding day and she had known the artist.

While I was talking to the Duke I asked him if he would be prepared to address the college. He asked when and what about and I said we would adjust our programme to match whatever day he chose and that the subject was entirely up to him. About three months later the Private Secretary rang to say that His Royal Highness would come on such and such a date and we agreed that he would arrive for coffee at 1030 hrs, talk from 1100 to 1145, answer questions for about forty-five minutes, and then take lunch with us. I asked what the talk would be about but this was not yet known. About a week before the visit we were told that the title would be 'Left, Right' but the Private Secretary did not know what this would mean. We discussed all sorts of possibilities: terrorism, politics, a naval dig at the Army, discipline, drill etc etc but reached no conclusions.

On the day Prince Philip arrived on time and after coffee I led him into the lecture hall. As we went down the aisle I pointed out his lectern and said that before he began I would just tell the students who he was. The students were amused by this impudence but I

On Deal front with my mother and father in 1945. On left is Lt Col Saunders, who pointed me towards the Army.

Passing-out at Palace Barracks, Hollywood, January 1948. Parade is led by Lance-corporals Charlie Small and Andy Nelson. JBA no 3 in nearest rank.

With Lt Col Houchin and the B Company Young Soldiers shooting teams, 1951

Wedding Day, 18 May 1955

LEFT With Alan Peckham, Kedah jungle, 1955 RIGHT Julian, aged ten

Headquarters personnel, Dhofar Brigade, Salalah, Oman, 1976

HRH Princess Alice, Duchess of Gloucester, plants a tree at Barnwell presented by the Northamptonshire Regiment to mark half a century as Colonel-in-Chief, 1987

Shirley, Michael and Penelope Barthorp, John and Sally Wetherall, JBA, Ypres 1988

Arrival at SHAPE, Mons, 1987

Welcoming our Colonel-in-Chief to the Royal Anglian Regiment, Colchester, 1989

First salmon: the Spey, 1989

Poacher and Poppy pose on a singular garden seat

Leaving SHAPE 1990. Left, Lt Col Andrew Stewart (AM), JBA,
Gp Capt Ian Dick (PSO), Capt Ian Gowdy (ADC).

Briefing the Prime Minister with SACEUR Gen Jack Glavin,
and German DSACEUR Gen Eberhard Eimler, 1989

JBA with Henry Cooper, Maj Gen Bill Cornock and Eddy Grimstead
at the Generals v. Variety Club Golf Match, Kingswood, 1993

am not sure that the Duke was. He began by saying: 'Sometimes I wonder why I have been asked, and sometimes I wonder why I have accepted; on this occasion both of these thoughts apply.' The talk turned out to be about the left and right sides of the brain and the tendency in modern times to be too calculating and mercenary, and not sufficiently appreciative of the finer, cultural side of life. The address seemed just to be getting into full swing when, after only fifteen minutes, it ended. Recovering from this surprise I called for a short break before questions and went over to talk to the lecturer who, before I could speak, said: 'Was Dyer right?' I stammered that I had not given the massacre at Amritsar much thought lately, but then got questioned in detail about the moral and ethical issues, the definition of 'minimum force,' and the historical effects of the incident on the sub-continent. I am afraid that nothing I said was useful to the debate and just as I was wondering what on earth this had to do with the price of fish, all was revealed. His Royal Highness had seen the film *Gandhi* the night before. No wonder he had the advantage of me.

Questions began badly. With an hour and a half stretching before us we were not encouraged when the first question, something about how the royal programme was constructed, was brushed aside with 'I haven't come here to answer silly questions like that.' Just as I was desperately trying to think up a question myself our bacon was saved by a Sudanese student who asked something about the mating of elephants and from that moment all went swimmingly.

The Commandants of the Staff College and RMA Sandhurst are *ex officio* church wardens of the Royal Memorial Chapel at Sandhurst and each has his own box just below the choir. One of the chapel's traditions is that field marshals, when they die, are commemorated by the installation of a window bearing their coat of arms, and there is a service of dedication. At one stage during the service the two generals, each bearing his wand of office, lead a procession down the long aisle to a point below the new window. Major-General Geoffrey Howlett and I had to be instructed by the Academy Sergeant-Major in the drill appropriate to the occasion when the late Field Marshal Sir Geoffrey Baker was honoured in this way. This was my last encounter with a regimental sergeant-major of the Brigade of Guards and, much like his predecessors of many years before, he thought we were pretty hopeless when time after time we failed to pick up a common step when we emerged from our boxes and set off down the steps. We thought this quite funny and the RSM, although he could not be scathing to generals as no doubt he would have been to cadets, had to grit his teeth, cast his eyes heavenwards and pretend to be amused. Rather more to his satisfaction we did get it right on the day.

One of my duties was to give the final address of the year and to leaven my sage, and probably boring, summary and advice I tried to make these entertaining. The RSM was a man called James, of one cavalry regiment, and he had an identical twin brother in another such regiment. In my first year I got both together, dressed them identically, and conducted a conjuring trick in which the RSM appeared to have been spirited magically from one cupboard on stage to another. It went down well and I have recently discovered that this is often the basis for professional conjurers' work. The following year I called 'Fore' as I approached the lecture hall and was preceded by a golf ball which appeared to run across the floor and into a hole in a model green for a hole in one. This was engineered with fine nylon fishing cast reeled in by a hidden instructor and it looked quite convincing.

The next move, on promotion, was to Headquarters United Kingdom Land Forces at Wilton, with a fine residence overlooking the polo ground at Tidworth. This was our eighteenth house in twenty-nine years of marriage and we were becoming accustomed to dealing with packers and movers; but I do not think we met the wag who was in the team who moved one of our instructors and his family from Camberley to the School of Artillery at Larkhill. One of the packers asked the wife why she was not wearing a headscarf. He explained that a headscarf was necessary dress for Larkhill, the high temple for Gunners. 'But I haven't got a headscarf,' said Cathy Lowe. 'Oh dear,' he sympathised, 'come up through the ranks then didja dear?'

16
Field Army and Inspector General

The Americans are well known for reducing as many titles as possible to acronyms but I was not sure whether or not a *double entendre* was intended when on first arrival in my office as Commander United Kingdom Field Army and Inspector General of the Territorial Army I found on my desk a signal from a former colleague in the United States. It read: 'Congratulations on command of FA, and good luck!' A less ambiguous message came from the historian Corelli (Bill) Barnet, which read: 'Your promotion offers proof that intelligence and a sense of humour need not be insurmountable handicaps in a military career.'

The Field Army was defined as being all operational units in the United Kingdom (less Northern Ireland) whose role was not static, administrative or training. Another lieutenant-general at the headquarters commanded most training establishments, and those with administrative responsibilities generally came directly under the Quartermaster General. In 1984 the Field Army numbered about 40,000 and the TA about 75,000 and expanding. It was a huge organisation but there was an efficient chain of command through nine Districts, two commanded by lieutenant-generals, the others (one of which, North East, was also a divisional headquarters) by major-generals and down through regular or TA brigades. Occasional directives could be issued and one could become closely involved from time to time, but mostly it was a matter of visiting and checking on standards. In just over two years I visited 124 major and 89 minor units, took off in aircraft 174 times, drove 86,000 miles, and slept in 143 different beds.

Resources, as ever in peacetime, were a constant worry and there was a continual need to determine priorities. Nowadays commanders have very direct and personal responsibilities for budgets and can adjust priorities by that means but then it was more a matter of detecting shortages in good time and then negotiating with the suppliers and purchasers. Mostly this came down to all forms of transport, spares, training areas, overseas exercises, and ammunition both live and blank. Blank was always in short supply and if there is one thing that everyone on tactical exercises and training enjoys, whether regulars, territorials or cadets, it is to be able to fire blank ammunition. All too often soldiers would be given five blank rounds to use during two days or more and this took away from them much of the realism and enthusiasm so necessary to effective training. It surprised me to learn that, because the production scale is so much smaller, blank rifle ammunition is more expensive than live, but this was a factor carrying little weight with Tommy Atkins who was not impressed when he had to shout: 'Bang! You're dead!' instead of pulling his trigger. The Americans had set up a very effective means of making exercises realistic and I went to Fort Irwin, not far from Las Vegas, to see it in action.

The system is well known in the British Army now and is in full use on Salisbury Plain but it was a novelty then. In effect both men and machines carried their normal weapons to which a laser beam was added. They also carried laser detectors which indicated a hit. This had two advantages. Fire, to be effective, had to be accurate whereas firing blank was just a noise and aiming was of no importance. The other advantage was in realism. Soldiers and their commanders, once properly motivated, developed a strong need to knock out the enemy and yet survive themselves. This taught invaluable lessons about movement and covering fire that had never been possible in training before, except perhaps in China on the two-sided live-firing exercises described by Mr Feng. I was greatly impressed at Fort Irwin and recommended as strongly as I could that the high initial capital cost of setting up such a scheme would quickly be recovered in the saving of training ammunition and would be very worthwhile. I know that many other visitors reached the same conclusion.

Essentially the Field Army had two roles. Most of the regular element and about half of the TA were to reinforce BAOR if war came and most of the rest were tasked to home defence, and to form the basis for expansion and reinforcement. It was important to impress upon home defenders, particularly in the TA, that their job was just as important as that of those who would set off across the Channel early in a time of crisis and that they were by no means the second eleven.

The TA, with its infectiously enthusiastic volunteers, took up much of my time and the two years I had spent as an adjutant in a TA battalion were useful, not only in my awareness of their characteristics but affording me an extra measure of credibility with the volunteers. With its central council in London and associations throughout the country, all including significantly influential members of the civil community, the TA could call upon a forceful and effective lobby. On a number of occasions during its eighty-year history it had thwarted Regular intentions for it by appealing directly to ministers, sometimes the Prime Minister. It had managed to survive many attempts to demolish or reduce it and was now as strong as it had ever been in peacetime. It was part of my job to convince doubting senior officers who had no experience of it that what it lacked in training it largely compensated with enthusiasm and would quickly learn if called upon. Front-line units might take up to six months to get themselves fit for general war, but they could quickly prepare themselves for lesser tasks and for many they were ready at once, as has been shown in the Falklands, the Gulf and Bosnia, where many TA members have been used.

Field Marshal Lord Carver had once coined the phrase 'One Army' to encompass both the Regular Army and the TA. What he meant at the time was simply that there would be one chain of command to manage both, but it has haunted those with responsibility for the TA ever since, being quoted *ad infinitum* as a reason for demanding equal resources, weapons and equipment.

I ran across TA sensibilities with a bang on my first visit away from the Wilton headquarters. It was to attend a TA study day in Perth and we travelled there in an HS125 executive jet, the first time I had been allotted a passenger aircraft to myself in the British Army. My excellent Military Assistant, Major David Montgomery, was so carried away by this symbol of power that when we arrived at Edinburgh Airport he rushed us from the jet into the waiting staff car and we were twenty miles down the road to Perth before he realised that our bags had not been unloaded from the hold. The next day I addressed a large audience of past and present volunteers and gave my first impressions of my new job. I referred back to my first meeting with the TA, at a time when, as I have described earlier, the battalion I stayed with was more of a drinking club than an operational unit despite a first class war record and its becoming a top class TA battalion later. Unfortunately my remarks were lifted out of context by an elderly retired Territorial who had commanded a Scottish transport unit in the fifties. He took my 'drinking club' remark to refer to the whole of the TA at that time. He wrote in high dudgeon to a local paper and, separately, to the Chief of the General Staff demanding my immediate resignation. Happily some senior serving volunteers rushed to my defence and there was an amusing sequel when a soldier who had served in the complainant's unit wrote to the same local paper to say that in his opinion that unit too had been a drinking club.

Not long before I had left Germany I had received a telephone call from Bishop Michael Mann, Suffragan Bishop of Worcester and later to be Dean of Windsor. We had met in Oman after a tragedy in which his only son was killed by a mortar bomb and had become friends. He was now chairman of the governors of Harrow School and asked me what my reaction would be if asked to join the board. Recalling my memories of my own schooling and academic record my first reaction was total disbelief. Michael explained that he thought a serviceman on the board would be a good idea and that I would fit the bill. Greatly flattered I accepted this honour with pleasure. The termly meetings took the form of an informal meeting on a Friday evening, followed by a governors' dinner successively for house masters and their wives, other masters, and the school monitors. Governors then stayed in one of the houses and attended a formal meeting on the Saturday morning which tended to go on for four hours or more. Overawed at first I rarely offered an opinion, and think I had been on the board for two years or so before I made a substantial proposal. This was that there ought to be a coffee break during the Saturday session. This was agreed, provided it could be served without interrupting the discussion.

It was the beginning of a very significant decade for Harrow. The school estate was seriously in need of refurbishment and if it was to keep its proud position high in the private educational establishment it urgently needed a modern theatre, of which more later, a state-of-the-art craft, design and technology centre, and an indoor swimming pool and gymnasium. All of this was going to be very, very costly and somehow the money had to be found – surprisingly to many, the school is not well endowed. A house refurbishment programme was first set in train and cost on average close to a million pounds a time. The next priority was the pool. The only one at the time was well away from the centre of the school and was out of doors. It was one of the biggest open air pools in the country and it was costing over £30,000 a year simply to keep it full of water, and a lot more cash to maintain it. There was opposition to the plan because for many, many years Harrovians had bathed in 'Ducker', as it was called, often naked, and it had a hallowed aura. A Buddhist sect wanted to buy the site to build a temple and offered for it almost exactly what it would cost to provide a fine pool and gymnasium complex nearer to the school which has become a very popular and fully used facility. There was opposition, particularly from the beaks who made good use of Ducker during the summer holidays, but few boys objected. When exams and cold days were subtracted from the short summer term they were not getting much use from Ducker. I believe the Buddhists are still awaiting planning permission for their temple but the sale had certainly been made in good faith.

With promotion came a knighthood in the Order of the Bath. Shirley and my mother (over eighty and almost overwhelmed with pride) came to the investiture and afterwards we three went to lunch at Wheeler's in St James's. There was a hush in the very small dining room when a pretty 'sing-along' girl, fortunately fully dressed and she stayed that way, suddenly burst in on the proceedings and, tunelessly, sang a dreadful ditty about me, and why I had been at an investiture. This had been composed by my Military Assistant and the ADC, Captain Chris Webster, who is now a senior manager on the Woburn Estate. My mother claimed later that this was the only time she had seen me seriously embarrassed and I have threatened one day to be avenged on the two jokers when they least expect it.

When the Ministry of Defence have senior visitors and run out of things to do with them they tend to send them out to the Army at large with instructions to entertain them in some way. Britain was seriously involved in major defence contracts, worth millions, with Saudi Arabia and a team of eight officers with interest in army aircraft visited Britain. For one night during their visit they were to stay with us, probably because of my Middle Eastern experience and my smattering of Arabic. The team arrived and there was confusion over who should occupy which room. One of the more junior in rank was of the royal family and therefore rated a better room than the officer wearing the highest rank on his shoulder. This seriously confused our house sergeant, Colour-Sergeant Harrington, and for some minutes there was a rushing from room to room not unlike a Whitehall farce. All was eventually settled when an officer in a disha-dasha gown suddenly appeared and said: 'Please, you tell me, which way is Mecca?' I pointed hopefully eastwards and calm was re-established. During dinner that evening it began to rain and all the Saudis leapt to their feet and rushed out of the dining room to enjoy it. It was a rarity for them at home.

It was about this time that the Prime Minister, Mrs Thatcher, visited Saudi Arabia and learned from King Fahd that he would like a British serviceman involved in the defence contracts being negotiated who would report back to the Prime Minister if any dissatisfaction arose. The appointment was given a title dreamed up by Brigadier Nick Cocking who was advising the Saudi National Guard and had once been my chief of staff in 4th Armoured Division. This was Senior Military Adviser to Saudi Arabia, or SMILVITSA, and I was given the job. Soon afterwards I was flown to Riyadh with the Chief of the Defence Staff, Admiral of the Fleet Sir John Fieldhouse, to be formally introduced. My instructions were that this would be additional to any other appointment I might hold and would continue indefinitely. In fact it lasted for only eighteen months because my next job was in NATO, where the additional position was unacceptable. My instructions were to visit Saudi Arabia from time to time and to get to know people of importance, especially members of the royal family. It was most interesting and I learned much about the contracts, firms involved and their business methods. On one occasion I was directly responsible for the dismissal of a Saudi senior officer who was promoting business with a rival country. But the time is not yet right to tell this or other stories in detail, although there is one that I cannot resist.

A vast contract, called Al Yamama, for the sale of Tornado and Hawk aircraft was being negotiated. A sticking point was the first delivery date, because aircraft supplied to Saudi Arabia on the date they sought would be at the expense of the Royal Air Force, who felt they had the higher priority. In due course their view prevailed and a signing ceremony was arranged to take place in Carlton House with considerable formality and I was present. With cameras flashing and television whirring the documents were placed before Michael Heseltine, the Secretary of State for Defence, and the Saudi Minister for Defence for signing. The Saudi prince went first, leant forward, looked at the body of the contract, and with the pen provided altered the month of delivery, bringing it forward six months, and then signed. With a large audience and media presence this was no time to start a dispute which might well have resulted in a walk-out, great embarrassment, and perhaps even the loss of multi-million pounds' worth of business, to say nothing of the associated jobs.

Michael Heseltine gritted his teeth and signed. Unfortunately I do not know the end of this story and whether the matter was satisfactorily resolved for the RAF but I do know the first deliveries to Riyadh were on time at the amended date.

I was asked to give a lecture on Reserve Forces to the Royal United Services Institute for Defence Studies and the afternoon before we were telephoned by a researcher for the 'Today' programme inviting me for interview at 0745 hrs the next morning. We were asked to help the researcher to prepare notes for the interview, which was to be conducted by Brian Redhead. It soon became clear that the girl had no idea about the subject and did not know what questions to ask. This was alarming, so David Montgomery and I said we would hasten to London and prepare a brief for her on the way. She was very grateful indeed and it was a comfort to me to have such a clear idea what the questions were likely to be. The next morning we waited in an anteroom with Lord Young who was off on a business mission to Japan and seemed sublimely self-confident, and a school teacher from North Wales who was practically paralysed with fright at the prospect of attacking an item of the Government's education policy. I hovered somewhere between these two extremes. When I was led to the little studio I sat nervously while somebody talked about football, and someone else about freak weather, and then a voice came from just behind me saying: 'You're on next. Don't be frightened, just think that there are three and a half million listeners out there longing to hear what you are going to say.' This was not exactly soothing but fortunately I had nothing controversial to say and Brian Redhead had no need to be confrontational or even argumentative. It seemed to end in seconds and without any gaffes.

As a guest of a Greenjacket battalion I sat between Field Marshal Sir John Harding, who had countless anecdotes from his long service which were by turns exciting and amusing, and Wilfred Thesiger, whose guide on his famous trek across the Empty Quarter I had met in Oman. Thesiger blamed most of the ills of modern society on the internal combustion engine, which he hated with all his being. Harding, at one point, was talking about the distress that loss of memory and absent-mindedness can cause as the years slip by. 'My boy,' he said 'you'll find as you grow older that there will come a time when you worry whether you have done up your flybuttons, But when you get older still you'll worry more about whether you've undone them.'

There were two major exercises during my time at Wilton. Exercise

Lionheart was a 1st British Corps exercise involving 131,565 personnel, of whom 56,500 were reinforcements from the United Kingdom. It was the largest exercise held since the war and took months of planning. Our job was to assemble the Regular and Territorial reinforcements and transport them to the Continent by all possible means. Most of the transport went through Dover and early on I asked for a meeting with the ferry companies and the Dover Harbour Board to ask how they would handle this sudden influx of about 5,000 vehicles of all shapes and sizes. The conference assembled but when I told them the scale of our requirement they wondered why we were meeting at all. The exercise was to be in October, as all major exercises in Germany were in order to keep crop damage to a minimum, and they told me that I was talking about smaller numbers than on a normal day in the holiday season and there would be no problem at all. In the event indeed there was not, although the Harbour Board were not too pleased when one of their JCBs was mistakenly taken by a sapper medium-wheeled tractor driver for his own and ferried across the Channel.

I had no responsibility for the tactical phase of Lionheart but decided to accompany part of the long convoy as it made its way from Calais to the north German plain. En route we came across a gigantic REME recovery vehicle being towed by another of its own kind. Asking the driver of the towed 'wrecker' where and when he had broken down he gave me the surprising answer 'Leeds, last month.' I asked him what it was doing somewhere in Belgium at that time. The answer this time was 'No bloody spares in Leeds.'

The exercise was hailed as a success. It may have been the largest of its kind but it was also the last, which was a relief to the staffs and the Treasury no doubt, but a disappointment to the TA and many soldiers who liked to be part of such an enterprise, even if it included occasional periods of inactivity and boredom for them.

The other major exercise was Brave Defender, which was not only the last and largest of its kind, it was also the first since 1944; and I had a primary responsibility for it. The threat, deliberately exaggerated, was limited to Soviet *Spetsnaz,* their highly trained special forces, acting offensively in the lead-up to general war and, in certain Districts, to conventional air attack. The aim was to exercise all military home defence forces with cooperation from police and fire services and civil defence. The exercise received good advance publicity and although there were no plans to involve the civil population, a number of people, mostly ex-Service, did pass on information to those taking part. 1,800 landowners generously allowed us to use their land. We did not practise higher control and there were in effect nine separate, simultaneous District exercises all working to a master plan. 70 per cent of the TA's total strength turned out for the training, which was a high figure historically. Whatever the notice given no date would suit all part-timers, who had to accord first priority to their jobs. In order to fulfil their commitment of two weeks' continuous full time 'camp' a year, which was necessary to qualify for generous bounties, volunteers could take courses or attachments to regular forces in lieu.

There was the usual pressure on cash and the extra costs amounted to only £3 million. This was good value for money, especially when the Director of Public Relations later estimated the value of the 'free' publicity for the Services at £6 million.

I gave a press conference to foreign correspondents a week before the exercise and during the question period the correspondent for Moscow's *Pravda* asked why we had chosen Russian forces as our enemy. Peterborough in the *Daily Telegraph* reported that I gave a disarming smile and said: 'Well, sir, on a military exercise somebody has to be enemy.'

I visited as much of Brave Defender as I could and flew over most of Britain by helicopter, accompanied by my very good ADC, Captain (now Lieutenant-Colonel) Nigel Burrell. Apart from some early cloud and rain which almost grounded us in the Lake District the weather was fine and clear, making this an unforgettable experience, especially flying over the Scottish Grampians. Later we flew from Inverness via some exercise action at RAF Lossiemouth to Fraserburgh and down the east coast to Edinburgh, leaving an impression that we had flown over continuous golf courses.

One little incident caused some amusement. A small SAS team were tasked to test the defences of an RAF station and kitted themselves out with the clothes and equipment of road workers. Setting up outside the station main gate they began to effect imaginary road repairs while covertly checking on guard and patrol routines, and possible points of entry. An alert RAF Regiment patrol spotted the deception because they noticed that the SAS never stopped working, thus identifying them as being untypical British working men.

One of the overseas exercises was in the United States where, with full American cooperation and support, a complete battalion used a training area near Seattle. 2nd Battalion The Royal Anglian Regiment were chosen for this experience and as Field Army commander and also Deputy Colonel for that battalion it seemed a natural for me to visit it. Lieutenant-Colonel Julian Browne was the Commanding Officer and because the battalion had recently trooped its Colour and laid on a re-enactment of a famous battle he thought this would go down well in the States. Off his own bat he hired the Tacomadrome, a huge arena about twice the size of Earl's Court, and appointed an agent for publicity and ticket sales. This was very enterprising, and risky too. It could have made substantial profits for the battalion, but Murphy interfered, as he so often does. The day of the show saw a swirling blizzard and the paying public mostly stayed at home. Fortunately enough braved the weather to enable the show nearly to break even.

In 1985 Michael Heseltine arranged for 250 former prisoners and war widows to visit the Far East in his company. John Chapple had been responsible for most of the arrangements and was to have been the escorting officer but, at the last minute, other duties prevented this and he asked me if I could get away. I could, and it was a wonderful and moving experience. The main group flew in a Tristar and Shirley and I went with the Secretary of State and his wife and staff separately in a VC10. The Tristar passengers included doctors and nurses and a supply of stretchers and bodybags. The medical advice was that in view of the age of the party and the stress that they would suffer, some casualties were inevitable, perhaps as many as eight deaths. The doctors had not taken into account that these were experienced survivors; there were no deaths and apart from one man who had a nasty turn in the Dubai duty free area there were no illnesses of any consequence.

The plan was that parties concerned with particular areas would go to Singapore, Thailand and Burma, and that we would go to all of those areas in turn, beginning with a diplomatic call in Kuala Lumpur. For some reason Heseltine's stay in Malaysia was extended and I was sent on alone to Bangkok, where I stayed the night in the embassy, and then was driven to Kanchanaburi, of *Bridge over the River Kwai* fame. Here a service was held in the Commonwealth War Graves cemetery and in the evening there was entertainment by Thai dancers in our hotel. One man was entering fully into the spirit of this and in one of the brief intervals when he was not dancing I sat with him to ask why he was there. His story was amazing. He had been a coal-miner in Yorkshire but in 1938 his mother, fearing the dangers of tuberculosis, had persuaded him to come above ground and join the Army. The first exciting thing to happen to him was to land with 18th Division in Singapore and become a prisoner of war without firing a shot. After a spell in Changi gaol he was sent north to work on the death railway for nearly three years. The Japanese then discovered he was a miner and shipped him to Japan, which he reached safely, although most ships on that route were being sunk. Soon afterwards he was standing in the open three miles from the ground zero of the Nagasaki atom bomb. He was dazzled and knocked down by blast, but survived to be sent, three days later, into the ruins with a shovel to begin clearing up. I had never thought I would meet someone with close personal experience of the bomb, but this man really was a survivor, having narrowly escaped death so many times, and here he was, at the age of sixty-eight, dancing the night away.

Before we left Kanchanaburi we visited the Jeath Museum in which there are few artifacts but many drawings, paintings and photographs of suffering, starving prisoners and their captors. We paid to enter and our widows and former prisoners were not best pleased to note that their entry ticket was printed in Japan. The museum had originally called the 'Death Museum,' but the Japanese had objected and the new title was created, and claimed, euphemistically, to be an acronym for Japanese, English, Australian, Thai.

One exercise that I visited was at the Hjörken training area in Norway. This was in winter and the area is 3,000 feet above sea level. I was being taken round by helicopter and one of the points of call was at a gun position. I happened to know that these particular guns had not been doing very well. After floundering through deep snow I eventually reached a gun, beside which stood a cold, dispirited gunner with a look on his face which positively dared the visiting general to ask a silly question. It is the only time in my service that I have found myself completely lost for words when facing a soldier. There was a pause lasting what seemed fully a minute before I asked about where he came from and similar questions unrelated to the performance of his gun.

Later on that visit we were taken for lunch to a warm, wooden building being used as a mess. I expressed surprise when the pudding exactly matched an unusual recipe used often by Shirley for dinner parties. The cook was summoned and he turned out to be a corporal who had worked for us in our house in Tidworth two years before.

Shortly before I was due to leave Wilton I was faced with one of the more difficult decisions. An infantry battalion had just left for a month's training in Kenya when the medical branch reported that the Aids level, especially around Nairobi, was dangerously high, verging on epidemic. The disease was comparatively rare in Britain at that time and it was easy to see the scandalous consequences if there were soon an outbreak in the area of the battalion's home base, and, worse still, some cases among wives. I sent a signal warning the Commanding Officer and putting Nairobi out of bounds to soldiers on 'R and R'. The battalion were furious and the High Commissioner sent a telegram of complaint that Kenya would take serious diplomatic umbrage at the false assumption on which my directive was based. A minister rang to say that I had exceeded my authority and there might be serious consequences. He would not listen to my reasoning, so I put it in writing and asked what the minister thought would be the consequences if an Aids outbreak arose in X's constituency. The following day I received an apology and was thanked for having taken the correct decision. So far as I know there were no diplomatic blips, although I did hear later that there was a temporary exodus of ladies of the night from Nairobi to the battalion's base camp area, despite which I know of no subsequent Aids casualties.

The time had passed quickly and I was soon to take up my final appointment as Deputy Supreme Allied Commander Europe, a very grand title for a job in which few decisions were possible because most of the important ones were the prerogative of the the American Supreme Commander. In the month before we left for Belgium we stayed in Warminster and I went for two mornings a week to the quarter of the French Liaison Officer at the School of Infantry, where his charming wife helped me to brush up schoolboy French which was mostly based on the written rather than the spoken word. By allowing no word of English for two hours or more of continuous conversation it came on quite well.

17
Winding Up

Supreme Headquarters Allied Powers Europe was originally established in Fontainebleau in France when General Eisenhower was Supreme Commander and Field Marshal Montgomery the first holder of the office I was about to assume. When the French withdrew from the military structure of NATO the headquarters were moved to Mons in Belgium. DSACEUR then acquired Château St Pierre as his very splendid residence. The *château* was nineteenth-century, large, rambling and, with its aged electrical wiring and temperamental central heating system, not without its drawbacks. The gardens were beautifully designed and a trout stream ran through them. The whole thing was very gracious and Shirley loved it, although I was more conscious of its defects and the consequent maintenance problems and expense. This view had been taken by the Property Services Agency a year or so before and it had already been decided that a new house would be built closer to the headquarters. This was to be a more modest dwelling, rudely referred to by Lady Burgess, wife of my predecessor, as a 'chalet-bungalow'. This was a bit unkind; the house was practical and efficient, but it certainly lacked the cachet of the *château* which we lived in for only six months, and I am convinced much more was paid to build it than was necessary. I was allowed to name the new house and chose 'La Belle Alliance', which was not only Napoleon's most forward position during the Battle of Waterloo but also, I thought, an appropriate, if flattering, name for the home of a senior NATO officer.

Mons is ideally placed for a military man, who is likely to have many guests with an interest in military history. Waterloo is evocatively well preserved, Crécy and Agincourt are within range, and many of the awesome battlefields of the First World War are nearby. We became expert tour guides to visitors who perhaps wanted to find a relative's war grave, or, more often, simply to see fields of the Somme, Cambrai, Ypres, Passchendaele, or Mons itself, where the first and last shots of the war were fired. The Commonwealth War Graves Commission's cemeteries were always a source of pride, and led me to lobby for a job for the only time in my life, that of War Graves Commissioner. I was appointed a Commissioner for five years soon after my retirement, and it afforded me much interest and pleasure. Guests could also be treated to the beauties of such towns as Bruges and Ghent, and entertained by the architectural attractions and gastronomic delights of Brussels, only forty miles away.

Another worthwhile port of call was St George's Church in Ypres, which had been built after the First World War and dedicated to the British regiments which fought in the area. The attractive little church is full of inscriptions and memorials of regiments and casualties but when we first saw it the interior decor was in a fairly sorry state and the small resident parish population could not afford the necessary refurbishment. I despatched an appeal to all the regiments of the British Army, and almost all made generous contributions so that all the necessary repairs and redecorations could be put in hand.

There were two DSACEURs, one British one German. Few decisions of any great consequence came our way and we both, especially my German colleague, General Mack followed by General Eimler, found this occasionally frustrating. Seldom lacking accord we usually found ourselves supporting, selling or interpreting SACEUR's decisions. One of my predecessors, General Sir Harry Tuzo, described himself as 'a sort of walking oilcan' and this was not far from the truth, nor was my own lighthearted description of it as being the perfect bridge between working and not working

There was no shortage of interest. One had carte blanche to travel throughout the NATO countries promoting ideas and seeking views and facts. I had always had a wanderlust and could now indulge it to the full; often Shirley could accompany me. I developed a visiting principle that for every day of military business I would also have a day of culture. This sounds to be an indulgence, and I suppose it was, but I found that it helped to put relations on a friendly footing for the serious business, because almost everyone we met was proud of what they had to show us and were grateful for our interest.

This was the swansong period of the Cold War. President Gorbachev was in full flow with his 'Perestroika' policies which were to lead to the end of that war and immense change to the face of the world. The threat which had brought NATO into existence and sustained the public subscription of money to arm and develop it was rapidly diminishing and economic pressures on defence multiplied everywhere. Arguments that the Soviets still had massive capability and their intentions could change at short notice mostly fell on deaf political ears because there were so many more vote-catching issues than defence on which to spend money. The United States was becoming the only superpower but its tax-paying public were resistant to the role of world policeman. With justification many Americans could see that Europe was quite wealthy enough to assume greater responsibility and pay for its own defence. The Europeans played hard to get on this one and although many European countries could certainly have paid more than they did, we, who had access the corridors of defence power, could see how important the American domination of NATO was. The Europeans could agree on so little and there were frequent fierce arguments between the leading powers, Germany, France and Britain, particularly on equipment, while such countries as Greece and Turkey were always at loggerheads and indefinitely unlikely to be reconciled. Americans could rise above all this and, when necessary, bang heads together.

Defence issues which generated the keenest debate during the last three years of the Cold War included Force Goals, or what SHAPE thought countries should do to enhance their defence and whose cost was always in dispute. Follow on Force Attack, or FOFA, was another. This was the effective use of developing technology to detect and attack advancing forces much earlier and further out than hitherto. It led to constant and often heated argument about the relative expenditure of resources on FOFA and the contact battle, the responsibility for a front that was much wider than the existing corps in the forward area, and the relative responsibilities of air and ground forces. Arms Control became a very complicated subject. The problem was to agree either equal reductions of conventional weapons on both sides, with the difficulties of not being able to compare like with like, or to effect reductions that would result in equal strengths. This would mean the Soviets having to make deeper cuts of most weapons than NATO, which did not appeal to them, especially when they took technical capability into account and not just numbers. Even when agreement on these matters had been reached, foolproof methods of inspection were necessary to ensure that promised reductions were verified. Yet another burning issue was so-called 'Star Wars,' or ballistic missile defence, which if not common to both sides could give the possessor of an effective system an unacceptable and provocative advantage. Another still was 'Right Mix,' a study which set out to reduce the field exercising, low flying and other activities which impacted on the civil population and caused much resentment. The recommendations from this study caused friction between nations and headquarters who felt that such matters were their own presrve. All of these things, together with the constant and powerful efforts of national defence industries and exporters to influence defence policies, kept us busy.

Before leaving England I paid calls on Admiral of the Fleet Sir John Fieldhouse, Chief of the Defence Staff, and General Sir Nigel Bagnall, Chief of the General Staff. The Admiral told me that it would be important to hit it off with General Galvin, the incoming SACEUR, to be international in style, but to ensure that the British head was held high despite forthcoming defence economies. The General did not want resources diverted from the contact battle to FOFA, and advised watching out for the ambassador to NATO, Michael Alexander, who was known to be a confidant of the Prime Minister, Mrs Thatcher, and met to brief her monthly.

The instruction to get on with General Jack Galvin was from a personal point of view easy and was accomplished, insofar as his American staff, who jealously protected their own influence on the commander, would allow it. Jack was, and is, a cultured and highly articulate intellectual who would be as happy on a university campus as in the thick of military business. Although not one to suffer fools, with whom he could be impatient, he was quiet and friendly and, like most of his countrymen, worked and worked and worked, taking little notice of my frequent advice to get away from it all from time to time. I liked and respected him very much indeed. We both arrived at SHAPE on the same day and were accorded the customary honour for senior officers of a guard of honour. Jack inspected his guard, went inside the front door, and then returned to greet me and escort me round the same guard, which was now for me.

Guards of honour are a constant hazard in NATO. Turkish ones, for instance, expect a shout from the inspecting officer when they present arms to him. I cannot exactly remember the obligatory cry, but it is something like: '*Marhaba Askar*' (which is Arabic for 'Congratulations, soldiers'), followed by something like '*Nastilziniz*', but I don't recall what that means. A different problem confronted me in Naples later. The guard was a mixture, both of nationalities and of sexes. Most NATO officers simply walk past their guards, sometimes not even looking at them, but the British style is usually to say something at least to some of the individual members of the guard. On this occasion I was half way down the front rank when I came upon an American girl soldier who was very obviously in the advanced stages of pregnancy. Stopping before her I simply asked 'When?' The lady glared at me and hissed: 'When what, General?' I blenched, and stammered 'Wh- wh- wh- when er when did you join the army?' and moved on quickly.

At SHAPE the guards were commanded by an Italian officer of the Bersaglieri who was a joy to watch with his flamboyant sword drill and exotic uniform topped by a long, flowing plume of feathers .On one occasion when he was awaiting Admiral Porta, the Italian Chief of Defence, and the senior SHAPE officers were lined up ready to be presented, Vice-Admiral Rosso, our most senior Italian staff officer, called across to the guard commander in a loud voice for all to hear: 'Eh! You screwa thisa one up and I posta you to the Anti-Mafia Squad in Sicily!'

One of the features of international organisations is the continuous provision of entertainment in the form of food and drink. Arguably not much would change if entertainment were confined to a few personal friends but, on balance, I am more or less convinced that it helps the wheels to turn. It certainly weighed heavily on us, with an average of three formal dinners and two luncheons somewhere every week and the statistic that we entertained 1,417 people to one thing or another in our house over two and a half years. Mostly all this was enjoyable, although it was often tiring and weighed heavily on the figure, the arteries and the cholesterol. Hosts, both private and official, tended to compete in both the quantity and the quality of their offerings and we certainly enjoyed some memorable meals during our stay. The British were almost alone in providing their senior officers with house staff so that they could entertain properly in their own houses, and we were lucky enough to have a house sergeant and corporal and two cooks. Other nations either provided cash to bring professional caterers to their officers' houses, or to enable them to take their official guests to restaurants.

Brigadier Bob Cook and his wife Jilly had been with us in Herford and had become friends, particularly during expeditions to learn more about wine. Bob was on the International Military Staff at NATO Headquarters in Brussels. Through the Cooks we got to know Christiane and Danielle Pol Roger, with whom we exchanged a number of visits and came to realise why Winston Churchill liked not only the champagne but also the family. They were kind, generous and entertaining hosts, both at their home at Epernay and in organising wonderful instructional visits to Bordeaux and Burgundy. On one of their visits to us we arranged a battlefield tour of Waterloo, which may not seem a friendly thing to do to entertain French guests but it made a splendid day and countered the balance struck for the casual visitor to the battlefield's souvenir shops and museums who, because of the local Belgians' eye to the main chance, might be led to believe that it was the French who won. In fact Waterloo, in my view, is a good NATO battle. The French can claim, not without justification, that their beloved Napoleon could have beaten Wellington if only those damned Germans had not intervened, the Germans can say they arrived and won the battle, Wellington claims the battle for the British because he was in charge and British troops were the hard core of his army, while the Dutch and Belgians can say they played a part with the victors and certainly chose the right allies.

One great trip with the Pol Rogers was to Bordeaux, where we were given private visits to several famous *châteaux*, including Lafite Rothschild, Lynch Bages, Pontet Canet and Cissac. At the latter house Bob, another friend and I were tested to become '*Commandants du Bontemps du Medoc et de Graves*', an honorary appointment of vinicultural distinction. The test was conducted in the cellars of Château Cissac by distinguished elderly gentlemen in flowing maroon velvet robes and funny black hats. We were each given a glass of red wine and invited to identify it. After a pantomime of tasting, spitting, and long debate in indifferent French we homed in on our collective decision, Château Cissac 1975, which was, after all, a reasonable guess, and was exactly right. The ceremony was followed by a magnificent dinner in the *château* accompanied by wines beyond price.

The following day we had lunch at Château Pontet Canet where the owner, Alfred Tesseron, was entertaining his fiancé. If for nothing else this pretty Bordeaux girl should have been won over by that lunch. Even now, ten years later, I can remember every detail: Roquefort tart, thinly sliced rare roast beef with a potato and aubergine omelette, and a pudding of baked peaches. These dishes were accompanied by the *château*'s own wines of 1975 (good), 1961 (superb), and 1945 (quite good). After lunch we were offered 1906 cognac. When we declared this delicious Alfred insisted we try the 1901 version. All of this set us up perfectly for our return to Bordeaux and a snack of oysters and Muscadet before preparing for dinner.

Tragically Bob Cook, who became a major-general before retiring, died in 1996, aged only fifty-seven, of motor-neurone disease, a dreadful end for a most delightful and capable man.

One of the very special features of my appointment was an invitation to a personal tour of North America, together with Shirley. We were asked what we particularly wanted to see in Canada and the United States and offered one or two suggestions, but mostly left it to what they would like to show us, provided it was not entirely military. I did want to visit Quebec, where both battalions which became the Northamptonshire Regiment had played a part in Wolfe's famous victory.

We began by recovering from jet-lag in Washington DC with our close friends Brian and Phyll Read, with whom we had served in Osnabrück. We then hired a car and, in company with Lieutenant-Colonel Brian Holt, Welsh Guards, our very good MA, drove through Baltimore, the Amish farming country, and past a small town with the evocative name of Intercourse to Philadelphia, where we paid our respects to the Liberty Bell. We continued to and through Manhattan to Greenwich, Connecticut, where we stayed in the charming house of Geoffrey Simmons, a Harrow governor, and his wife Doreen.

Then came a long drive through New England, perhaps a week early for the full splendour of the fall, but beautiful for all that, and on over the border to Gagetown. This houses a Canadian training area where we were allowed to fire a variety of weapons, but made to realise that the Canadian army was being seriously starved of resources and had little faith (justifiably) in political promises of major reform during a fifteen-year programme.

Next we went to Quebec via Montreal and got a sharp taste of a single nation divided by two languages and cultures. The cost of government paperwork all being duplicated bilingually and of training personnel to use two languages must be enormous. We walked the Quebec battlefield with interest but the steep cliff scaled by Wolfe and his men to achieve surprise must either be seriously eroded, or the story has been glamourised over two centuries of telling.

We then flew to the air base at Goose Bay regularly used for low-flying training by aircraft of several NATO countries. Having survived an initiation ceremony calling for a speech and the compulsory drinking of an appalling local brew known as 'Screech', which tasted like jet fuel, we were briefed, amongst other things, on the problem of the local Inuit people who were milking whatever sympathy (and cash) they could get for the loss and noise pollution of their homelands. One claim was that aircraft noise was stopping the caribou from breeding, but official figures were produced to show that the caribou population was actually on the increase. It must have been because the poor creatures couldn't sleep at night. The Inuit campaign was highly successful. A year later their 17,000 people were given an area half the size of France, including rights to fish and hunt, together with a large cash payment in compensation for lost land. We also learned how flyers had to seal all ways into their clothing with sticky tape so that should they have to eject they would not be bitten to death by the lethal blackfly.

In Ottawa I had a long and frank discussion with the Chief of Staff, General Paul Manson. I will not record the details here, but can offer a funny story from it. Part of the Canadian Ministry of Defence had recently moved and one feature of this event was the sensitive matter of shifting highly classified material contained in two huge safes with countless locks, keys and combinations. When they pulled the safes out from the wall against which they stood they were found to have no backs.

On to Winnipeg where as winter now approached we learned why a certain crossroads by our hotel was known as the coldest in the world. An air base called Moose Jaw is not far away and here we were given a guard of honour. Keen not to leave their guardroom a minute too early in the biting cold there was a blip in their communications which meant we had to wait at the barrier while the guard ran out putting on their hats and other items of clothing and equipment. Not many senior officers have been to Moose Jaw I think, although many pilots were trained there.

The Canadians had been wonderfully hospitable throughout our travels, but we were now handed over to the Americans, who most generously provided a C20 executive jet for our exclusive use during the next seven days. First it took us to the B52 and Minuteman missile base in seriously remote Minot, North Dakota. The weather was as bitter as the welcome was warm, but of special interest were 450 miles bumpy, noisy, low-level flight in a huge B52 aircraft, and sight of the awesome inter-continental ballistic missiles ready in their silos for immediate launch.

Next stop was Nellis Air Base where we were shown the realities of *Top Gun* as fighter pilots of NATO nations took part in the testing competitions known as 'Red Flag'. For one of our two nights here we stayed in Caesar's Palace, Las Vegas. Our comfortable suite, complete with jacuzzi and an enormous television, was ridiculously inexpensive. Our VIP status earned us this accommodation which was cheap because the usual occupants would be high rollers, most of whom would be spending fortunes in the casino on the ground floor. We high rollers put up twenty dollars each and lost them in minutes before going out to dinner and a theatre extravaganza. In daytime we were taken to look at the Grand Canyon and, at its head, the Hoover Dam. The following day when we took off the aircraft steward said we ought to use the aeroplane's telephone. I said we had already called all the numbers we knew in the States. 'Never mind that,' he said, 'from this baby you can call anywhere in the world.' 'Right,' I said, 'I'll call my mother.' 'No problem, sir,' and within moments he was telling my mother she had a call from America. Although I was comfortably looking down at the Grand Canyon, this was not the best moment for this indulgence. My mother not only feared the worst, her first thought was that we must have suffered an accident, but it was also exactly the moment that the infamous 1987 storm hit Leatherhead, where she lived, and the noise was terrifying. We could even hear it in our aeroplane.

We arrived at Fort Hood, Texas, late in the evening to be greeted by Major-General John Brown and fitted with a flying suit for night flying orientation in an Apache helicopter and shown its amazing powers of target acquisition at night. 600 of these machines were shortly to be sent to Europe and I was greatly impressed with the power that such a force would create. The beginning of the end for the tank perhaps?

After dinner an aide said the first item on our programme next day was a working breakfast and asked what we would like to eat at it. I said 'Eggs Benedict,' not realising what a stir this would cause. The aide had never heard of it but said he would ask the cook. The cook didn't know but rang a friend who also didn't know. I said I had last had it in the Captain's Paradise in New Orleans. American aides do not give up easily. The Captain's Paradise was telephoned, a recipe obtained and, lo and behold, 'Eggs Benedict' for twelve served at breakfast. The next morning I was flown over the Fort Hood tank park. Row upon row upon row, each over a mile long, of tanks. This really put Britain's puny armoured force into perspective for me.

We now flew back to Washington and spent an exhausting day visiting many offices in the Pentagon. To be honest there is not much I can remember about the various briefings, but one thing stands out clearly. This was a haircut by a US Marines barber who, if I had not shouted instructions every few seconds, would have removed every hair of my head. The two Marines on either side of me were getting exactly this treatment and clearly thought I was a wimp.

The delights of this wonderful tour were still not over. The next day we were flown by helicopter to the Gettysburg battlefield for an escorted tour of that wonderfully preserved memorial to courage at the turning point of the Civil War. I had seen it before, but not in such detail, and in any case it is something of which I could never tire. There was a tricky moment in the briefing centre when the lights were dimmed and we were shown the progress of the battle on a model with a series of little torchlight bulbs. Sitting in the second row I relieved myself of an opinion that Pickett's famous last charge had been launched at what was tactically an unsound objective, namely a saddle. Even if it had been taken it would have been dominated by higher ground at both ends of the ridge. I still believe this to be true but would not have mentioned it had I known that just in front of me was a group of Southerners, for whom the Civil War was clearly not yet over and for whom General Lee could never possibly be wrong – and even if he was it would be sacrilegious for a 'damn Brit' to say so. I narrowly escaped with my life.

Our final call was on the US Marines base at Fort Lejeune where, like everywhere else, we were made warmly welcome and pride was taken in showing off whatever they wanted us to see.

It had all been a glorious tour. We had seen so much, learned so much, and been treated throughout with lavish but warm hospitality. I am aware that it reads like the sort of 'freebie swan' that is so rightly criticised when undertaken by some politicians, but that would not be fair to our hosts. In order to understand the attitudes, the power, and the capabilities of NATO's senior partner who wielded decisive influence on the Alliance's policies and finances it was imperative that a Deputy Supreme Commander should visit the country itself. The briefings, discussions and the contacts were of inestimable value in the years that followed, and I was immensely grateful that a number of important and busy people felt able to give me so much of their time and attention. It was an unforgettable experience, but also a necessary and thoroughly worthwhile one.

Other visits could occupy pages of description, but might equate to showing endless family snaps to uninterested visitors. I will confine myself to two or three snapshots.

In Rome, at dinner, a companion was the only British cardinal in Rome, Monsignor David Lewis. He explained that a plot for his body under a stone in his church, St Mary's Basilica, was assured whatever he might later do with his life. No crime could deprive him of the right to be laid to rest there. The problem was that it seemed that this privilege might be exercised sooner rather than later. He looked awful and had visited his doctor that day to be told that his blood pressure was astronomical and he would have to go on a diet. He explained that his only pleasures gastronomically were going out to dinner, as this evening, and, when on his own, eating little other than baked beans, to which he was addicted. His opinion of dieting was that it was 'eating as if you were sick in order to die healthy'. I have not heard of him again and hope he has survived, but his chances looked slim on that evening.

We love Venice and have visited a number of times privately, twice by Orient Express, but an official visit is unbeatable. With contacts organised by our good friend Doctor Luigi Sartori, met during a SHAPE occasion, we wined and dined in style, were given privileged visits to all the prize cultural delights and throughout had Carabinieri launches at our beck and call. We were also able to visit Rossetti Barracks in Trieste where I had begun my commissioned service, this time greeted by a guard of honour, given a full tour and, for three of us, offered a buffet lunch that would have satisfied the hunger of ten times our number. Still in Italy we stayed in Verona and saw *Aïda* in the famous amphitheatre, and went on to Florence to suffer a mild case of 'Stendahl Syndrome', defined as 'a surfeit of cultural opportunity impossible to satisfy'. Our apartment in the Officers' Club in Florence deserves a mention. It was palatial, beautifully furnished in impeccable taste, and the kitchen had been stocked with a week's food just for our one night's stay. Looking around the large sitting room I had the temerity to ask why there was no television. Our guide coughed discreetly, went to the wall, pressed a switch, and a huge screen suddenly arose like magic from the parquet floor. My new MA, Lieutenant-Colonel Andrew Stewart, 13th/18th Hussars, was hugely impressed, and later spent ages in one of the enormous jacuzzis in the apartment.

A Spanish admiral who had stayed with us in Tidworth declared Istanbul to be the most interesting place he had ever visited and I was delighted to get an early opportunity to do so myself. I have come largely to share the admiral's opinion. There is so much to see and do in this extraordinary city which has changed hands so many times and is truly where East meets West. A real Turkish bath is not to be missed. It is a very physical business and takes courage and endurance, but one comes out walking on air. The mosques and the Topkapi Museum are just fabulous.

It was while visiting a NATO exercise in Turkey that I had the opportunity to fly by helicopter to Gallipoli. This is the most remarkable battlefield whose total area is so small that it is hard to credit that, in eight months, there were a quarter of a million casualties on each side. We flew in over 'W' beach where the Lancashire Fusiliers suffered so dearly and won six Victoria Crosses before breakfast. In seconds we were flying up the cliffs of Anzac Cove where the Australians and New Zealanders were mistakenly landed. Almost immediately we reached the limit of their penetration over months of cruel fighting. On landing we laid wreaths and then visited a Turkish museum filled with the ugly detritus of war – skulls with bullet holes, smashed dentures, odd bones, and many badges, brass shoulder titles and various scraps of uniform. As we left I was invited to make an entry and sign in the VIP visitors' book. The last entry before mine was signed 'Elizabeth R.' and above it in the Queen's handwriting: 'In memory of the battle in which our two nations developed such respect for each other'. This was not easy to follow. I wrote: 'Through bitter fighting and appalling slaughter it is arguable that three proud nations were born here.'

Admiral Sandy Woodward, with whom I had once shared an office at The Royal College of Defence Studies, asked us to dine on HMS *Victory* on Trafalgar Night, when the toast to 'The Immortal Memory' is proposed. To dine on this famous little ship is a moving experience. Some years later I was myself invited by the officers of HMS *President*, the London base of the Royal Naval Reserve, to propose the toast myself at a Trafalgar Night dinner held, because they were volunteer reservists, on the nearest Saturday to the actual date, which happened to be 23 October, the anniversary of the Battle of Alamein. This gave me a chance to begin my address by questioning whether I was to toast the immortal memory of Field Marshal Montgomery which did not amuse everyone. The prospect of this speech had launched me into a frenzy of research about Nelson. I discovered two points I thought worth including in my speech. One was that the celebrated wounds which caused the admiral to lose his eye and his arm were actually suffered not at sea but on land. The other was that after the battle of the Nile Nelson and his men had been fêted in the City of London with many a dinner and showers of gifts. But after Copenhagen nothing was offered. The businessmen of the City disapproved of his 'cowardly attack on those nice Danes who were at anchor at the time and with whom we enjoy such good trade'. Nelson was furious and never accepted another invitation to the City. 'So,' I said, turning to the Lord Mayor, who was present, 'you should consider yourself pretty lucky to be invited tonight.'

Many well-known international figures visited SHAPE while I was there, but none involved me quite so closely as that of Mrs Thatcher. Good news seldom arrives in a brown envelope and the one that contained the announcement that the Prime Minister would like to call on us in February 1988 filled many, especially the American staff who were well aware of the lady's formidable reputation, with panic. The American staff it was who produced the first draft programme. The visit was to last two hours and the proposal was an hour's staff briefing, half an hour for questions, and finally half an hour privately with SACEUR and his deputies. When I saw this I rushed in to Jack Galvin to say that from what I knew of the Prime Minister there was no way she would sit through an hour's continuous briefing and she would soon have the programme in ruins. I asked if I could prepare an alternative design. This would be to pick eight or nine subjects of importance, allow the staff three minutes to brief on each one, and immediately follow with questions. I said I would be surprised if, in an hour and a half, we would get through more than four subjects. In laying out the briefing room I ensured that Malvern water, not 'that French muck', was beside Mrs Thatcher, together with a small bowl of jelly beans, which 'her friend' President Reagan liked, and to balance them a bowl of British Smarties. Interestingly she ate all the jelly beans and did not touch the Smarties.

The briefing went well and everyone was impressed by Mrs Thatcher's grasp of the subjects and her penetrating questions. When we adjourned to SACEUR's office for tea and private conversation Jack Galvin opened with: 'Now, Prime Minister, as you know we are seeking a three per cent increase in defence spending this year and it is important that your country and mine should lead the way. Will you be making this increase?' Mrs Thatcher replied: 'Yes, I think we are, aren't we Charles?' turning to her private secretary, Charles Powell. 'Well, actually, no, Prime Minister, we are reducing the defence budget slightly,' said Powell. The eyes flashed and the atmosphere was suddenly electrified as Mrs Thatcher launched into an amazing diatribe: 'It may seem like a decrease, but if my Chiefs of Staff would not waste the money that I [sic] give them in the way that they do it would really be an increase. They have squandered three billion pounds on various projects in the last five years.' She then reeled off without pause and without notes six projects with their precise budget and actual costs, including Nimrod, EH101 helicopters, two missile systems, a torpedo and, her voice rising to a shout, 'THAT GUN!' referring to a planned self-propelled medium gun. This was a terrifying *tour de force,* showing a quite remarkable feat of memory, and we all sat stunned until Jack, in a hushed voice, whispered that he wished he had not asked the question. Everyone laughed, calm was restored, and it was felt that the visit had gone well.

One visit caused a mild panic. I gave an 'on the record' press conference to a visiting group of defence journalists. One of these was the *Guardian*'s Hella Pick, whose birthday it was. In the evening she went out for a celebratory dinner in Brussels and I was awoken after midnight by a friend who told me that he had just overheard Hella Pick telephoning her copy from a restaurant and he thought I ought to know about it. During the conference I had given personal views on two subjects. One that negotiations on the abolition of short-range nuclear weapons could begin as soon as agreement was reached on conventional forces, and second that although there could be no foolproof system of verification, any treaty with the Soviets on the possession and use of chemical weapons would be better than no treaty. I had always thought the latter problem to be NATO's Achilles Heel because of the terrifying effect of such weapons on civilian targets. Western Europe's high density population, unprotected by any form of respirators, was desperately vulnerable to chemical attack. Hella Pick latched on to these two opinions and declared them to be at variance with Mrs Thatcher's from whom I had 'distanced' myself. Public relations staffs were alarmed by this and feared the Prime Minister's wrath, but I warned the Downing Street press office in advance and they were relaxed about it. There were no repercussions.

One was able to indulge one's enjoyment of golf at SHAPE because the Royal Golf Club du Hainault is nearby and generously extends membership to the transient SHAPE population. It is a good course and the golf was fun, but probably more important was the opportunity it afforded to meet local Belgian people. We made a number of friends there, especially Colonel Jean Hottois and his charming wife, Francine, who had endeared herself to the RAF during the war by helping, despite her youth at that time, to run an escape route – at extreme personal risk. Looking at a diary I seem to have played more often than I had thought, usually in the company of Belgian members or Major-General Bill Cornock who had been my deputy at Staff College and was now commanding Live Oak, the international contingency operation to counter any new attempt to isolate Berlin. Bill and Kay became great friends, as they still are. His deputy in Live Oak was Brigadier-General Wayne Lambert, of the US Air Force, who was a golf addict. He and his wife Pee-Wee were as Georgian as could be, both in what they said and the way that they said it. Wayne chewed 'Red Man', a lethal tobacco, as he played and could spit with all the power and accuracy one could expect of a true Southerner. He was very funny, and claimed to have a friend called 'George' who lived in the woods whose duty it was to bounce any wayward shot back onto the fairway. As a slice headed for the forest Wayne would shout 'Come on George' at the top of his voice, and it was remarkable how often it worked. My ADC, Captain Ian Gowdy, was also a keen and competent golfer so there was never any difficulty in finding playing company.

We were protected from terrorists throughout our tour by a Royal Military Police Close Protection Team who, of course, had to be with me when playing golf. The most unobtrusive way of achieving the objective was for them to act as caddy, which was most acceptable for me. Few, if any, of my playing companions were aware that my golf bag contained a sub-machine gun.

I was, at this time, chairman of the Army Golf Association, which was expanding rapidly with ever-increasing numbers of soldiers taking up the game. This gave me opportunities to attend golf meetings and support the Army team on several occasions, when I could usually fit in a round or two myself, and this together with such events as the annual Admirals, Generals, Air Marshals matches (during one of which I had an expensive hole-in-one), and captaincy of the Army Benevolent Fund's team of generals to play the Variety Club Golfing Society, meant plenty of golfing opportunities. Practice did not make perfect, however, and my handicap remained unchanged throughout.

The Variety Club match is always a special treat. The match is for the Baker Plate, presented by Field Marshal Sir Geoffrey Baker. The competition is fierce but playing with famous names from the media and discovering that they are not only good golfers but very good company is a pleasure indeed. After the match there is a dinner, at the end of which the entertainers in the Variety Club team tell their stories, to everyone's delight.

Although by now an experienced trout fisherman I had never before fished for salmon, but during this tour three opportunities came up. The first was on the Alta river in northern Norway, famous for massive fish. Sadly my two days there were fruitless, although for sixty heady seconds I was in contact with a monster which my escort estimated at twenty kilogrammes. He did not break me but came unhooked. Later, together with an invitation to chair the Council of Territorial, Auxiliary and Volunteer Reserve Associations (TAVRAs, of which more later) after I retired, Colonel Lord Ridley, President of the Council, asked me to join him on the Spey in early August. My general experience of salmon fishing is that it is always marvellous last week and next week but never this week. However, on this occasion I did land my first, and, shortly afterwards, my second.

Soon after the war a Canadian Chief of Staff sought a means of getting senior officers of American and Canadian services together in informal surroundings, in order to have totally private, unscripted conversations without eavesdroppers or note-takers, on defence matters of mutual interest. To this end a camp was built miles from anywhere on the Eagle river in Newfoundland, where salmon were plentiful and the natural beauty outstanding. Groups of officers assembled each year in late summer to fish and to talk. Later the invitations were extended to other NATO countries and, in 1989, I was lucky enough to receive one. The weather, the fishing, the accommodation, the food and the company were all first class. Much important business was done in congenial surroundings and without the fetters of minute-taking staff officers. On the way back, which should have been via Ottawa and Kennedy airports, we had the alarming experience of an engine dropping off our twin-engined aircraft, causing a few moments of seriously asymmetric flying, and we had to put down in Quebec, where the temperature was 30°C, and negotiate for any flight to get me to Kennedy on time. It was a slow process and meant much walking, trundling a trolleyful of luggage and rapidly melting frozen salmon. The fish refroze in the flight across the Atlantic and I did not admit to anyone that it had ever melted, but I was a bit nervous about the first dinner party at which it was served. Happily it was delicious and there were no ill effects.

Retirement began to loom and I looked into the possibilities for further employment. I was encouraged to put my name in for the governorship of Gibraltar and the lieutenant-governorship of Jersey, but did not do so because we felt we had had enough of the continuous entertainment circuit, we wanted to live in our own house, and I had already accepted the voluntary post of chairmanship of the Council of TAVRAs. I nibbled at the possibility of one or two non-executive directorships but none came to fruition and, as most people find when they retire, there was plenty to fill my time and my pension was sufficient for our needs. I was entitled to a short course to prepare me for civilian life, the criterion being that it must be something that could help me to earn a living if I fell on bad times. I think my choice was, and remains, unique. I spent a fascinating week in Eastbourne learning some of the art of tying trout and salmon flies from a leading expert, Peter Deane.

My last duty was a pleasant one inaugurated by Field Marshal Montgomery when he had the job. He arranged that, when leaving, the incumbent would normally be granted a personal interview by the Queen, and on 16 March 1990 I went to Buckingham Palace. Her Majesty received me in a private drawing room and we had a totally informal conversation, some of it including the Queen's views on current issues which might have caused considerable surprise to members of the Government and the general public.

So ended my service. One of the attractions of service life to me is the continual change of employment and environment but if one marries one must find a wife who can bear, even enjoy, the many moves and vicissitudes involved. I had been fortunate indeed in this, and lucky too in my various postings and wide variety of interesting jobs, none of them disagreeable. Almost everyone with whom I worked had been congenial, and the few that were not were never with me for long. Throughout I had been quite extraordinarily favoured in personal staff and those who had worked closely with me. In the last decade we were fortunate enough to be in appointments that rated official residences and with them went drivers and house staff. Here, too, we were lucky. Colour Sergeant Paul Harrington for eight years, Sergeant Steve Baldwin, a superb driver, for ten, and Corporal David Pearson for eleven gave us unstinting and loyal service, for which we are both eternally grateful.

I had certainly chosen the right career, coming in as the Cold War began and leaving shortly after its end with the collapse of the Berlin Wall. The only sadness has been to see the way in which Britain's incomparable army has been gradually whittled away in the 'piping days of peace', a process which never ceases.

18
Retired

It has become a cliché that retirement is the busiest time of one's life, and to me it feels that way. I suppose the lack of staff to do the office work and make travel arrangements contribute to what is probably an illusion. I must also confess that more time is taken up by indulging one's pleasures – golfing, fishing, gardening, holidays and so forth, but although I did not take up any paid employment I have found plenty to occupy myself.

It was an exciting new experience to live in our own house, indeed to live anywhere for more than three years. Warminster having been an army garrison town for many years, we have plenty of friends and acquaintances around, not to mention the pleasure of Shirley's sister, Brenda, and her husband, Barny Cottam, living a hundred yards away.

Warminster is a good place to live. It is only two hours by car and an hour and a half by train from London but has 'country tempo'. It is a historic market town and many of us want to keep it that way, especially the Civic Trust, of which I am currently the president. The Trust also works with other organisations and the planners to preserve architectural taste, common sense and integrity. There are those who for commercial reasons alone seek expansion and development on the lines of Basingstoke and Andover but this would rob it of many of its attractions as a place to live. Despite a bypass there is still too much traffic through the town and there is a chicken and egg situation over building new houses. The developers argue that if new citizens occupy their houses there will automatically be new trade and therefore jobs. In an area of high unemployment already I am more persuaded by the need to create the jobs first and fill them with those who are here now before raising the population any further.

There are other benefits to living in Wiltshire, on the western edge of Salisbury Plain. There is quick and easy access to Bath and Salisbury, two of our favourite towns. Good trout fishing is readily available on the local chalk streams, and the countryside offers endless walks, which is an asset much appreciated by Poppy and Poacher, our two Cairn terriers.

Chairmanship of the Council of TAVRAs took up a good deal of time but the objective of raising the profile of the Reserve Forces, especially the TA, seemed entirely worthwhile. A reasonably logical argument is that as the Regulars contract, as they have continuously done for fifty years, so the need for Reserves should rise. They are a framework for expansion should the need arise. They have other advantages too; they are a bridge between the diminishing Regular military community and the civil population. They promote fitness, teamwork, patriotism and public-spiritedness and they offer useful and paid spare time occupation to many who might use that time less worthily. Reserve Forces are good value for money, costing a tiny proportion of the whole defence budget, but even that is begrudged by Regular staffs who see anything spent on Reserves as being at the expense of the Regulars, who are themselves already strapped for cash. For this reason, when sharp cuts were in prospect during the early nineties we targeted ministers, including the Prime Minister himself, for support, keeping the Chiefs of Staff informed but effectively bypassing them. The political arguments, we felt, were more compelling than the military ones.

This policy did not win us many military friends but it worked twice. In the first instance Defence Secretary Tom King was supportive and grateful for the effects of our wheeling and dealing, and in the second Malcolm Rifkind refused to accept the bulk of the cuts proposed for the TA, leaving such a small reduction that we understood John Major to say that he was certainly not going to take the political fallout from cuts of three or four thousand volunteers. Strengths were therefore left virtually unchanged. I believe the present Government, with its Strategic Defence review, is not so easily persuaded and is likely not to relent on the substantial reductions being proposed. I think this will be sad and a loss both to defence and to the country.

I first got to know Malcolm Rifkind in an unusual way. A NATO Reserve Forces shooting meeting was to be held near Edinburgh and was to be followed by a Beating of Retreat and dinner, for which mess kit and other finery would be worn. The dinner was to be in the central barracks cookhouse, but it would be fully decorated with parachute silk and there would be 'the whole nine yards', as the Americans say, of damask table linen, regimental silver and the best cutlery and crockery. There would also be a large number of speakers as the leaders of every country's team was given his chance to speak after dinner.

I flew to Edinburgh by British Airways from Heathrow. The problem was that my luggage flew by British Airways to Glasgow. When I arrived at mid-day British Airways assured me that they would get my bag to my Edinburgh hotel well before six o'clock, the deadline by which I had to leave for dinner. They failed, and later claimed that their driver had been held up by traffic. I decided to go as I was and found myself, wearing sports jacket and flannels surrounded by mess dress uniforms of fourteen different countries, second to speak and seated next to Mr Rifkind. I found him very good company, and was able to rehearse a number of arguments in the Reserve Forces' favour. When I came to speak I began with: 'I would not wish you to think that generals' pensions are so mean as to prevent me from wearing clothes appropriate to this grand occasion. In any case, as we are seated in a cookhouse, don't you think that perhaps you are all slightly overdressed?' Writing later in protest to Colin Marshall, head of BA, and citing my embarrassment at sitting beside a cabinet minister when improperly dressed in international company, I received a handsome apology, a fare refund and a discount off my next flight.

Under existing legislation it was very difficult to enable Reserve servicemen to give a period of full-time service in the Regular forces. Either the whole of the Reserves had to be mobilised or, for individuals, there was a cumbersome procedure of resigning from part-time and then signing on for full-time service. For nearly two years the Council, with others, fought to hasten the introduction of a new Reserve Forces Act which, amongst other things including job protection and employer compensation, would enable individuals to serve with Regulars and assume the same rights. There was much consultation about the content of the Act and eventually, the day before it was published, Field Marshal Lord Bramall and I were summoned to the office of Nicholas Soames, the minister responsible, to be given advance news of its content. As Mr Soames ploughed wearily through the small print I felt I had to say: 'Forgive me, Minister, but I think, having worked on it for months, that we know more about the content of this Act than you do, and we could spare you the tedium of going through it in detail. Perhaps you could give us a drink instead.' This was well in line with Mr Soames's style and he readily agreed.

The Council's donkey work is done by the Secretary and his Assistant. The latter was the hard-working and dedicated Brigadier

Tom Sneyd throughout my chairmanship, but the Secretary, Major-General Mike Matthews, died suddenly and unexpectedly after only a year of my five-year tour. He was very good at the job and universally popular, a hard act to follow; but luckily for us all the right man was at hand and Major-General Andy Evans has filled the post admirably. We always enjoyed unfailing support and good advice from our presidents, Lord Ridley followed by Lord Younger.

I travelled widely around the country visiting and addressing TAVRAs, of which there were fourteen, and Reserve Forces units, encouraging them to make use of every influence they could bring to bear in their own defence. One of the units was the Honourable Artillery Company, with its distinguished history and long line of important members and powerful advocates, mostly from the City of London. Speaking at a dinner in Armoury House, their mess, I told them how delighted I was to learn of a rumour that they were to be disbanded. If anyone could defend themselves the HAC certainly could and it was good news for the campaign that they would be galvanised into action.

One of the principal interests of the Reserve Forces Association, of which I became president, is the Confédération Interallié des Officiers de Réserve, or CIOR. This is a monster organisation which promotes cooperation between the various reserve forces, NATO and Partnership for Peace countries. With most of the countries having some form of conscription the potential membership is huge and it enjoys the influence of many individuals who served conscription as young officers but then went on to positions of importance in many fields.

Each year the CIOR holds a Congress, which 1,000 or more delegates attend for discussion about topics of mutual interest, military competitions for the younger officers, and seminars specifically for serving young officers. The Congress lasts for a week and the countries take it in turns to host it. Spouses usually attend with the delegates and although there is much discussion there is also a bit of a holiday atmosphere as each country tries to outdo its predecessors in the entertainment it provides. The United Kingdom was host in London in 1988 when, as DSACEUR with a responsibility for Reserve Forces, I was invited to give the opening address. Ten years later I found myself with a similar responsibility, this time as president of the Reserve Forces Association, when the Congress was hosted once again by Britain. This time it was be at Brighton.

The Council brought the United Kingdom's forthcoming turn to host the event in 1998 to the attention of the Ministry of Defence three years in advance, when I was still chairman. The predictable MOD reaction was that it was only a summer holiday jamboree which did not significantly affect the conduct of defence and, in sum, would be a waste of money. We argued that their view was both prejudiced and parochial, and that trying to pull out of the job would be a very un-NATO act. It might be acceptable for a small country but Britain was a leading member of the Alliance and should not be seen to be pulling the plug. Ministers accepted this view, but directed that the event should be made as inexpensive as possible.

We did not want to be in London, travel times from hotels to centres of presentation or entertainment were made too unpredictable by the traffic, so we investigated possibilities at the well-known conference towns, Birmingham, Blackpool, Scarborough, Bournemouth and Brighton. Brighton, with the best access to airports and London, would be good if a reasonable deal could be struck. We learned that in return for occupying their hotels the conference facilities would be provided free of charge. No other town could offer anything similar so we went proudly to MOD to tell them that with Brighton's help, some sponsorship and after attendance fees had been paid the event should be very inexpensive indeed. The thought of offering its facilities for nothing completely fazed the civil servants and they demanded that we obtain three competitive tenders. Eventually the Minister, Lord Cranborne, forced common sense to prevail and Brighton it was. The military competitions were held in the Aldershot area and there was a major military exhibition at Minley, near Camberley. With a Government reception at Arundel Castle and visits to Portsmouth Dockyard, Hever Castle and other places of interest, and plentiful opportunities for shopping in both Brighton and London, all our hopes for a spectacular and successful Congress were realised. In making a video inviting delegates to the Congress I had promised an 80 per cent chance of good weather at that time of the year on the South Coast but a 100 per cent chance of a warm welcome. This came back to haunt me several times during the week because the weather was simply dreadful. Fortunately the welcome and the arrangements made up for it.

Another spectacular event was a Beating of Retreat by a Royal Marines band in the forecourt of Arundel Castle. This was to be attended by George Robertson, the Secretary of State for Defence. The day before I was telephoned by one of his private secretaries and

and warned that a speech prepared for the Secretary of State was pretty dull, and could I think of any way of brightening it? I suggested references to the terrible weather and to Bastille Day, which it was, and the recent French victory in the World Cup, but was soon telephoned back to say that the department which had prepared the original speech would brook no amendment. When I met Mr Robertson I had a few minutes at his side before he was due to speak and strongly advised him to keep his prepared speech in his pocket. It was mostly about the forthcoming Strategic Defence Review. I warned that there were thirty-one countries represented at the Congress, that thirty of them did not give a damn about the review and that the one that did give a damn was very unhappy about its rumoured content, which boded ill for the TA. I recommended a light-hearted speech such as come easy to practised politicians and Mr Robertson brilliantly did just that. I later received a letter from him thanking me for my 'sage advice'.

After visits to a number of CIOR gatherings we have come to expect the occasional administrative hiccough, but none could beat Washington DC in August 1993. It was ferociously hot and at four o'clock in the afternoon Shirley and I were resting in the Crystal Marriott hotel after a busy day. Shirley was in the bath and I prostrate in slacks and T-shirt when the hotel fire alarm sounded and we were instructed to make our way down the stairs, not the lifts, at once. Shirley threw on a housecoat and slippers, I grabbed a book and down twenty-eight flights of stairs we rushed in fear for our lives to assemble in the forecourt with more than 1,000 other worried guests. No smoke could be seen but firemen carried out two or three casualties on stretchers into waiting ambulances. Eventually we learned that the firm who maintained the swimming pool had allowed a box of chlorine crystals to get wet and the resulting gas had affected some guests and made the hotel uninhabitable for the next four hours. We were due at a formal British Embassy reception at six o'clock but could not return to our room to get the right clothes to wear.

There seemed to be two alternatives. One of them was to wait in the steaming hot forecourt for four hours. The other was to telephone the embassy and warn them that we were coming as we were. We chose this option but our troubles were not yet over. Another British officer, Brigadier Michael Brown, had obtained the use of a staff car and offered us a lift. We gladly accepted but were not so sure when we heard the driver, who did not know Washington and had been drafted in from Florida, being given very complicated instructions about how to find the embassy. Needless to say he was soon lost and after driving north west for much longer than we should we found ourselves in a very dangerous area indeed. There were car wrecks in the streets, more boards than windows on the houses, and a number of sinister-looking men leaning against walls and lamp posts. At this point I asked the driver if he had a map. He told me it was in the 'trunk' but he was damned if he was stopping here to get out of the car to fetch it. He then effected a handbrake assisted 180-degree turn and we roared back the way we had come. Fortunately we eventually came alongside a police car which kindly escorted us to our destination. It was almost an anticlimax to drink at a reception in housecoat and T-shirt amid a crowd of guests in their elegant best.

Shortly after Saddam Hussein invaded Kuwait in August 1990 I was putting on Little Aston golf course just north of Birmingham when a long-haired youth appeared and asked for me. He said he had a message from Peter Snow who would like me to appear on 'Newsnight' that evening. I said I was committed to dinner after the golf and was a speaker at it, and therefore must decline. 'When is the dinner?' demanded the youth, and discovered from my playing companions that it would all be over by ten o'clock. 'Fine,' he said, 'please come to Pebble Mill at a quarter past ten.' This I did and found that at that time in this extensive BBC broadcasting centre the total staff on duty numbered two. One was the doorman, who called up the other, an engineer, who guided me to a tiny studio and sat me down before a large camera and a small monitor screen, both apparently inert. He told me to sit and wait and before long the telephone would ring and 'Newsnight' would tell me what to do. Asked about make-up he said he thought there was some powder in a tin in the corner, and with that he left.

After a few minutes the monitor and the camera came on and Peter Snow was on the telephone telling me that an interesting debate was in prospect. There would be Caspar Weinberger in Washington, a Saudi Minister in Riyadh, Akehurst in Birmingham, and he would chair it from London. I asked him what was required of me. He said we would be discussing the situation in the Gulf, I could play that by ear, but would I please note that once Weinberger started talking it was difficult to stop him. With that the credits and signature tune began to roll and I could see myself being introduced on the monitor. I can remember little about the debate except that at one point Weinberger was indeed banging on, which made me smile. The producer evidently thought this a good moment to catch me and there I was on screen grinning disdainfully and expected to interrupt the American's flow.

Soon after this while driving back from a Sandhurst Sovereign's Parade I had an uncomfortable feeling in my chest to the extent that I felt I had to undo the car seat belt. Stupidly, I now know, I did not heed the warning and see a doctor. The following week we spent three days with the Pol Rogers in Epernay, with the usual wonderful eating and drinking. On one evening after going to bed, I was up with what I assumed to be indigestion. The thought of anything more sinister did not occur to me. On the morning after our return there was more discomfort while I was sweeping the drive, and this time, at last, I did go to the doctor, who said she did not think anything was seriously wrong but recommended that I should go to the RAF hospital at Wroughton to check. I drove there with Shirley for company, filling up with petrol on the way and carrying a note from the GP. With this note in my hand I wandered around miles of corridors until eventually finding the duty physician. Within minutes I was flat on my back, wired for sound, and the nurse and the consultant were exchanging the sort of look that is familiar to watchers of medical drama on television. The consultant then told me that I had had a heart attack that morning and took some time telling me frighteningly what this meant. He then turned away and talked to the nurse until Shirley called to him saying she thought I did not look at all well. My heart had stopped, Shirley was led away for hot sweet tea, and the consultant banged my chest, happily with immediate success. I had no knowledge of all this and came round none the worse for it all. As it turned out it was not a particularly serious heart attack, but it was all very frightening and after ten days in hospital I was very absorbed with care for myself for a while. However, with Shirley's help I made a full recovery and was able to return to golf and appearing on television after six weeks.

In September Peter Snow rang to say that 'Newsnight' would like to place me under contract for the duration of the Gulf crisis. He explained that this did not mean I must come whenever I was called, but only that I must not appear for anyone else. He said that the contracts branch would be in touch offering a weekly contract fee. Actual appearances would be paid for separately. When the contracts people rang they asked me for how long I thought the contract should run. The only answer I could think of was that we were already booked on a holiday in Zimbabwe in the first week of the following March, so, without mentioning that, I suggested that the last week of February would probably be a reasonable guess. When the final programme on the war appeared in that particular week I won the totally undeserved reputation with 'Newsnight' of being extraordinarily prescient.

I quite enjoyed the sixteen programmes on which I appeared, although made nervous by the lack of any preparation. Peter Snow felt that spontaneous reaction was much better television, but it could often be alarming. I was always very careful to comment on the day's events and never to speculate on what might happen next. If a forecast was right I would be accused of using my military experience and expertise to help the enemy, and if wrong, could be made to look silly. I tried to keep whatever I thought as brief as possible and imagined myself talking not to military experts and pundits, but to the mother of a soldier serving in the Gulf who wanted to know what was going on. This approach seemed to work. It protected me from exposing technical ignorance and, to my surprise and satisfaction, earned me ten out of ten in a *Sunday Times* poll about the pundits pontificating on the media. The proceeds were fairly modest but they certainly helped to pay for the Zimbabwe holiday.

Since then I have often been asked to appear on radio and television about defence issues but have seldom accepted. I consider myself past my sell-by date and would only appear if I felt I knew enough about the subject. One such was commentary on the rash of books written by members of the SAS, of which I strongly disapprove. Any single one might be defended, but collectively they provide very detailed information about this highly secret organisation and tell a potential enemy much too much about how they operate and how they are likely to react to any given situation. Secrecy was one of their trengths and gave them psychological power over their opponents but, like the Royal Family, I believe they were much more effective when people knew little about them and simply respected their mystique.

School governorship has taken up a lot of my time and captured my interest. After ten years as a governor at Harrow I was invited in 1991 to assume the chairmanship of the board, to follow Sir Robin Butler, who felt that his responsibilities as Cabinet Secretary to varying political masters might make chairmanship of the board of a top private school potentially difficult. Flattered but considerably daunted, I accepted and became the first chairman who was not an old boy since 1823. I often said that it took the school 168 years to recover from the last one and wondered how long it would be in my case. In an attempt to make up for my lack of a Harrow education I stayed at the school and immersed myself there as a pupil for three days, which provided very useful background for me.

In fact it was a fascinating and challenging appointment in which most of the time I drew pleasure from things that went well, met countless distinguished and interesting people, and attended many enjoyable functions. One pleasure was to have a box at Lord's for the Eton/Harrow cricket match, and to which I could invite personal friends. I also went twice to the Far East to support rugby tours and to help drum up support for Harrow's highly successful and lucrative summer schools programme.

Throughout our time at Harrow Shirley and I were both the recipients of generous hospitality from many people, especially my deputy, Roger Boissier, and my successor as chairman, Sir Michael Connell, and two head masters and their wives. I was also especially grateful to Andrew Stebbings, the Clerk to the Governors, for his efficiency and endless patience which made the machinery of governing run as smoothly as it usually did.

There were difficulties too. A school like Harrow is automatically news for the media when anything happens there, particularly if something goes wrong. Fortunately not much did but with a community of nearly 1,000 boys, masters and staff one feels constantly to be sitting on a keg of gunpowder waiting for the first spark. Of course it is much more stressful for the head master and I had great respect for the aplomb and resilience of Ian Beer and Nicholas Bomford who were the heads in my time. One of a school chairman's prime duties is to be in close accord with the head master and happily this was easy for me to achieve.

The only major contentious issue during my time in the chair was the building of a theatre for the school. The site for this was fiercely opposed by the many residents on the Hill and they forced the plans to public appeal. This was won by the school but there was much ill-will and permanent rifts between town and gown were forecast. Certainly the residents, despite superhuman efforts to reduce it to a minimum, were put to considerable stress and inconvenience from noise and traffic congestion during the eighteen months it took to build the theatre, but the end product is magnificent and the strained relations from the exercise have largely been repaired as the original villains, like me, have departed. I am one of these because I took it upon myself to field most of the flak in order to protect the head master, Nicholas Bomford, who had arrived after all the decisions had been taken and was therefore blameless. Despite the fuss I am proud of the theatre. One lady, particularly vigorous in her opposition, wrote to me after the building was completed to tell me that I had ruined her life, that she had sold her house for much less than its former worth, and that she had moved to a village in Norfolk where she had a view across fields to a Norman castle. 'No one' she wrote 'is going to ruin that.' In reply I sympathised, but wondered what the villagers had thought when the Normans built their castle.

An opportunity arose in 1996 for Harrow to help in the establishment of an international school in Bangkok which would bear Harrow's famous name. There was little doubt about the potential to fill the school and there would be benefit for Harrow in contributing to such an enterprise. A board of shareholders were to fund the project and Harrow's responsibility, which included no financial liability for the school, would be to find a head master, help him to recruit staff and then to set and monitor the educational curriculum. Unfortunately some management problems in the shareholders' company and the crisis of confidence in Far Eastern markets and devaluation of currencies there in 1997 created serious difficulties for the school. It is still viable and has survived a number of crises. It started up on a small scale but quickly earned a glowing reputation, thus attracting a wealthy backer to see it through its difficulties. It is expanding rapidly and Harrow International School seems set fair to emulate its mentor.

When General Sir Timothy Creasey died in 1986 I became Colonel The Royal Anglian Regiment, a signal honour and one which, as I visited the battalions, the reunions and the dinners, gave me great pride in what had been forged from the former regiments. Naturally their disappearance on amalgamation had caused deep distress and disappointment but the affection and loyalty of those who had to adjust to the new regiment never wavered. It was not easy for those who had left before the Royal Anglian Regiment came into being to generate anything like the same devotion; some never did but many adjusted successfully and gave this young creation their full support. The quality of all the battalions, including the TA ones, was never in doubt and it was good to hear commanders sing their praises wherever I went. The regiment could not be called 'smart' or fashionable but it always did its work professionally, efficiently and without fuss.

Recruiting mostly went well and units were usually close to their proper strength when others in the Infantry were desperately short. It therefore came as an unpleasant shock when in the next wave of cuts the Army Board again failed to back the 'large' regiments in favour of the 'small' ones and we lost a battalion. This was a time of anguish and it was my responsibility to decide how to handle the loss. I went for amalgamation of the whole regiment into two battalions, 1st and 2nd. I felt, and still feel, that with nine counties to represent it was grossly unfair that we should be cut, but although the 3rd Battalion will not forgive me I think the business was managed sensibly and correctly. As much as possible of all the former history and tradition has been retained. Later we also lost a TA battalion, when it was converted to a transport regiment, and this, too, was felt to be unfair in the light of their record and their recruiting strength; but again the bullet was bitten and the best made of a bad job.

One service I was able to effect for the regiment during my colonelcy was to arrange a special association with the Poulters' Livery Company. This has proved to be to our mutual benefit and is a small but useful way in which to bridge the civil/military gap and enable officers from time to time to learn something about the City of London. I have been privileged to be given honorary membership of the livery in recognition of having initiated this association.

The Northamptonshire Regiment still sports a thriving Comrades Association, which reunites in strength every year. It should be getting ever smaller but is showing resilience and even getting in new members. Each year we have a dinner in Northampton on a Saturday evening and on the following morning a church parade and service followed by a march past. All of these events are well attended and it is a humbling but uplifting experience to talk to the soldiers of yesteryear to relive shared experiences and discover what they have made of their lives since service together. One always leaves reinforced in one's views that the British soldier rarely wears his heart on his sleeve but he is a man of unsurpassed patriotism and loyalty to his former comrades and his regiment. For so many men the regiment becomes their family and others will criticise it at their peril. There is nothing in civilian life to compare with the lifelong bond, affection, comradeship and belonging that comes from joining a British regiment.

As an aside, I attended this weekend while serving in Belgium and was unwise enough to park illegally. A ticket to this effect caught me up on my return. Instead of paying I wrote to the Chief Constable telling him I was abroad and asking if a parking offence was extraditable. Luckily he proved to have a sense of humour and wrote to say that the offence would be ignored for now, but that I would be ill-advised to return to Northampton for the next twelve months. We were able to laugh about this when he came to lunch with us after the parade the following year.

Another regimental occasion which snowballed from small beginnings was organised by former RSM Knight in Felixstowe. 'Lofty' Knight put an advertisement in an East Anglian newspaper suggesting that men who had served in the 'Poachers', nickname of the 2nd Battalion The Royal Anglian Regiment, might like to reunite at a hotel in Felixstowe, where the battalion had served and to which area a number had retired. The response was astonishing and it became a beautifully organised annual event attracting more than 200 former soldiers. This sort of thing is the essence of the British Army's regimental system which has been a prime foundation for the Army's successes and standards over so many years. Those of us who have known it believe it to be a prize of untold worth which must be preserved at all costs, however many reviews, studies and economies occur.

In 1991 I was elected to the Senior Golfers' Society. This is an organisation to which men over fifty-five may be invited, provided they are supported by three members who must each write in detail to describe why the candidate will be an asset to the society. It has given me much pleasure. The members, who come from all walks of life all over the country, are congenial people who are all good golfing company. There are over 100 fixtures a year, all at good courses with good lunches, and the format is usually a foursome in the morning followed by another after lunch. Shirley thinks I am crackers but I am prepared to drive long distances to play in a number of these events. Each one is a happy reunion. Conversation in the changing room among this ageing community can be amusing. I have heard, for instance:

> 'Don't you find your feet get further away every time you put your shoes on?'

'My father always said to me: "1 Always live east of your golf club so you don't get the sun in your eyes on the way there or on the way back. 2 Never make love to your wife in the morning in case a better opportunity comes up later in the day." '

A favourite course is Little Aston which has a wonderful record of hospitality to the Army, and has been run with a rod of iron for many years by Mr Norman Russell, the honorary secretary. I arrived at the Army championship one morning to find Norman not in his office. When I asked a sergeant-major if he knew where Mr Russell was he told me that he was in hospital. I asked what the trouble was and the sergeant-major said he believed it was something to do with an insect bite. I went to the hospital and found Norman, already the terror of his ward, suffering from *phlebitis!*

With Army officers' golf fixtures, the Variety Club match, the annual tussle between admirals, generals and air marshals, and regimental golfing dates, to say nothing of my own golf club, I have more than enough play, though not much in the winter. I shall be sad if and when I am too infirm to follow that silly white ball.

In 1990 we loyally went to a local British Legion dance and I was quietly sitting in a corner drinking a beer, nursing my raffle tickets and minding my own business when a large lady bore down upon me and demanded a dance. Propelled around the floor by this lady, who was like a galleon in full sail, I eventually found my way back to my seat nominated by the local council as a governor of Princecroft County Primary School in Warminster, which has just under 200 children. This did not seem as if it would be too demanding but it has certainly taken more time and effort than I expected. In my first four years the head teacher took early retirement and three chairmen resigned. Each time I was asked if I would take the chair because of my Harrow experience. I declined on the grounds that Harrow was rather different, that I was too old for a primary school, that I knew hardly any parents, and that I had enough to do already thank you. When the next chairman walked out in the middle of a meeting I again refused to take the chair, but, asked if I would be vice-chairman, I stupidly agreed. 'Right,' they said, 'we have no chairman so please take the chair.' At this point I felt guilty about the way in which the governors were failing to support the school properly and took it on.

The former head teacher had been a nice and popular man, but his forte was in teaching and the ever-increasing bureaucratic load being forced upon him by the authorities was proving too much. Mr Graham Ball, a dedicated and efficient professional, had been selected as a replacement and knew that if he was to sort out the mountain of administrative and bureaucratic problems he would have no time to teach. This increased the workload on the other teachers, which did nothing for Mr Ball's popularity, and when he applied the many reforms demanded by the Government and local authority which further burdened the teachers he became very unloved. This sort of situation becomes a critical problem for the governors, particularly the chairman. I pointed out to my colleagues that they had chosen the head and they had but two alternatives, to back him or sack him. With only unpopularity to support the latter course I insisted on full, unqualified support and gradually we conveyed this message to the teachers.

After a sticky period the teachers came to recognise that their head was exceedingly hard-working and totally dedicated to the good of the school, and with changes in the staff and the governors things gradually came right, culminating in a successful OFSTED inspection. This came at the end of a very stressful few months for the head and the teachers and they deserved much credit for coming through it so well. Princecroft is a happy, thriving little school. We do our best to cope with inadequate budgets and the ever-increasing weight of paper that descends upon us from the authorities. Most of this paper, which people are being well paid to write, print and post, is either irrelevant or is designed to ensure that if anything goes wrong it will be the fault of the voluntary governors or the teachers and never theirs. I wrote to *The Times* to this effect and received not only support from a minister, but also a large bundle of correspondence agreeing with my arguments. We now await the fruits of the Government's promises to increase funding, reduce class sizes and cut down the amount of paper generated. As the demands on governors' time increase so it is going to become more and more difficult to find the right sort of people who are prepared to take it on.

In 1997 my heart caught up with me again and a bypass operation was recommended. When I was told that it would take National Health fifteen months or so to get around to it I thought I might well die of fright, if nothing else, before a surgeon could get at me. I therefore decided to invest in my chap, my place, and my time. In August Mr Charles Pattison did the business with commendable efficiency at the Harley Street Clinic. Six days later I was able to walk around Paddington Station to catch a train home and recovery has gone well since then. Mr Pattison gave my heart a ten-year warranty, although he did not explain how I was to claim if necessary.

19
Reflections

A consistent feature of the Labour Party's lead-up to the 1997 election, and in due course included in its manifesto, was an intention to hold a detailed defence review which was not solely to save money but to decide what capabilities and forces Britain should take into the twenty-first century. Every aspect of the Services and their management was to be examined and the end-product should reflect a balance between the roles and risks agreed with the Foreign Office and the resources provided by the Treasury. I have no particular political affinity and support or oppose political matters as I find them, but this project was one with which I found myself wholly in agreement in principle. Whether I would agree with the findings would be another matter altogether but the concept was one which I felt had been sensible ever since the end of the Cold War when the Wall came down in 1989. There had been two Tory reviews since then, *Options for Change* and *Front Line First*, but neither, in my view, was sufficiently radical in coming to grips with an entirely new situation.

I am not, by nature, an 'I-told-you-so' sort of person, but I confess to being gratified when I look at the script of my final address at the annual conference of the Chief of the General Staff in January 1990. I find that I made the following points:

1 We face a new defence world.

2 There is no early prospect of another world war.

3 There is only one superpower for the foreseeable future. We would be wise to be allied to it.

4 It is in our national interest to support NATO. Alternatives, such as WEU, do not include American power and Europeans alone seldom agree on anything.

5 German training areas will come under increasing pressure and we would be wise to withdraw from that country, which is not threatened, as fully and as soon as we can. To remain is only a very expensive and unnecessary gesture to NATO.

6 The days of the heavy tank are numbered. Our forces should all be capable of transportation by air.

7 Our firepower should be based on the missile and our battlefield mobility on the helicopter, which we, the Army, should command and control.

8 A nuclear deterrent is justified, but should be confined to submarine missile delivery.

9 A comprehensive defence review, taking all this into account, is needed soon.

This, I feel, was quite prescient and I have not changed my opinion on any of the points, although I know there are strong arguments for the heavy tank. I cannot foresee nuclear war on a global scale but I think it is important to be able to say to a dangerous dictator that if he uses a nuclear weapon against our interests we will simply obliterate his country. This creates no guarantee, of course, but diplomacy is much more effective when it is backed by an overwhelmingly powerful threat. The Strategic Defence Review itself was thorough and I find myself generally able to support most of its findings, with two important exceptions – the Territorial Army and the Eurofighter.

It is fairly easy to identify situations in today's world in which Britain might need to deploy troops for peace-keeping or other United Nations operations, and some where it might well be desirable to evacuate British citizens from dangerous places. It is not so easy to predict where operations on a larger scale or of a more belligerent nature might be required. This, indeed, has seldom been the case, and many such conflicts have come unexpectedly and at short notice. Nationalism, dangerous dictators, chronic Middle Eastern unrest, and Muslim Fundamentalism are ever-present threats and who is to say which, if any, will present a vital British interest to be defended? The Government has to assess risk and then tailor and arm its regular forces taking account of what can be afforded, but reserve forces are a necessary insurance against what cannot be forecast and I consider that severe reductions, such as are planned for the Territorial Army as I write, are therefore dangerous.

Overall the TA faces cuts of nearly 20,000 and the majority of these are targeted on the yeomanry, the infantry and the Royal Engineers. The former two, in particular, sadden me and I believe them to be wrong. These units are the very heart of the TA and bear most of the territorial connections and titles. Quite apart from the distress that their demise will cause the volunteers who serve in them, it must surely be a shortsighted policy. The justification, quoted by the

Secretary of State, Mr George Robertson, is that all TA units must be 'relevant and usable'. I believe this to be a cop-out expression overused by politicians, civil servants, and sociologists and had a letter published in *The Times* pointing this out. The inference is based on the readily foreseeable future, not taking into account the longer term and the unexpected, which, as the cliché has it, is what always happens. Reserves, by their very nature, represent an early reinforcement for understrength and overstretched Regular forces, and also a basis for expansion if and when those forces have been deployed. In peace and war they have an important recruiting function and this at a time when regular recruiting is already in trouble.

I have dealt with the characteristics and strengths of the TA in earlier chapters but there is another feature here which is important. The Review acknowledges the importance of the cadet forces in value to the country and in recruiting for the services. An intention to increase the size of the Army Cadet Force by 10,000 is mentioned in the Review. I believe this to be pie in the sky anyway, but quite impossible if the planned TA cuts are made and many drill halls, or to give them their proper title, TA Centres, are sold off. The TA was decimated before, in 1967, but wiser counsels prevailed and like a phoenix it rose from the ashes. This was possible because the decision to recreate it was taken before the drill halls were sold for a one-off Treasury bonus. Once they have gone they will never be replaced. Many of them provide centres for the cadets and cadet units can not only use all of their facilities but also borrow instructors from their local TA units. Many of these units also often provide the cadets' adult instructors when their TA time ends. There is talk of 'reprovision of accommodation' by setting up cadet huts, but these will not fill the bill because they lack so many of a TA Centre's features. A cadet unit by its very nature must be essentially local. Cadets cannot be expected to travel far and a local TA Centre is an important attraction.

I believe the new Eurofighter devours a disproportionate share of the defence budget. It is hugely expensive, made more so and long delayed by the collaboration with other countries, and it is an aircraft designed in the Cold War for General War operations. I do not consider that it has the characteristics required of an aircraft for our stated primary roles of peacekeeping, evacuation of British nationals from endangered areas, minor national operations or major operations in conjunction with allies. The aircraft is a technological marvel no doubt but I believe its adoption has much more to do with jobs than operational requirements. I do not know enough about the industry to speak with authority, but I would have thought that to develop and enhance the Harrier, which has such desirable characteristics for what we may have to do, would have been less expensive, offered export potential, and safeguarded just as many jobs – perhaps more because we could have built the whole aircraft, not just parts of it. It would have been entirely British.

Turning to more personal matters I was remarkably lucky in my choice of a career. I often say that I enjoyed every minute of it, and this is broadly true, although one of the characteristics of the military memory is its capacity for forgetting the bad bits. I am often asked whether I can commend an Army career to young people today. I can, although I have to follow up with a number of warnings.

Today's Army is very different from the one that I joined, indeed from the one that I left. There have been endless studies, reviews, and economy drives over the last half-century and in my experience most of them have meant a drop in the quality of life for some or often all of us. This is not a whine from a sybarite. Although pay is much better than it was, the Army offers no opportunities to make a fortune and quality of life therefore becomes an important factor in attracting the high grade officers and soldiers that the armed forces demand. There are plenty of frustrations, which weigh in varying degrees upon the individual. There has to be subordination of self to discipline and a hierarchical structure. Initiative must often be tempered by rules and discretion. Long hours of work, separation, frequent moves, uncomfortable and uncongenial stations, all take their toll. I omit danger and the rigours of active soldiering because for most of us that has been an attraction not a drawback.

For much of my early service sport in many forms was a feature of Army life, and it was beyond question an attraction to potential recruits. Except on operations, for instance, Wednesday afternoons were devoted to sport, but now that is very rare indeed; the time can not be spared. To some extent this is a product of the demands on time of training for a far greater variety of weapons and equipment, but there are penalties in fitness and teamwork at the lowest levels, and in unit *esprit* when there is so little opportunity to support unit teams.

Today's soldiers work harder and are more widely proficient than yesterday's. They may not be more basically intelligent but they are much more widely informed through advances in education and through the continuous assaults of all forms of the media. In society generally there is a certain readiness to question authority. Forty years ago officers were usually accorded a right to respect and obedience simply through holding a commission. Now, to a much more significant degree, respect has to be earned through leadership and professional competence, which is to be applauded.

I view most of these changes either with mild regret or with admiration, but I am more seriously concerned with the creeping effects of what is called 'political correctness', an unattractive and usually destructive import from the United States. Throughout society I believe that pressures for such issues as feminine equality and racial harmony, highly desirable though these may be, have reached ridiculous lengths which are largely counter-productive because by their very extremes they harden the attitudes of the people they hope to oppose or curb. A law about harassment, for instance, may reduce it marginally but it makes potential harassers more, not less, resentful and thus provokes actions and gibes.

It is far from clear why political correctness achieved such prominence and influence. I suppose at first it chimed with the aspirations of various groups who felt disadvantaged or disrespected and some of its objectives were not unreasonable, but, as so often, it gathered unstoppable pace and it became politically incorrect to oppose it, whatever the extremes. Perhaps, with luck, there will be counter-moves in due course, but there seems little chance while the 'ambulance-chaser' type of lawyers can make so much money for themselves and their clients from politically correct courts, and wealthy companies will usually pay rather than risk any adverse publicity being aired in open court.

It is one thing to direct that the Army must recruit from ethnic minorities but the publicity accorded to such a directive arouses opposition among soldiers who, if the policy could be put into effect quietly and without media ballyhoo, would be much more ready to accept it. Those regiments, like mine, that have quietly assimilated many coloured soldiers have experienced little difficulty. Tabloid headlines generate an awareness that can quickly turn to resentment which, particularly when drink releases inhibitions, can find repulsive or aggressive expression.

Another dangerous trend, imported from America, is the award of substantial damages for what would once have been thought laughable or, at least, petty affronts. People are becoming more and more aware of the financial rewards available from successful lawsuits and one can even see advertisements inviting anyone who feels in the slightest wronged to get in touch with unscrupulous law firms to find out if they have a case. The motive for this is invariably mercenary and it has unattractive effects both socially and in the soaring costs of professional insurance. A number of Services grievances have won cash at British and European courts and although it is not for me to question whether all of them have been justified I believe it is a disturbing trend which chips away at authority and makes leadership and management more difficult.

Many stations and situations offer few opportunities for nubile company and the constant moves put stress on romance and, later, marriage. A soldier needs to find a mate who is prepared to accept moving house every two or three years and equally frequent periods of being left on het own, with all the disruption and stress thus caused. Again, in Shirley, I have been much blessed in this; it does not suit everybody. During our marriage we have also seen a substantial change in the style and expectations of military spouses, some of which may be fairer and an improvement for the individuals but a loss for the unit generally. There is much less of following the drum today. Wives now are often career girls and their own jobs will often determine where they will live and the degree to which they will accompany their husbands. This, together with the sensible policy of early investment in a house of their own, is breaking up the cohesion of the unit family. Gone is much of the free and dedicated devotion that generations of Army wives have put into accompanying their men, supporting their careers, and taking a close and helpful interest in the wives and children of those under their husband's command.

There are still plenty of attractions. Comradeship, teamwork, regimental spirit, physical and mental challenges, a wide variety of jobs and locations and the ever-present possibility of exciting action are all hackneyed expressions well used by recruiters but they are none the less important for being hackneyed. Many civilians would envy the thought that if a particular place, job or boss was unlikeable one or more of them would be likely to change within a short time. Above all, for the officer, there is the British soldier. He can be difficult, he can be bloody-minded, he can be stubborn, he can be uncommunicative, he can use the most appalling language, but he responds to good leadership and training. When the chips are down he is one of the best in the world. The basic characteristics of resilience, determination not to be beaten, and an indomitable sense of humour and fair play are today backed, more than ever before, by a professionalism and mastery of an ever more technical and varied requirement, even for the most junior infantryman. No more the cannon-fodder or the dour, dull footslogger beloved of the cartoonist and the satirist. Today's soldier is alert, intelligent, proud, fit, and usually articulate. He is so good at adapting to whatever is required of him, and this, in my view, is what gives him the edge over other soldiers. He fights doggedly and courageously, he keeps the peace without taking sides, he communicates with everyone no matter whether they do not speak his language or he theirs, and others criticise his regiment or unit at their peril. One has only to admire the way in which he has coped with the immensely difficult situations in such places as Northern Ireland and former Jugoslavia and to realise that no other soldiers could have coped so well. In the case of United Nations operations the British soldier almost invariably earns nothing but praise from all sides and is therefore much in demand. This is not only because he is a Regular volunteer when so many other countries still rely on conscription. Finally, I have always enjoyed his ability to identify pomposity (sometimes mine!) and skilfully deflate it, sometimes in ways that the offender does not himself recognise.

As I write, British servicemen, and many others, are deeply embroiled in the tragic turmoil in Kosovo and the surrounding countries. It is hard to see how this conflict may end but I feel sure it will end in tears. Interference in civil wars has been shown historically almost always to be seriously counter-productive and the Balkans present as intractable and dangerous an area in which to interfere as one could find. Wars are not won by air attack alone and the bombing has so far not only caused innocent casualties and terrible destruction but has hastened the dreadful ethnic cleansing. Whatever the outcome hatreds are being inflamed that will last for centuries. The operations are hideously expensive and someone will have to pay for repairs to physical damage and economies when the fighting stops. Operations are being conducted which do not have United Nations authority and seem to be contrary to the spirit of NATO's charter. In my view the situation is deplorable and decisions appear to me to have been taken more for prospective electoral popularity than to be based on responsible diplomacy and practical military common sense.

There are two organisational aspects of the British Army that set it apart from many others. One is the regimental system. Since the fifties the system has suffered many blows. Successive cuts have continuously reduced the number of battalions required. At first regiments had to be amalgamated as, increasingly, the number of battalions fell below the number of counties who had once given their name to their own regiment.

The first and worst mistake in this process may be laid at the door of the Army Board of 1958, when Mr Duncan Sandys wielded his axe as Secretary of State. After endless wrangling about which regiments could stay and which must go, a mixture, as I have described earlier, of 'large' and 'small' regiments was created, based mostly on the influence individual regiments could bring to bear. Those, like Queen's, Royal Anglian, Light Infantry and Greenjackets, who followed Army Board advice and became large regiments, were assured that the decision would stand them in good stead in any future reorganisation, because battalions could be added to them or taken from them without affecting cap badges or regimental spirit. This was the time when all regiments should have been directed to this course, but the nettle was not grasped. Over the years the large regiments have been disproportionately reduced because it was found to be easy, and smaller single-county regiments have usually survived either through senior pleading or because it was thought too emotive and politically unattractive to deprive them of the identity for which they had worked so hard. In the Royal Anglian Regiment our four battalions have been whittled down to two to represent nine counties, while Yorkshire alone, despite a very similar recruiting record, has three regiments. Gradually the small regiments are being chipped away and eventually I hope all regiments will be 'large' so that the infantry can speak with one voice. Hitherto it has been easy to divide and rule it, especially when the butchers' knives are out. Incidentally I do not support a Corps of Infantry, which would be a serious blow to the regimental system.

Despite all this the regiment is still what the infantry soldier joins and it is to the regiment that he devotes his loyalty. History and tradition are a small part of this but most of it is the pride of wearing its badge and the privilege of belonging to an exclusive club in which he finds his closest mates. After his service he will continue to belong to his regiment and for the rest of his life will enjoy meeting the friends he made and reminiscing with tales that become more inaccurate and more enjoyable as the years pass.

The second unusual organisational difference from many other armies may seem minor but I believe it to be important. The chief of staff, or chief executive at every level above company (even that if one considers the special position of the sergeant-major), is two ranks junior to the commander, and therefore one rank junior to the next tier of command. In a battalion the lieutenant-colonel commands, the next level is the company commanders, who are majors, but the chief executive is the adjutant who is a captain. This means that the commanding officer's mouthpiece has to be deferential and persuasive to those to whom he is conveying the commander's requirements. They, in turn, feel it easy to let the adjutant know their ideas and criticisms which can be passed on without nervousness or loss of dignity or face, often to the common good. It does not always work like this, because of personalities, but it should and the system is there to enable it.

My answer, therefore, to the inquiry about whether or not to join the Army is: 'By all means try it, but treat it as a trial rather than necessarily a final career. You may not like the Army, it takes a particular sort of person, and the Army may not like you. But if you stay for only three years or so you will have grown up and matured more quickly than in most professions, you will have gained wide experience of dealing with, serving, and even commanding, people from all walks of life. You will have enjoyed real responsibility from a very early stage and you may have travelled widely. You will have forged close, lasting friendships and made contacts which may prove useful later wherever you go. You will be physically strong and fit. Three years may seem an age at your time of life but the experience and self-confidence gained should prove much more valuable than any loss of time in another calling. If you stay I hope you enjoy the life and the luck that I have.'

One of the features which has made Army life so enjoyable for me is my having what I like to think is a keen sense of humour and of the ridiculous. I have had many more chuckles than tears and I wonder if that could have been true in any other profession. Some of the eccentrics have provided endless enjoyment and I deplore the fact that the modern demand for professionalism, worthy and important though that certainly is, has left no room for the particular and sometimes narrow talents of the slightly dotty but often creative nonconformists who can devise imaginative training, are often courageous, and whom soldiers will follow through thick and thin, if only because they do not want to miss what the boss may do or say next. There seems to be little room for such characters today and I fear a time when the services and the civil service may be indistinguishable. Ambition may be commendable but in excess it can be corrosive and selfish.

Writing a book such as this and thus looking back on one's life to date, one inevitably considers whether one has any regrets, what one might have changed and what one might wish to have been different. My list under these headings is quite short, and I suspect much shorter than most. I have virtually no regrets about anything I could have changed but just a couple of wishes. I wish I had gone to university, not so much for the academic education but for mixing there with a much wider group of people than were offered at school or in the early years of the Army. I am sure that this would not only have been interesting, it would have developed maturity and broad, questioning attitudes much earlier, and would also have brought lasting friendships with people in widely varying walks of life. Perhaps Sandhurst did me more good than university would have done; I do not know.

Secondly I wish, as we both do, that we could have had children who survived.

However, generally speaking, it has been a good life, although one life does not seem to have been enough.

Index

Many of the people in this book have progressed to higher rank or title since the time at which they are mentioned and some are still progressing. To include their subsequent honorifics in the text disrupts the flow; so in the book they are given the rank or title relevant at the time but the index shows the current style where this is known. The index is also selective; it excludes many place-names and events judged to be of only passing interest.

Adamson, Paul, 21
Aden, 118, 150
Akehurst, Caroline, 94
Akehurst, Geoffrey, 11-12, 16-17, 33, 87, 89, 90
Akehurst, Julian, 95, 97, 108, 118, 136, 148-9
Akehurst, Shirley, 9, 59, 69, 81, 83, 85-6, 91, 109, 136, 149, 155, 158, 177-9, 186-8, 200, 205, 207, 214, 231, 233-4, 236-7, 247
Al Yamama Contract, 201
Alor Star, 59, 61, 69, 70, 80, 83
Alexander, Sir Michael, 211
Alice, HRH Princess, Duchess of Gloucester, 131
Amery, Rt Hon Julian, 163
Amritsar, 193
Anderson, Brig David, 119
Arab/Israeli War 1967, 120
Arengo-Jones, Brig Tony, 126
Aris, Brig Michael, 134
Armour, Col Billy, 103
Armoured Division, 4th, 170-83, 201
Army Cadet Force, 244
Army Golf Association, 137, 222
Army Officers' Golf Society, 137
Asprey, John, 163
Australia, 143-5
Austria, 39, 43-4, 108, 178

B Specials, 22
Backscratcher Affair, 14-15
Bagnall, Maj Basil, 99
Bagnall, FM Sir Nigel, 99, 180, 211
Baker, FM Sir Geoffrey, 194, 223
Baldwin, Ssgt, 171, 225
Balkans, 248

Ball, Graham, 240
Baluch, 153
BAOR, 100, 102, 104, 110-11, 170, 176, 180, 197
Barber, Col Ali, 98
Barnett, Corelli, 196
Barthorp, 9, 45-6, 48-9, 115, 117
Barthorp, Penelope, 46
Bath, Order of the, 200
Beach, Gen Sir Hugh, 132
Beer, Ian, 236
Beetham, ACM Sir Michael, 118
Begg, Adm of the Fleet Sir Varyl, 126
Belfast, 19
Belize, 168
Benison, Sadie, 21, 33-4
Bethell, Brig Drew, 102
Bickford, Maj Jack, 108
Birrell, Maj Bob, 148
Bisley, 42-3, 52
Boissier, Roger, 236
Bomford, Nicholas, 236
Bonallack, Michael, 185
Boorman, Lt Gen Sir Derek, 99
Bramall, FM Lord, 228
Brave Defender, Ex, 203, 204
Bridge, Brig Jack, 137
(British) Corps, 1st, 100, 107, 174, 176, 203
Brittain, RSM, 27-9
Broke-Smith, Maj Bill, 33
Brooke, Brig Frank, 62-4, 65
Brooking, Maj Gen Patrick, 173
Brown, Maj Gen John, 216
Brown, Brig Michael, 232
Browne, Brig Julian, 205
Bryant, Miss, 14-15
Bryers, Brig Dick, 82

Index

Buchan, Hon Alastair, 138-9, 141
Burgess, Gp Capt Gordon, 124
Burgess, Lady, 208
Burgess, Maj Gen Rodney, 116
Burma, 205
Burrell, Lt Col Nigel, 204
Butler, Gen Sir Mervyn, 110, 120-1, 141
Butler, Sir Robin, 235

Cadet Company, Helen's Bay, 21, 24
Cairn terriers, 179-80, 226
Callaghan, Rt Hon Lord, 161
Camberley, 98-9, 112, 182, 195
Cameronians, 1st Bn, 104
Carrington, Rt Hon Lord, 135
Carver, FM Lord, 142, 198
Castle, Rt Hon Lady, 67
Chambers Lt Col Dick, 114, 117
Chapple, FM Sir John, 110, 205
China, 191
Christie, Brig Ian, 157
CIOR, 229
Clark, Col Wake, 42
Clements, RSM, 39
Close-Brooks, Lt Col Neville, 63
Clutterbuck, Maj Gen Richard, 140
Cocking, Brig Nick, 201
Cockram, Capt, 23, 28
Colchester, 37-8, 128
Colombo, 170
Connell, Sir Michael, 236
Conway Williams, 36-7
Cook, Maj Gen Bob, 212-14
Cooper, Gen Sir George, 129, 132
Copp, RSM, 25, 30
Cornock, Maj Gen Bill, 222
Cottam, Maj Barny, 226
Cottam, Brenda, 59, 81, 226
Council of TAVRAs, 198, 223-4, 227, 230
Craig-Adams, Maj Ian, 54, 58, 65
Cranborne, Rt Hon Lord, 230
Cranbrook School, 13, 15-16, 54
Creasey, Gen Sir Tim, 155, 169, 237
Cumberbatch, Pte, 128
CWGC, 208
Cyprus, 111-18, 155

Daily Express, 128
Daily Mail, 11
Daily Mirror, 23, 91, 104, 122
Daily Telegraph, 125, 204
Dalzell-Payne, Maj Gen Harry, 120
Dartmoor, 92
Das, Topi, 109

Davies, Cfn, 49
Deane, Peter, 224
De Bretton Gordon, Maj John, 125, 132
Denny, Col Reggie, 95, 111
Dhofar, 149-65, 185
Dick, Jimmy, 13
Dickson, Brig Jimmy, 74
Dickson, Lt Col Seton, 54, 57-9, 64-6
Dinnin, Maj Richard, 123
Dodd, June, 17
Dover, 203
DSACEUR, 207-25, 229
Durban, 91-2

Earle, Maj Charles, 30
Eaton Hall, 25-7
East Anglian Bde Trg Centre, 37-8
East Anglian Regt, 2nd, 1st Bn, 103, 111
Economist, The, 133
Edinburgh, HRH Duke of, 192-4
Egypt, 188-9
Eimler, Gen, 209
Eisenhower, President, 208
Elliott, Harvey, 133
Ellis, 33-4
Elphinstone, Elizabeth, 69
Erskine, Gen Sir George, 94
Erskine-Crum, Maj Gen Vernon, 139-40
Erskine-Tulloch, Brig Pat, 111
Essex Regt, 38
Evans, Maj Gen Andy, 229
Eurofighter, 243-4

Fahd, HM King, 201
Farndale, Gen Sir Martin, 174
Felixstowe, 12-13, 129
Feng, Mr, 191, 197
Fieldhouse, Adm of the Fleet Sir John, 201, 211
Firqat, 155, 156, 157
Fletcher, Brig Jack, 165
Fletcher, Mary, 164
FOFA, 210-11
Ford, Gen Sir Robert, 159, 160
Fort Benning, 186
  Bragg, 187
  Hood, 216-17
  Irwin, 197
  Lejeune, 217
Fowler, Maj, 27-8

Gallipoli, 219
Galvin, Gen Jack, 211, 220-1
Garrett, Maj Gen Len, 106
Gerrard-Wright, Maj Gen Dick, 136

Index

Gettysburg, 217
Gibraltar 124-7, 167
Gibraltar Regt, 126
Goodale, Lt Col Mike, 87
Goodwin, Lt Gen Sir Richard, 125
Gorbachev, Mikhail, 209
Gordon-Lennox, Maj Gen Bernard, 175-7
Gore, Brig Francis, 142
Gowdy, Capt Ian, 222
Gowing, Capt, 131
Graydon, ACM Sir Michael, 185
Greenfield, Richard, 61
Griffiths, Revd Jack, 80-1
Griffiths, RSM, 59
Guardian, The, 105, 221
Guernsey, 93
Gurkha Rifles, 2nd/10th, 73
Gurney, Sir Henry, 51

Hackett, Gen Sir John, 110
Hamdi, President, North Yemen, 162-3
Hammond, Col Trevor, 190
Harding, FM Sir John, 202
Hardy, L Cpl, 131
Harrington, C Sgt, 200, 225
Harrow International School, Bangkok, 237
Harrow School, 199, 235-7, 240
Harter, Maj Gen, 35
Haycraft, Lt Col Ian, 123
Hazan, Capt Ray, 131
Healey, Rt Hon Lord, 133, 138-9
Heath, Rt Hon Sir Edward, 134-5, 138
Hedley-Dent, Capt, 25, 27
Herford, 170, 179 182, 212
Heseltine, Rt Hon Michael, 201-2, 205
Hickey, Col Mike, 61-2
Hipkin, Maj Guy, 115
Holland, Bandmaster, 97
Holt, Col Brian, 214
Hong Kong, 85-90
    1957 Riots, 88-9
Hottois, Col Jean, 222
Hottois, Francine, 222
Houchin, Brig Derek, 41, 43-4, 46-7, 50, 84
Howard, Maj John, 122
Howard-Dobson, Gen Sir Patrick, 165
Howlett, Gen Sir Geoffrey, 194
HQ UKLF, 195, 198
Hudson, Mark, 14
Huitfeldt, Gen Tonne, 140
Hunt, Gen Sir Peter, 133
Hunt, Sir Rex, 184
Hussein, HM King, 153, 164, 169
Huxtable, Gen Sir Charles, 164

IGTA, 96, 196
Indonesia, 142-3
Iranian Army, 153-4, 156

James, RSM, 194
Japan, 206
JDSC, 146-9
Jones, Gen Sir Charles, 109

Kanchanaburi, 205-6
Kennedy, President, 109
Kenya, 125, 129-33, 207
King, Rt Hon Tom, 227
King, Sgt, 19
Kitchin, Maj Ted, 42
Kitson, Chiggy, 148
Kitson, Gen Sir Frank, 82, 147, 148
Knight, RSM 'Lofty', 239
Knox, Maj Terence, 43, 51
Kosovo, 248
Kota Bharu, 54, 56, 57

Lancers, 9th/12th, 108
Lancers, 16th/5th, 103
Lambert, Brig Gen Wayne, 222
Lancashire Fusiliers, 103, 105, 107
Leach, Adm Sir Henry, 158
Lee, Gordon, 133
Leng, Gen Sir Peter, 171, 177
Lewis, Msgr David, 218
Lionheart, Ex, 203
Lord, RSM, 30
Lord, Riley, 31
Lovat, Lord, 122
Lovelock, J.O., 16
Lovesey, Maj John, 39, 51
Lowe, Cathy, 195
Luck, Brian, 13
Lück, Col Hans von, 122
Lupidi, Velleda, 48

McCance, Maj Neil, 33
McColgan, RSM, 114-16
MacIntyre, Brig Donald, 126
Mack, Gen, 209
Majid, Sgt, 61
Malay Regt, 51-3, 57, 63, 76
Malaya, 51, 53-84, 107, 119
Malaysia, 125, 129, 133, 205
Man, Brig Pat, 103-4, 109
Manchester Regt, 63, 68
Mangham, Maj Gen Desmond, 142-3
Mann, Rt Rev Michael, 199
Manson, Gen Paul, 215
Margaret, HRH Princess, 21

Matthews, Maj Gen Mike, 229
Mayhew, Maj Niall, 127
Mons Officer Cadet School, 27
Mons, Belgium, 208
Montgomery, Brig David, 198, 200, 202
Montgomery, FM Lord, 208, 220, 224,
Morgan, Maj Gen, 40
Morgan, Col Geoffrey, 38
Morgan Line, 40, 48
Morony, Maj Gen Tim, 149, 168
Morton, Adm Sir Anthony, 142
Moss, Stirling, 50
Murphy, Superintendent, 63-4

National Service, 16, 21, 38, 41-2, 45, 61, 63, 67, 95, 113-14
NATO, 100-1, 108, 125, 139, 141, 173, 201, 208, 210, 212-13, 215, 217, 221, 227, 229-30, 242, 248
Nelson, Adm Lord, 220
Nelson, Maj Andy, 20
Nelson, Capt (REME), 87
New Zealand, 142, 145
Newell, Lt Col Peter, 179
'Newsnight', 156, 232, 234
Nigeria, 189-90
Northampton 38-9, 73, 93, 238
Northamptonshire Regt, 37-52, 73, 85-94, 214, 238
Northamptonshire Regt (TA), 43, 94-8
Norway, 206

Oborne, Brig John, 147
O'Connell, Bandmaster, 126
Ogle, Maj Nick, 43
Ogle, 2 Lt, 19
Oman, 138, 148-50, 163, 165, 169, 179, 185, 199
Osborne-Smith, Brig Robert, 50-2
Osnabrück, 103, 108, 214

Palace Barracks, 19, 21
Parachute Regt, 67, 111, 127, 141
Pattison, Charles, 241
Pearson, Col Alastair, 121
Pearson, Sgt, 225
Peckham, Lt Col Alan, 54, 78, 80-1, 83, 147-8
Perkins, Maj Gen Ken, 157
Perkins Diesel Ltd, 96
Peterborough, 43, 95-6, 98
Pick, Hella, 221
Pincher, Chapman, 128
Pol Rogers 212-13, 233
Pond, Maj Ray, 131

Pople, Maj Gordon, 76, 78, 80-1
Porta, Adm, 212
Poulters Livery Company, 238
Powell, Sir Charles, 221
Pratt, Maj Gen, 26-7
Princecroft Primary School, 240-1
Prince of Wales's Own Regt of Yorkshire, 103
Princess Royal, HRH The, 230-1
Princess Victoria, mv, 20
Pritchard, Lt Col Monty, 96
Profumo, Rt Hon John, 105
Pyne, Cpl, 11, 23, 24

Qaboos bin Said, HM Sultan, 151, 156-63
Queen, HM The, 181, 192, 219, 224

RAF Regt, 151, 204
Rawlins, Lt Col John, 47
Read, Col Brian, 108, 110, 214
Redhead, Brian, 202
Reece, Col Peter, 177
Reserve Forces Association, 229
Reynolds, RQMS Ned, 47-9
Regular Commissions Board, 20-1, 26
Ridley, Lord, 223, 229
Rifkind, Rt Hon Sir Malcolm, 227-8
Rifle Brigade, 90
Riggall, Col John, 33
RMA Sandhurst, 21, 26-37, 57, 61, 99, 120, 159-60, 194, 233, 251
Robertson, Rt Hon George, 231, 244
Roche, Maj Rocky, 92
Rootes, Lord, 16
Ross, Lt Col Donald, 185
Rosso, Vice Adm, 212
Rowson, Revd Philip, 39
Royal Anglian Regt, 114, 237, 248-9
 2nd Bn, 122, 127-31, 205, 239
Royal Artillery, 6th Fd Regt, 103
Royal College of Defence Studies, 137-45, 219
Royal Engineers, 151, 176
Royal Fusiliers, 20, 23, 28, 35
Royal Highland Fusiliers, 125
Royal Irish Rangers, 127
Royal Welch Fusiliers, 177
RUSI, 202
Russell, Norman, 239-40

SACEUR, 207, 209, 211, 220-1
Salalah, 151, 153, 155, 157, 160, 161, 164
Said bin Taimur, HM Sultan, 150
Sandys, Rt Hon Duncan, 248
Sarfait, 152

Index

Sartori, Dr Luigi, 218
SAS, 68, 96, 151-2, 155-6, 161, 204, 234
Saudi Arabia, 200-1
Saunders, Lt Col H.F., 15-16, 20
School of Artillery, 195
Scott, Russell, 15
Scott, Sonia, 173
Scotter, Gen Sir William, 129
Senior Golfers' Society, 239
Shah of Iran, 152-3
Shailes, Csgt, 128
SHAPE, 139, 208-24
Sibbald, Maj Gen Peter, 129
Simmons, Geoffrey, 214
Singapore, 73-5, 78, 80, 87, 90, 133, 142-3, 205-6
Singapore *Straits Times*, 133
Small, Charlie, 19, 20
Sneyd, Brig Tom, 229
Snow, Peter, 155-6, 232, 234
Soames, Rt Hon Nicholas, 228
Somerton-Rayner, Maj Mike, 107
Spearpoint, Ex, 174
Staff College Camberley, 130, 183, 191, 194
   Directing Staff, 118-22
   Entrance exam, 95, 97
   House, 183
   Student, 99-102
Standen, Jack, 18-9
Staniforth, Maj Norman, 56-7
Stanmore Golf Club, 137
Stebbings, Andrew, 236
Stewart, Brig Andrew, 219
Stibbon, Gen Sir John, 166
Stockwell, Gen Sir Hugh, 57
Strategic Defence Review, 242-3
Sultan of Oman's Air Force, 152
Sultan of Oman's Navy, 154
Sultan's Armed Forces, 152
   HQ, 153-4
Sunday Times, 107, 234
Sweden, 189
Sword, Operation, 64, 67-70, 73

Taurus House, 172
Taylor, Col Terry, 117
Teague, Col Tony, 35
Templer, FM Sir Gerald, 51, 53, 68-9, 73, 75-6, 114
Tengku Ahmad, Gen, 66
Territorial Army, 95-8, 196-9, 203-4, 227, 231, 237-8, 243-4
Tesseron, Alfred, 213

Thailand, 71, 205, 237
Thatcher, Rt Hon Lady, 201, 211, 220-2
Thesiger, Wilfred, 202
Thorpe, Rt Hon Jeremy, 19-20
Tidworth, 195, 207
Times, The, 241, 244
Tippen, Maj John, 108
Todd, Richard, 122
Toh Kar Lim, 63, 67-8, 73
Tomlinson, Brig Mike, 165
Topol, 120
Tower, Maj Gen Philip, 102-4, 106, 110
Trieste, 37, 39-52, 84, 108, 179, 218
Trolley Trials, 93-4
Turnill, Lt Col Teddy, 50
Tuzo, Gen Sir Harry, 209

UK Field Army, 196
United Nations, 119, 243, 248

Variety Club Golfing Society, 137, 223, 240
Vickers, Lt Gen Sir Richard, 171
Vincent, FM Lord, 165

War Office Selection Board, 21, 23
Warminster 146, 148-9, 181, 207, 226, 240
   Civic Trust, 226
Warsaw Pact, 101, 110, 173-4
Watchet, 90-1
Waterloo, Battle of, 208, 213
Watkins, Maj Gen Guy, 166
Watts, Maj Gen Johnny, 151
Wayper, Dr, 131
Webster Capt Chris, 200
Weinberger, Caspar, 233
Weston, Pte, 125, 126
Wetherall, Maj John, 45-6, 74, 87-8
Wheeler, Gen Sir Roger, 126
Whelan, RQMS, 21, 28
Wilford, Col Derek, 67-8, 114
Wilkes, Capt Tim, 171
Wilkinson Sword of Peace, 127
Wilmott, RSM Willie, 49-50
Wilson, Lt Gen Sir James, 107
Winder, Brig Bill, 147
Wood, Cpl, 19
Woodburn, Brig Bill, 121
Woodward, Adm Sir Sandy, 138, 219
Worthy, Col Peter, 38, 47, 51, 73

Young, Rt Hon Lord, 202
Younger, Rt Hon Lord, 229

Zainal, Cpl, 68